GLASSFIBRE BOAT MANUAL

GLASSFIBRE BOAT MANUAL

Practical Repairs, Maintenance and Improvements

Supervising editor: Bo Streiffert

Macdonald
Queen Anne Press

GLASSFIBRE BOAT MANUAL
World copyright © 1989 is the joint property
of Johnston Co-editions, Gothenburg, and
Streiffert & Company, Stockholm, Sweden.

Idea, design, and production by Johnston
Co-editions and Streiffert & Company.

First published in Great Britain in 1989 by
Queen Anne Press, a division of
Macdonald & Company (Publishers) Ltd,
Headway House, 66-73 Shoe Lane,
London EC4P 4AB
A member of Maxwell Pergamon Publishing Corporation plc

Editors: Turlough Johnston, Bo Streiffert
Designer: Nils Hermanson
Copy editor: Jon van Leuven
Authors: Dave Gannaway, Loris Goring, Peter
Milne, Dag Pike, Bo Streiffert, Jon Winge

Illustrators: Anders Engström, Hans Linder,
Lennart Molin, Tuire Tepponen

Filmset by Bokstaven, Gothenburg.
Lithography by Repro-Man, Gothenburg.
Printed and bound in Italy by Grafedit,
Azzano San Paolo, Bergamo, by arrangement
with Graphicom, Vicenza.

British Library Cataloguing in Publication Data
Streiffert, Bo
Glassfibre boat manual.
1. Fibreglass boats–Maintenance and
repair.–Amateurs' manuals
I. Title
623.8'207   VM321

ISBN 0-356-12357-X

Contents

CHAPTER 1
THE GLASSFIBRE BOAT 7
General building methods 8
Materials 10
Laminate moulding 12
Sandwich construction 13
Reinforcements 18
Joinings 21
Built-in reinforcements 24
Boat survey: the racer-cruiser 26
Boat survey: the motor cruiser 30

CHAPTER 2
**WORKING WITH
GLASSFIBRE** 33
The tool box 33
Repairing damage 40
Moulding a storage box 42
Fastening wood to
laminate 44

CHAPTER 3
THE UNDERWATER HULL 45
Iron keels 46
Lead keels 47
Antifouling 48
Blistering 51

CHAPTER 4
THE HULL 53
Repairing damage to gel coat 54
Marking the waterline 55
Painting the boot top 57
Gel washing the bilge 57
Repainting the hull 58

CHAPTER 5
**DECK AND SUPER-
STRUCTURE** 61
Deck hardware survey 62
Stanchions and lifelines 63
Fastening heavy fittings to
sandwich 66
Fastening lighter fittings to
sandwich 67
Fastening light fittings to
sandwich 68
Fastening fittings to
laminate 69
Non-skid surfaces 70
Laying teak 71
Windows and portlights 74
The cockpit 76
Cockpit drainage 77

Cockpit gratings 78
Grabrails 80
Headlinings 82
Cabin insulation 84
Heating and ventilation 86
Plumbing 88
Gas installation 90

CHAPTER 6
RIGGING 91
Rigging tool kit 92
Rigging types 93
Masts and booms 94
Fastening fittings to alloy
spars 96
Rods and wires 99
Rigging screws and
toggles 100
Sail-handling systems 101
Setting up the mast 104
Sailing from the cockpit 107
Ropes and ropework 108

CHAPTER 7
SAILS 111
Sail cloth 111
Sail types 113
Maintaining sails 114
Emergency repairs 116

CHAPTER 8
ENGINES 117
The diesel 118
Diesel-engine fault
finding 121
The petrol engine 122
Petrol-engine fault
finding 128
Cooling 130
The exhaust 132
Air cleaner/flame trap 133
Engine ventilation 134
Lubrication 136
Rocker adjustment 136
Starter motors 137
Power transmission 138
Propellers 142
Engine beds 144
Engine noise 145
The outboard 146
Engine instruments 148

CHAPTER 9
ELECTRICS 149
Electrical circuits 150
Batteries 153
Expanding the electrical
system 157
Fault finding 159
Maintenance and care 160
Alternative charging
methods 162
Installing electronic
equipment 163

CHAPTER 10
**SAFETY AND
MAINTENANCE** 163
Firefighting 166
Liferafts 166
Lifejackets 167
Maintaining and repairing
deck equipment 169
Dinghies and inflatables 170
Winter lay-up 171
The boat ashore 172
Winterizing the boat 177
Spring overhaul 180
The woodwork 181
Leaks 181
Corrosion 183
Drastic engineering 185
Emergency repairs at
sea 186

INDEX 191

CHAPTER 1

The Glassfibre Boat

Molten glass has a very high degree of viscosity, and it is this characteristic that allows it to be drawn into the form of an exceptionally fine fibre (about one-sixth the diametre of a human hair) and which is the basis of all glassfibre woven or mat material. Because of glass's excellent tensile properties, it has also come to be used as a strengthening laminate in items made from synthetic resins. The plastic resin with which the glassfibre reinforcement is combined is usually polyester.

One of the earliest commercial applications of a glassfibre-reinforced laminate was the manufacture of radomes for military aircraft during the Second World War. The object was to produce a lightweight, streamlined, protective shield for the radar scanner. The resins used had to be heat-cured, however, and this made them susceptible to workshop conditions, which had to be strictly controlled. Almost invariably, items of this kind had to be pressure-moulded in matching metal moulds and then heat-cured. This type of tooling is expensive and only worth considering if the item is to be mass-produced.

Because of the shortage of traditional materials after the Second World War, the boatbuilding industry was one of the first to begin to produce large, yet relatively simple, mouldings. This became easier with the introduction of laminating resins that would cure at ambient temperatures and did not require pressure in the moulding process. This meant that much larger mouldings could be made and from relatively cheap glassfibre tooling.

Since those days, the plastics industry has refined and developed the production of glassfibre-reinforced plastics to a very high degree, and most modern sailing-boats and motorboats are made from this material—and not just hulls, but also superstructures.

A glassfibre hull is normally built up in a female mould which is first covered with a releasing agent, to make it possible to lift the finished hull from the mould. The releasing agent is coated with a thick layer of epoxy·resin, known as the gel coat, and then with successive layers of glassfibre and polyester resin.

Correctly engineered, glassfibre can produce structures that are light, exceptionally strong, and puncture-resistant.

GENERAL BUILDING METHODS

Laminate and sandwich construction are the two most common methods of building boats in glassfibre. On the following pages, we explain how hulls are built using these methods, so that the boat owner will get an idea of how his boat was built. This information is important, as many of the methods for repairing and improving the boat depend on the basic construction. Laminate hulls are by far the most common type, but these usually have decks and superstructures built by the sandwich method.

Laminate moulding

Contact moulding in a female mould is used first and foremost for moulding solid laminates, although the method can be used for producing the skin for a sandwich laminate. Laying-up the glassfibre by hand is the most commonly used production method. Contact moulding on male moulds functions, in principle, in the same way, differing only in details.

To keep things as simple as possible, we can describe laminate moulding in the following way. First, the mould is built (almost always a female mould) which is an exact copy of the hull plus its thickness. Great attention is paid to detail during the making of the mould, which must have an absolutely fair surface, as the hull's outer surface will be moulded against it. The mould is coated first with a releasing wax, so that when the laminate has cured, the hull can be released from the mould by applying pressure between the laminate and the mould. The gel coat is applied first (this forms the hull's almost waterproof outer armour and colour, so it is coloured as required). Then follows the lay-up of the various layers of glassfibre. Each layer is saturated with resin as it is laid-up, and this binds together the layers into a laminate that has a strength-to-weight ratio greater than that of steel. When the material has cured properly, the hull is removed from the mould.

The cost of building the mould is high, as the finish has to be exact, so this method is used for long production runs. The mould is laminated directly either on an existing hull, very often the prototype which has been used to test the design, or a temporary, cold-moulded wooden plug which is specially built for the purpose. If the finished boat is a commercial success, the plug will be kept

to produce a new mould when the first becomes too worn for use.

Sandwich construction

Glassfibre laminate can be given extra rigidity and additional buoyancy by means of sandwich construction, which is also known as core construction. An additional advantage over laminate hulls is that the sandwich hull is lighter. A core of foam plastic, balsa, plywood, honeycomb, or suchlike is contained between two "skins" of laminate. A male mould, made from wooden battens, is erected, and this type of mould is, of course, considerably cheaper than the mould required for laminating. The male mould produces the inside of the hull, so extra attention does not have to be paid to fairing the surface, etc. The low cost of the male mould makes this method ideal for one-off productions or for small series.

The sandwich core material, be it foam plastic, balsa, plywood, or honeycomb, is then applied, whereupon layers of the various glassfibre materials are laid-up and worked-out with resin. When the skin and core have cured and bonded together, the hull is taken off the mould, and a similar skin is applied to the interior of the hull.

Recently, some manufacturers have altered the order in which they build the skins and begin by laying-up the inner skin directly on the mould. Then follows the core material and finally the outer skin and gel coat, so that the entire hull is ready when it is lifted from the mould.

Glassfibre as a boatbuilding material

Even if its strength-to-weight ratio is high and it has many other advantages over more traditional boatbuilding materials, glassfibre laminate has a comparatively modest rigidity (resistance to bending). Therefore, glassfibre-laminate panels are usually stiffened by the use of stiffeners, such as longitudinal stringers.

Among fibreglass's other advantages are the fact that the same panel can be moulded in two different curvatures. Unlike wood, it is immune to marine borers, is resistant to weathering, abrasion and corrosion, is easy to maintain and repair, and can be easily coloured during manufacture.

Female mould
A typical female mould being laid-up
by hand.

Mould plug
A typical plug from which the female
mould is laminated. The plug must be
built with great exactitude in order to
produce the specifications of the hull.
The appearance of the final hull or
deck moulding depends entirely on the
standard of finish of the plug.

Male mould
A male mould for sandwich construction, built from timber and plywood or
hardboard. It is being covered with
foam sheets.

Bonding to the hull
The detail (*a*) shows how an internal
structural member (for example, a
bulkhead) is bonded to the hull shell.
Note how the edge of the member is
prevented from resting directly on the
inside of the hull (this would result in a
"hard spot"), by an intervening strip
of polyurethane foam or balsa. The
edges of the intervening strip are
bevelled, because this helps the bonding (in the form of strips of CSM) to
lie more snugly into the angle between
the structural member and the hull.

Internal stiffening
A longitudinal stringer (*b*) built over a
lightweight core is bonded internally to
the hull to provide stiffening.

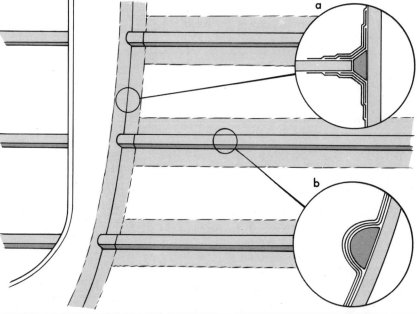

MATERIALS

Nowadays, boatbuilders have a wide choice of glassfibre matting and fabrics with which to build.

Polyester resins

Polyester laminating resins are easy to handle. A catalyst, or hardener, must be added in order to make the resin cure.

For maximum strength, the polyester resin MUST wet-out the glassfibre roving or mat as thoroughly as possible and then bond to each individual filament. In practice, it is very difficult to coat the entire surface of every filament with resin and to work out the air bubbles from every crevice. But if the resin does not bond securely to the surface of each and every filament, the strength of the laminate will be impaired.

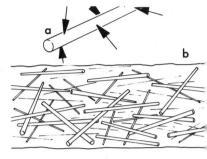

(a) Magnified view of single strand being wetted-out on all sides by the polyester resin.

(b) Magnified view of glassfibre cloth completely wetted-out.

Chopped strand mat (CSM)

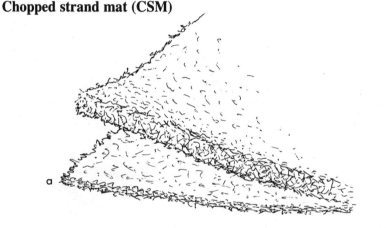

The most common type of reinforcement is chopped strand mat (CSM). It consists of strands of glass filaments chopped to about 35 mm (1½″) long and held in a random pattern by a binding agent of polyester-resin powder or polyvinyl acetate emulsion. Powder-based CSM is less sensitive to moisture and is to be preferred.

The material is supplied in rolls and weighs a known number of grammes per square metre.

A fine powder-bound surfacing tissue should always be used in conjunction with an isophthalic resin directly after the gel coat to separate this from the first substantial layer of

CSM. A laminate made up only of CSM does not possess particularly good directional qualities, so the surfacing tissue noticeably improves them.

(Right) The strands of CSM are shown strongly magnified. The surfacing tissue *(a)* prevents the strands from piercing the gel coat.

Woven roving

Woven roving is not as easy to wet-out with the resin as is CSM, but it produces a laminate which is much stronger, particularly when put in tension in the direction of the solid arrow. Its performance at right angles to the main run of rovings is less impressive, because there are fewer rovings running in this direction. To provide a satisfactory inter-layer bond, successive layers of woven roving must be laminated with intervening layers of CSM.

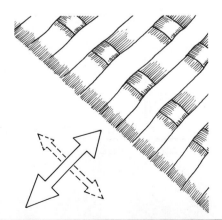

Glassfibre cloth

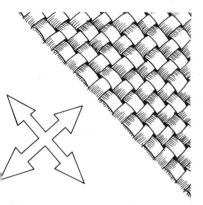

Combination material

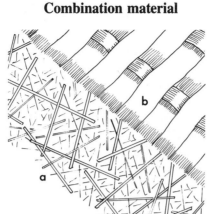

Unidirectional roving

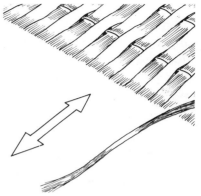

Glass cloth, or fabric, is tightly woven from strands of glassfibre. It provides good resistance to tensile loads in two directions at right angles to each other. Resistance to deformation on the bias is not good.

Cloth is not easy to wet-out because the strands are packed tightly together during the weaving process. As with woven roving, successive layers of glass cloth must have intervening layers of fine CSM surfacing tissue.

Combination material, consisting of a layer of CSM (a) bound to a layer of a directional material, such as woven roving (b), cuts down the time needed to laminate a hull. Modern combination materials wet-out well, but again, it is essential that all air bubbles are worked out during consolidation.

Unwoven unidirectional rovings, made up of long tows of glass filament, are available loosely stitched across the direction of the tow. The material is very strong and resists stretching in one direction only. It is useful for bonding along the inner face of hull-stiffening members.

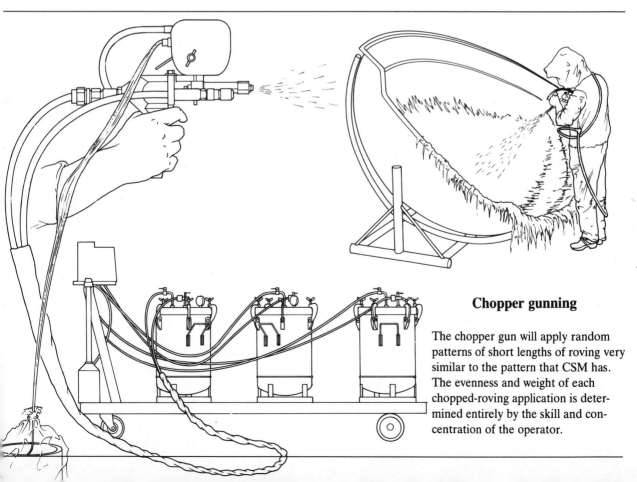

Chopper gunning

The chopper gun will apply random patterns of short lengths of roving very similar to the pattern that CSM has. The evenness and weight of each chopped-roving application is determined entirely by the skill and concentration of the operator.

LAMINATE MOULDING

Unfortunately, all polyester laminating resins are permeable, and, inevitably, the hull will take up water, usually very slowly. The first line of defense is the gel coat; this must be applied evenly and carefully, so that the formation of air bubbles is avoided. A layer of surface tissue is applied next to prevent the fibres of the first layer of CSM from penetrating the gel coat. It is essential that both resins and glass materials are free from impurities, as these can also lead to the problem of bubbles forming.

Almost all highly detailed mouldings feature some sharp corners. Accommodation-hatch slide guides are an example. If the builder does his job properly, he will lay a tow of unidirectional fibres right in the corners before the first lamination of CSM is applied.

Stiff short-bristled brushes are used when positioning a section of glassfibre cloth in an area that has been wetted with resin. A lamb's-wool roller is then employed as a first step to get the resin to wet-out the cloth. Both brush and roller are worked quickly to discourage aeration of the resin in the initial stages of the operation.

Once the material is thoroughly wetted-out, it is consolidated by the careful use of a metal-disc roller. This presses the filaments of the glassfibre against the preceding layer, improves the wetting-out and encourages trapped air bubbles to work their way up to the surface.

Woven rovings and glass cloth use more resin for a given area than does CSM, and the resin tends to pool at the crossover points between the strands. Care has to be taken to ensure that the air is expelled from these areas. Woven materials should not be used adjacent to the gel coat, because its pattern will "print through".

It is essential that all moulding operations are carried out under conditions of carefully controlled humidity and temperature. Variations in temperature will result in erratic curing. If the humidity rises much above 40 per cent, there is a chance that the moulding will achieve only a partial cure.

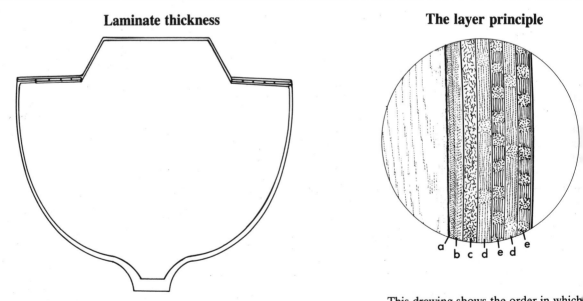

Laminate thickness

The layer principle

A typical mid-section showing how the lay-up is graduated so that the maximum thickness lies in the region of the centreline. The whole of the hull bottom, up to a height about 150 mm (6″) above the waterline, carries additional layers of glassfibre. The topsides above this are the thinnest part of the moulding (about 6 mm, or 1/4″).

This drawing shows the order in which the different glassfibre materials are laid against the gel coat. The layer of surfacing tissue is sometimes omitted, but this is not recommended.
(a) Mould surface.
(b) Gel coat.
(c) Surfacing tissue.
(d) Chopped strand mat (CSM).
(e) Glassfibre cloth.

Laying up the first layer

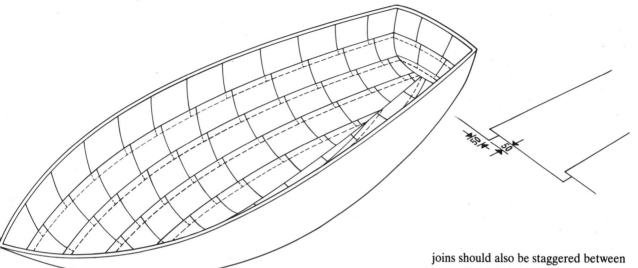

The female form in this picture has been prepared with releasing agent and a gel coat of about 25 micron has been applied. The first layer, of surfacing tissue, has been laid up in the mould. Note how the joins between the individual pieces have been staggered, so that there is little likelihood of there being any weak spot due to joins coinciding. For the same reason, joins should also be staggered between succeeding laminations.

The pieces of cloth and mat which form a laminate should be cut to fit the mould into which they will be placed, so that the laminator has a kit of pieces with which to work. When in position, they should overlap their neighbours slightly (see detail).

Deck mouldings

Because a deck has more detailed shapes than a hull, great care must be taken to ensure that the glassfibre laminations are thoroughly worked into tight corners to prevent the laminations from becoming air-rich. Sharp exterior angles encourage the glassfibre to pull away from the area immediately in the vicinity of such a feature. Wherever possible, mould details should be finished with large radii.

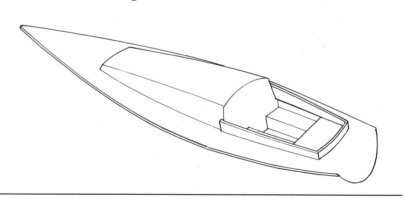

SANDWICH CONSTRUCTION

Sandwich construction is both strong and easy to achieve, but it is important to carry out the process accurately to ensure that delamination between the outer glassfibre skins and the core material does not occur. Should it do so, the strength of the structure will be severely diminished. Sandwich construction is an economical method to use for the construction of one-off hulls and decks. It is too slow and too labour-intensive to be a useful application for series or mass production.

For a given area, a glassfibre sandwich can provide excellent panel stiffness for a low structural weight. The stiffness of a cored panel is a function of the cube of the total thickness of the sandwich. In other words, a panel with a thickness of 20 mm will be eight times as stiff as a panel just half the thickness (10 mm):

$$\frac{20^3}{10^3} = \frac{8000}{1000} = 8$$

The function of core material is to hold the skins of the sandwich a prescribed distance apart. The skins themselves must be able to resist puncturing. Apart from this, they must be able to accept both compressive and tensile loads without failure or distortion.

A good material for a sandwich core must be light and be capable of being bonded firmly to the inside of the load-bearing, surface skins, without fear of delamination occurring under load. It is also imperative that the core material does not disintegrate within itself when panels are subjected to shock loadings or, inevitably, some distortion. Core material is cellular. It is essential that unicellular substances are used so that, if one of the skins is ruptured, water is prevented from saturating the core material, which is what would happen if the cells were interconnected.

Airex is a polyvinyl, unicellular core material, supplied in sheet form, which has been used in sandwich constructions for many years. It bonds well to glassfibre laminates and has the property of being capable of being bent around relatively tight radii without being substantially reduced in thickness. In order that it can be used in double-curved panels or worked around really tight radii, the material may be supplied with a "grid" deeply incised on one side—this being the side to lie adjacent to the concave side of the panel.

Nomex is the trade name for an aramid, honeycomb core material which has been used with varying degrees of success in high-performance racing yachts. It is compatible with glassfibre laminates but, because only the edges of the honeycomb come into contact with the surface skins, the total area of adhesion is low and it is essential that bonding is most conscientiously carried out. Large, flat panel areas must receive additional stiffening to prevent deformation of the cellular structure, which might lead to core failure.

End-grain balsa is sometimes used for the core of sandwich constructions laid up over a male mould, but more usually it is used in the construction of decks—and sometimes hulls—laid up within a female mould. End-grain balsa is supplied in sheet form and consists of small blocks which are attached on one side only to a fine mesh, the purpose of which is to hold the material together temporarily while it is being handled. The most common thickness used is 13 mm (½").

Boards of unicellular, polyurethane foam are the most common material employed in one-off, sandwich construction. Judicious use of a hot-air gun can be employed to give the material some double curvature when it is being fitted over strongly shaped parts of the hull or deck. The material bonds well to glassfibre and is resistant to degradation, should a panel pant unduly. The material is easily cut to shape and subsequently faired.

Glassfibre sandwich construction

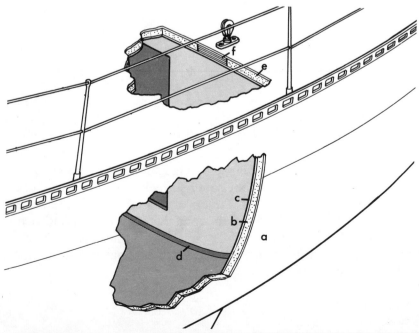

Sandwich construction consists of a lightweight core material "sandwiched" between thin skins of laminate. Although the skins are thinner than the single-skin laminated construction described on the previous pages, the overall hull is thicker, stiffer, and often lighter.
(*a*) Outer skin comprising gel coat, surfacing tissue, and laminates.
(*b*) The core material. It can be bonded to the skins by the laminating resin or by a suitable adhesive.
(*c*) Inner skin.
(*d*) Frames. These are moulded to the inner skin.
(*e*) The deck is also a sandwich construction.
(*f*) The sandwich core is reinforced in areas where fittings will be fastened (see page 66).

Polyurethane closed-cell board is the most satisfactory core material for sandwich hulls when it is important to achieve a fair finish on the exterior with the minimum of effort. The foam can be applied to the mould in any convenient shape and area, commensurate with ease of handling and speed of construction. Long, flexible fairing boards surfaced with coarse garnet paper may then be employed to give the exterior of the core a fair surface upon which to lay the exterior sandwich skin. Detail shapes can be carved and sanded quickly to shape before being cemented to the main surface of the core with polyester paste.

A selection of fairing boards is used to get the required finish. In strongly convex areas, flexible boards of, say, 700 mm × 100 mm × 3 mm (24″ × 4″ × ⅛″) are used. In flatter areas, which are always difficult to fair, stiffer boards about 8 mm (⅜″) thick are used. Small sanding blocks are only used for small details. A *fair* finish on the core surface is needed, not just a *smooth* and maybe undulating surface.

Before the first layer of CSM is applied, it may be necessary to fill shallow depressions with a polyester filler paste made up from resin and microballoons. This produces a cured material similar in hardness to the sandwich foam, so the two materials fair well together. A strong, beamed light, such as a flashlight, held close to the faired surface of the filled foam will give a good indication of where hollows and bumps exist.

After the initial layer of CSM has been applied, the remainder of the laminate for the outside of the sandwich is completed—this will almost certainly consist of layers of combination mat or woven roving interspersed with CSM. The outside is finished by first sanding fair and then covering with a *thin* skin of polyester filler paste. By this stage, it is important that only minor imperfections remain or too thick a build-up of paste will be required in places. It is easier to fair the hull while it is upside down and before it is removed from the building mould. The hull is then turned up the right way ready to receive the inside skin of the sandwich.

The sandwich core

A section of sandwich construction, showing the core (*a*) between the two outer skins (*b*). Good adhesion is essential between skin and core, and the skins must be puncture resistant.

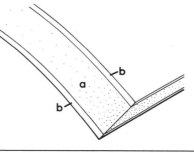

End-grain balsa

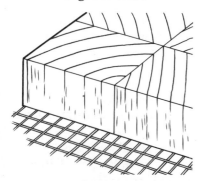

A good insulator for both sound and heat, end-grain balsa is, however, relatively heavy, and it can absorb too much resin during bonding, because it is rather porous. Its low cost makes it popular. Usually, it is delivered attached to a fine glassfibre mesh.

Foam core material

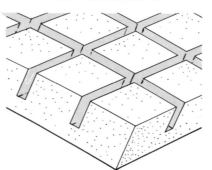

Polyvinyl, unicellular core material is often scored with a deep grid pattern on one side, to make it easier to form it against curved areas. The bonding resin, filling the scores, will inevitably increase the weight of the sandwich. A hot-air gun can be used to shape the curves.

Honeycomb core material

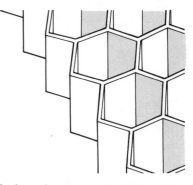

The latest in core material, this can be made from glass, carbon or nylon fibres, from light-metal alloys, and even from cardboard, kraft paper or aramid paper. The adhesive which bonds the skin to the core must work its way a little up each cell wall, to ensure an adequate bond.

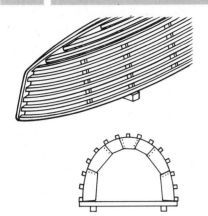

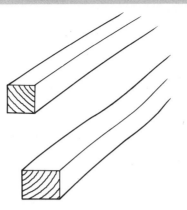

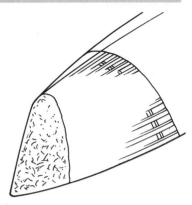

A simple, spaced-battened mould is all that is required to produce a satisfactory former for either a hull or a deck. The battened mould, or former, is a male shape whose dimensions take into account the thickness of the sandwich to be laid over it. It is important to fair the mould to a good standard before skinning it with the core material, or too much fairing will have to be done.

It is good practice to use square-section battens to cover the mould longitudinally, as these will take up a compound bend more accurately than will battens of rectangular section. In the interests of fairness, it is worthwhile using as clear timber as possible for the battens. The clearest pieces are used for the most strongly shaped areas and for the sheer batten.

Should a batten run incorporate a join, the join should be scarfed so that the full run remains fair.

The male mould partly covered with the core material. When finished, the surface will be faired.

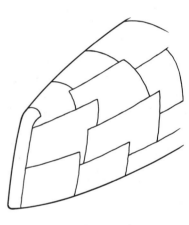

The outer skin is laid-up as usual. The outside is sanded fair and grounded with a thin coat of polyester paste.

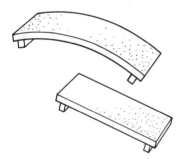

Fairing boards, covered with coarse garnet paper, are used to fair the core material before the outer skin can be applied.

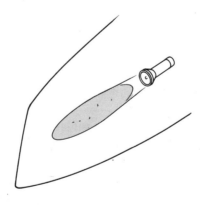

(*left*) Lighting the sides with a flashlight shows up any unfairness on the surface.

The sandwich material is held tightly to the male mould of either hull or deck in such a way that the workpiece can be removed and turned over prior to the inside of the core being smoothed off and the back-up laminate being applied. It is essential that the hull or deck is well-supported and held true so that no distortion is "built in" when the back-up laminate is applied.

The internal laminate "balances" the laminate that was laid-up on the outside of the sandwich. As the performance of the sandwich depends upon the skins being correctly matched and on the integrity of the sandwich remaining intact, it will be realized that just as much care must be taken when laying down the back-up laminate as when working on the exterior surface.

For the very best finish, final fairing is left until hull and deck have been assembled and all internal stiffening and bulkheads have been installed. Again, a lamp shining close along the surface shows up any unfairness. Work must be done quickly and accurately. If the fairing process is carried out over too long a period, there is the likelihood of the section already faired losing something of its excellence before the job is finished.

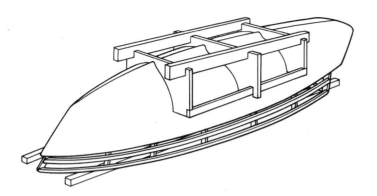

Before the hull is turned over, a receiving cradle has to be fitted over. The hull and cradle are then lifted off, and the hull is placed right side up.

The bulkheads and stringers are now installed.

The deck, which has usually been laid up as a separate unit, is now lifted into position and the two parts are bonded.

Finally, the boat is given a surface coat of gel.

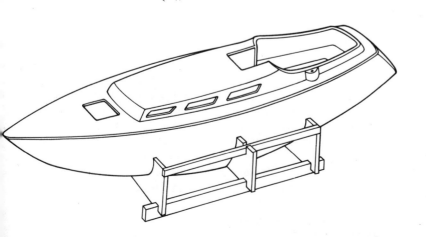

REINFORCEMENTS

It is often necessary to increase the strength of a laminate locally, so that it is more resistant to tensile and compressive loads as well as more resistant to impact loads—such as occur when the hull is bumped against a corner of the jetty. This is not quite the same as simply increasing the stiffness of the laminate where the object is to reduce deformation.

Where it is known that a laminate must accept high tensile loads in a particular direction, then it is possible to reinforce it by laying down a section of unidirectional rovings with the rovings aligned in the direction of the greatest expected loads. Because a yacht is subjected to hydrostatic, hydrodynamic, and rigging loads, its structure is subjected to infinitely variable stresses, so no basic structural laminate should consist solely of unidirectional rovings.

In many high-performance yachts and in a number of performance-oriented production yachts, the tough, aramid fibre (marketed under the trade name of Kevlar) is finding increasing favour. Kev-

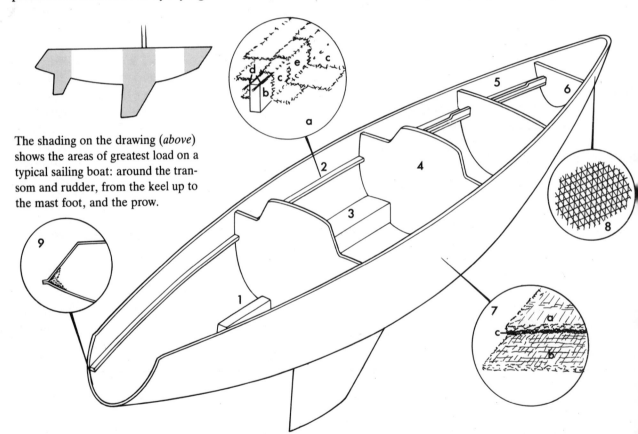

The shading on the drawing (*above*) shows the areas of greatest load on a typical sailing boat: around the transom and rudder, from the keel up to the mast foot, and the prow.

The big drawing shows the various parts of the glassfibre construction that have a stiffening effect on the structure.
1. Engine bed.
2. Longitudinal stringer.
(*a*) Hull.
(*b*) Foam.
(*c*) Glassfibre cloth.
(*d*) Tow of unidirectional fibres.
(*e*) CSM.

3. Berth.
4. Bulkhead.
5. Shelving.
6. Bulkhead for anchor box.
7. Local reinforcements built up of several layers of glassfibre cloth (*a*) and woven roving (*b*). These must be interspersed with CSM (*c*) to make a good bond. Note that the corners of reinforcing patches are always rounded before application, preventing the build-up of localized stress.

8. A combination glassfibre cloth, with tri-directional rovings, spreads forces evenly, thus reducing stress on an area that needs heavy reinforcement.
9. A well-built boat will have reinforcing glassfibre laminate covering the join between panels that are at an angle to each other, such as where the transom meets the shell of the hull.

lar is only 58 per cent of the density of glass. The material must be worked very carefully to ensure thorough wetting-out. Kevlar cloth requires special shears when cutting and trimming.

A build-up of several layers of woven rovings or cloth may be required when creating a local reinforcement. In order that these materials are securely bonded together, it is essential that they are interspersed with CSM to improve the bond performance.

When applying reinforcement to a basic laminate, it is essential to have a clear idea of the forces that are acting in the area. Localized stresses build up at the corners of reinforcing patches, so these are rounded off to relieve the stress. The edges of any reinforcement are securely bonded to the base laminate to discourage delamination.

Where more than one layer of woven roving or glass cloth is added, make sure that the layers are staggered—the smallest piece being overlaid by increasingly large pieces—so that the change of thickness of laminate is made gradually to avoid the creation of a sudden change in inertia of the laminate at the edge of the reinforcement.

Rigging and mast loads create a complex pattern of loads when the yacht is sailing in rough water. These are greatest in the region of the mast(s) position and the attachment points of the standing rigging. Directional reinforcement should be used. A combination material with directional rovings aligned in three ways is available, and this makes for a reinforcement which has good directional stability and resistance to stress all round.

Where what are essentially large panel areas are joined at a sharp corner—the corners on cockpit coamings or where the transom meets the shell—the bending stresses in the corner may be very high. A small amount of reinforcement along the angle between the panels will reduce distortion at the corner itself and prevent undue flexing and gel-coat cracking.

It happens that local reinforcement has to be applied after the base laminate has cured. Invariably, this will occur when a repair is being effected. Fresh resin will not form a chemical bond with resin which has long since cured. It is, therefore, of the greatest importance to create as effective a *mechanical* bond as possible. The area to be covered by reinforcement must be abraded thoroughly by coarse (80 grit) garnet paper.

Fitting a bulkhead

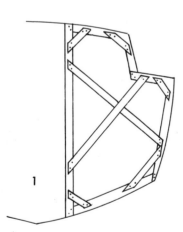

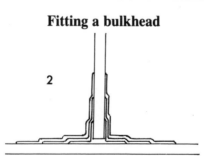

2. On small craft, up to 7 m (20 ft) or so, the bulkheads can be fitted directly to within 15 mm (⅝″), but they must not be a tight fit.

Bulkheads are a main structural reference point within any craft. They must be perfectly plumb and square, so you must begin by ensuring that the boat is perfectly upright and level.
1. Make a template of the exact shape required. This can be made first in cardboard and then the shape can be transferred to a proper template, built from battens and thin hardboard.

3. On larger craft, the bulkhead (*a*) is prevented from resting directly on the inside of the hull (*b*) by an intervening strip of polyurethane foam (*c*). Bevelling the edges of the foam strip helps the bonding to fit snugly in the angle between the bulkhead and the hull. The polyurethane strip helps to distribute the loads, thus preventing hard spots.

Heavily score the hull surface and the bulkhead where the glassfibre laminate is to bond with it. Use the coarsest abrasive paper.

Drill some holes through the bottom of the bulkhead to allow the resin to seep through. If the bulkhead is plywood, strip it of a layer of laminate in the fastening area, to increase adhesion.

Prime the area with a slightly over-catalyzed coat of resin.

Laminate in the normal way, increasing the width of each lamination.

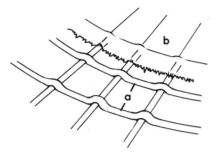

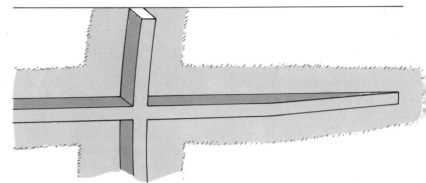

Where low weight and stiffness are paramount and cost is of secondary importance, a grid of carbon-fibre tows (a) may be incorporated on the inside of the panel and then overlaid with CSM (b) to lock it in position. It is essential that this work is very carefully carried out. Should the bond between the grid and the laminate break down, panel stiffness will be seriously degraded.

Where it is unavoidable that a stiffening member terminates inside a panel area, it is essential that the end of the stiffener is reduced gradually until it tapers into the back of the panel. This will ensure that point loading is reduced to a minimum. Wherever possible, extend stiffening members to meet with similar features running across their path.

When siting shell-stiffening members, it must be remembered that they all produce some degree of hard spot. On the whole, longitudinal stiffening members create less of a hard spot than do transverse members.

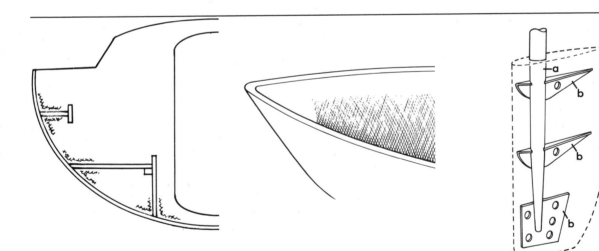

Some hulls are of monocoque construction—all the required stiffness is included in the hull shell. The alternative is to provide the required stiffening by careful siting and bonding in of such features as bulkheads, berth fronts, berthtop margins, and shelves against the topsides. The stiffness and strength of the resultant structure depends directly upon the standard of workmanship.

It is possible to build in inherent stiffness by giving panel areas some double curvature. It is the flat panel areas (shaded in the illustration), such as the bows of an IOR hull, that require additional support. In these areas it may well be an advantage to combine a cored laminate with additional stiffening on the inside.

Some items, such as spade rudder blades, may be very highly stressed from time to time. They must be both strong and very stiff. These characteristics are reinforced by fitting the rudder with an adequately strong rudder stock (a) to which are welded spurs (b) which transfer the torque of the stock over the entire blade area while, at the same time, providing additional stiffening.

JOININGS

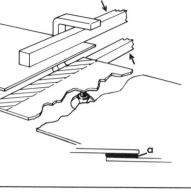

Two pieces of glassfibre laminate can be joined in a number of ways.
1. Here, the mating faces of two mouldings are cemented together using a neoprene rubber adhesive (*a*) with slight pressure being applied to the join by a straight, stout batten cramped to each side. In order to improve the performance of the bond, the glassfibre on both sides of the join (shaded in the drawing) should be abraded thoroughly with 80-grade garnet paper.

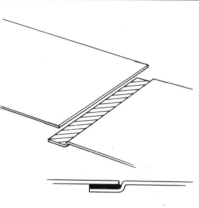

2. In order to make a good location in the region of a lap join, one section of laminate may be shaped with a land which not only helps to register the join in the correct alignment, but also allows a level surface to be presented. If possible, use battens and cramps to close the join. Excessive pressure is never used, or the adhesive will be squeezed out of the join to the extent that its performance is seriously diminished.

It is not always possible to use battens and cramps to close a join. In this case, it may be necessary to use mechanical fastenings such as stainless-steel self-tapping screws or, maybe, short stainless steel machine screws. Both improve the security of the join, but machine screws are the better choice. The fastenings along each side of the lap must be staggered, as shown, and not over-tightened.

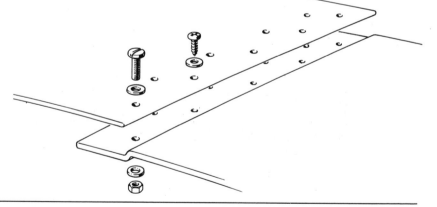

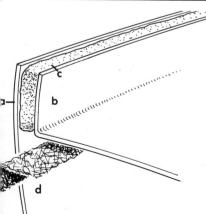

One of the most important joins between two mouldings is that between hull and deck. Here, the top of the hull shell (*a*) and the edge of the deck (*b*) have been shaped to form a low rail. The space between the two mouldings is filled with polyester paste (*c*). When excess paste has been cleaned away, the underside of the join must be glassed across with CSM (*d*), and the top of the rail will have to be capped. The fastening of the rail must be taken down into pads of solid timber embedded in the polyester paste.

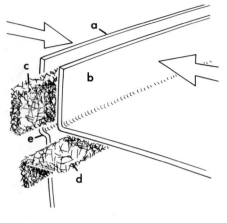

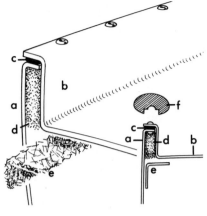

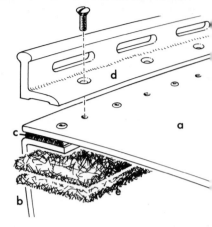

This join of hull (*a*) to deck (*b*) calls for closer alignment between the mouldings than that already shown. Wet CSM (*c*) is packed in the join, and the upstand that will form the rail is cramped together. CSM is applied as a bandage (*d*) to the underside of the join. Note how initial assembly may be assisted by allowing the deck and side to register in a land (*e*) moulded in the hull.

An alternative way of forming a rail and joining the hull (*a*) to the deck (*b*). This is the easiest join to assemble. Either pop rivets or short machine screws may be used to make the initial join, with neoprene-rubber adhesive (*c*) providing the watertight integrity. Polyurethane foam (*d*) fills out, and a CSM bandage (*e*) is applied to the underside of the join. A wooden or plastic rail cap (*f*) completes the job.

Probably one of the most common and strongest joins between hull and deck, this method is popular with builders of high-volume production yachts. Deck (*a*) and hull (*b*) are pop-riveted together with neoprene-rubber sealant (*c*) in the join. The slotted aluminium-alloy toe rail (*d*) is then bolted or machine-screwed in place, the excess thread cropped, and the inside of the join bonded with a bandage of CSM (*e*).

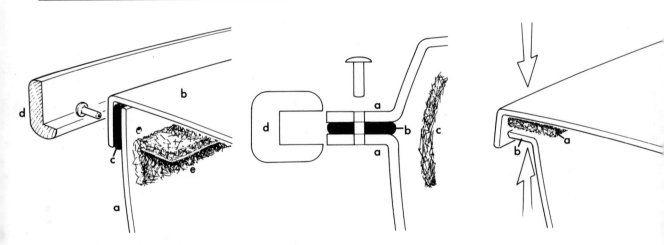

The "tin lid" join in which the hull (*a*) is sheered down correctly and then the deck (*b*) is registered over. Neoprene sealant (*c*) is paid into the join, and then the two mouldings are pop-riveted or machine-screwed together. Finally, a timber rub-rail (*d*) may be attached by through bolts which intersperse with the initial fastenings. Watertight integrity is assured by glassing over the inside of the join with CSM (*e*).

A hull/deck join may be effected using two out-turned flanges (*a*) which are pop-riveted together with sealant (*b*) between. The inside of the join is then glassed over with CSM (*c*), and a neoprene-rubber 'C' section extrusion (*d*) heated and stretched around the cleaned-up flange to form an effective rubbing band.

A variation of the "tin lid" join that is often employed during the assembly of small dinghies. Wet CSM or polyester paste (*a*) is placed upon the trimmed hull flange (*b*) before the join is made. It is easy to use cramps and battens to apply suitable pressure during assembly. The resulting join is strong and the trimmed edge of the deck moulding forms an effective lip which facilitates lifting.

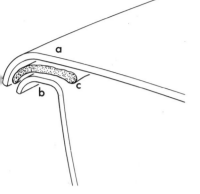

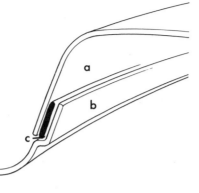

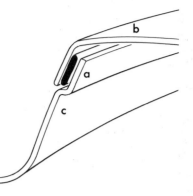

Here the edge of the deck (*a*) and the outboard edge of the hull flange (*b*) have been rolled to mating curves. This produces a greater area for adhesion (which makes the join stronger) and a more pleasant finish than above. The edge of the lip is also better able to withstand wear and tear. (*c*) Polyester paste.

In yachts where a selection of cabin tops may be available, it may be possible to retain a standard deck and change just the coachroof and cabin trunk (*a*). One way of achieving this is to mould the deck with a rebated upstand (*b*) into which the trimmed bottom edge of the cabin trunk fits. The cabin top is usually fitted at a late stage in assembly, so that easy access to the inside of the boat during assembly is allowed for as long as possible. (*c*) Neoprene rubber sealant.

Here the upstand (*a*) illustrated in the previous picture is continued up to the underside of the coachroof (*b*) itself, the cabin trunk (*c*) being moulded as an integral part of the deck. This is not so versatile a system, but it may be employed if it is ever necessary to open up the yacht so that a large piece of machinery can be replaced.

Another form of the "tin lid" join. Here, the land (*a*) is featured in the deck moulding (*b*) and it allows the deck (*c*) to be conveniently aligned over the hull (*d*) when the latter has been taken down to the correct sheer line. A neoprene rubber sealant (*e*) is laid into the join before the two mouldings are pop riveted together. A timber or aluminium extrusion rub rail (*f*) is then through-fastened through the join, and a CSM bandage (*g*) is applied over the inside of the join to complete the job.

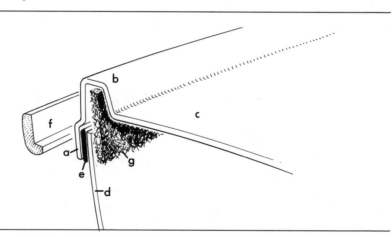

Minor bulkheads (*a*) may be of glassfibre, and the edge (*b*) is often flanged in the interests of rigidity and a correct fit. These features are glassed in using overlapping layers of CSM (*c*). This process may also be employed when bonding in the margins of modular items such as head compartments and galley units.

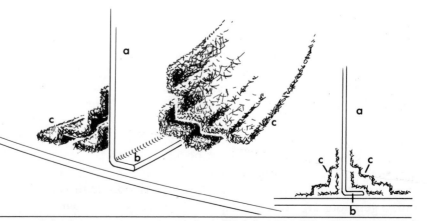

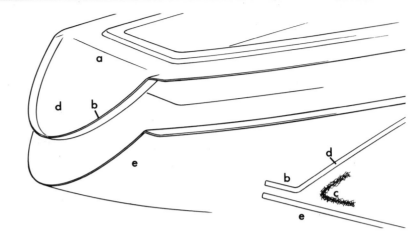

Most modern hulls with retroussé transoms are moulded with the transom integral with the hull. Several, however, have the deck and transom moulded as one unit (*a*), and the join with the hull is usually typified by an outturned flange (*b*). The inside of the join must be bandaged securely using CSM (*c*). The raw edge of the outturned flange is trimmed and coated with gel coat to prevent water soaking into the edge of the laminate. (*d*) Transom. (*e*) Hull.

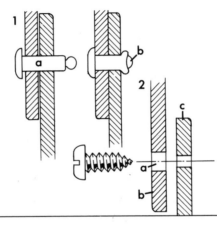

1. Where pop rivets are used to pull a join together, it is essential that the body (*a*) of the rivet is long enough to pass right through the join, so that the two pieces can be pulled together by the rivet as the mandrel (*b*) bells it out. The hole to take the rivet must be snug. Slackness allows the tail of the rivet to open inside the second laminate. Mechanical security is impaired and the expanding tail may crack the resin around the hole.

2. Where self-tapping fastenings are used, it is essential that a clear hole (*a*) is made in the first laminate (*b*) through which the fastening passes. It grips by cutting its own thread in the second laminate (*c*). Make sure that the smaller hole drilled in this laminate is not so small that the actual body of the fastening tries to burst through the laminate as it is pulled in by the thread. Use a drop of grease to ease the cutting action of the thread.

BUILT-IN REINFORCEMENTS

Where a permanent fitting, such as a chain plate, is subjected to a lot of stress, it must be bedded in the hull in such a way that the load is spread over a wide area. Because glassfibre is a fairly brittle material, it will not, once it has cured, adapt to the distortioning forces that arise from stress. Therefore, it is usual to mould stress-spreading reinforcements, such as metal plates or hardwood pads, into the hull and deck at lay-up stage. If the area of the stress-distributing reinforcement is too small, cracking will appear, and this will eventually lead to hull damage, leakage, and if the worst comes to the worst, a serious problem while at sea in heavy weather.

Where fittings such as cleats, sheet blocks, winches, genoa tracks, etc. are to be fitted to a sandwich-construction deck, it is essential that the foam-core material is omitted and the space filled with a generous area of marine-grade plywood of suitable thickness. This will take the required fastenings without the sandwich construction being crushed and will also spread the loads transmitted by the fittings when in use. Some core pads may be fitted direct to the building mould, so that they are incorporated while the foam core of the sandwich is being laid-up. More often, however, it will be found that the job is easier to keep fair if an area of foam somewhat larger than that of the intended support pad is removed when the deck has been taken off its building mould, and the plywood support pad bedded in its place on polyester paste. When all the pads are bedded in, the inner skin is applied.

Hull reinforcement
Some details on a hull need to be reinforced with extra layers of CSM matting. These are laid-up as shown on page 18.

Deck fittings

All deck and superstructure fittings, such as stanchions, cleats, winches, fairleads, and handrails, must also be well supported from within by load-distributing pads or plates of hardwood, aluminium, stainless steel or solid fibreglass laminate. These plates are laminated into the hull or deck during lay-up.

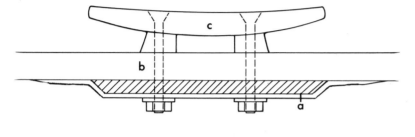

Here we see a reinforcing plate *(a)* laminated into the deck *(b)*, so that the stress from a through-bolted cleat *(c)* will be distributed over a large area of the deck. On pages 66–67, we show how repairs to glassfibre sandwich that has been damaged due to the fact that not enough reinforcement was available can be carried out.

BUILT-IN FASTENINGS

Forestay fastenings

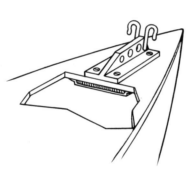

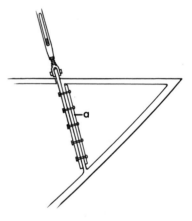

This forestay fastening is a through-hull fitting, with a stainless-steel plate on the outside of the hull, through-bolted to a forged plate in which there is a sturdy holding ring.

A forestay fastening through-bolted to a sandwich deck. Note the sturdy backing pad that was laminated into the deck during construction.

Here we see a common method of securing the forestay. It is fastened to a stainless-steel plate that in its turn is through-bolted to the anchor-box bulkhead *(a)*.

Chain-plate fastening

(Left) Extra-strong chain-plate fastening, secured both on deck and to a longitudinal stringer.
(Centre) A chain-plate fastening that consists of plywood moulded in glassfibre and then laminated to the hull during lay-up.
(Far right) This chain-plate fastening is bolted to the topside *(a)* through a large backing pad *(b)*. Note how the above-deck part of the fastening is angled to be in line with the rigging.

BOAT SURVEY: THE RACER-CRUISER

The standard sailing-boat can be improved in literally hundreds of ways. There are plenty of ideas around, not to mention a wealth of extra equipment, that will improve performance and make the boat safer, more comfortable, and simpler to handle. Many of the measures that the boat owner may take will usually improve the boat's appearance, too, as well as give it that personal touch which identifies the boat even more with its skipper.

This survey presents just a few of the measures that can be taken to improve, maintain, and repair your boat, but it will probably help you to think out new measures that will make the boat even more suitable to your needs and your kind of sailing.

Later in the book, we will show how you can carry out many of the suggestions.

Fitting out and improvements

1. A terylene net, attached between the lifelines, prevents a headsail from going overboard, when you are changing headsails, especially if you are shorthanded (see page 65).

2. Two or three lengths of shock-cord on each side, fitted with simple, plastic carbine hooks, are handy for temporarily stowing a headsail that is being changed (see page 65).

3. If the deck's non-skid surfacing is worn or in otherwise poor condition, it must be exchanged for non-skid material with a sturdy pattern (see page 70).
   On hatch covers of acrylic glass or similar slippery surfaces, anti-skid strips can be glued on (see page 71).

4. A safety line stretched along the cabin roof or across the top of the deck, from the cockpit to the beginning of the foredeck, is an extra safety measure—you don't need to unhook your safety line to make your way forward.

5. Hauling halyards and control lines from the cockpit also increases safety and makes it easier to trim the boat when you are short on crew. Using a number of stoppers means that you don't require several expensive winches (see page 107).

6. Stowage bags of sailcloth for the stowing of halyards and control-line ends mean a neat and ordered cockpit and allow instant action and function (see page 81).

7. Give your boat an individual look by adding a new waterline or boot top (see page 57), or by adding a name plate or symbol.

8. An extra winch for the spinnaker sheet is necessary, and it can also double as a winch for the genoa sheet, if you are sailing alone. The deck must be strongly reinforced where the winch is fastened (see page 69). This winch is difficult to fit without a jointed socket spanner (wrench) and a lot of patience.

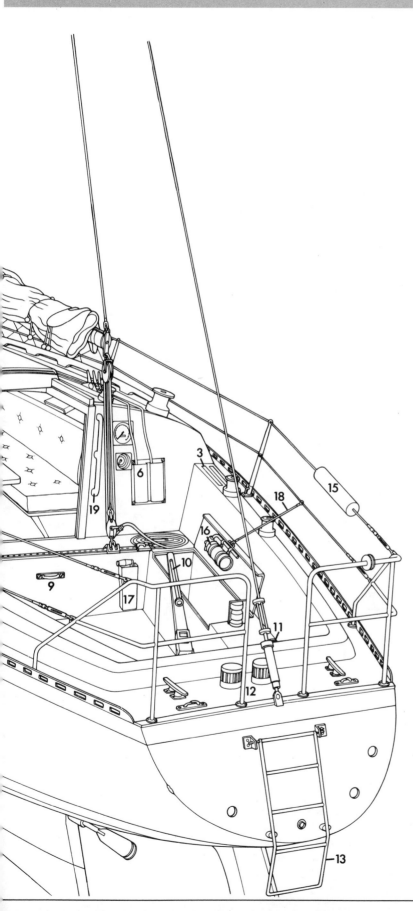

9. A stainless-steel eyebolt for fastening one end of the crew's safety line. Another one is necessary at the aft of the cockpit, for the helmsman. Fit these as low as possible with through bolting.

10. If your boat is equipped with a tiller, it can be fitted with an extension for more comfortable handling.

11. Drainage holes in the cockpit seats (see page 77). These need a drainage pipe or tube to the bottom of the cockpit or through a skin fitting in the hull, if there is enough fall.

12. An extra air intake for the engine. Often, standard boats are not equipped with a big enough air intake.

13. A fold-down rescue/bathing ladder which should be held with a rope from the pushpit which can be reached from the water and from the cockpit.

14. A stemhead roller for the anchor rope spares your back and prevents chafing.

15. A fender fitted over the lifeline enables the helmsman to sit comfortably, leaning against the lifeline with the fender under his armpit, when you are sitting in the lee (see page 65).

16. A good place for the fire extinguisher: out of the way but still near at hand in an emergency.

17. Winch handle box, made from soft plastic.

18. A cord with a plastic carbine hook in the end can be fastened to the locker lid, so that it can be held open when the hook is attached to a lifeline.

19. An extra grabrail on either side of the companionway and preferably on both the inside and the outside (see page 80). This makes cabin and deck access easier and safer.

Maintenance

These measures are numbered in squares on the illustration. Maintenance of your boat is covered on pages 167–183 and is an important part of boat owning, not only because regular maintenance keeps a boat's outside, inside, and equipment shipshape and looking good, but also because maintenance prevents problems occurring or, once occurred, becoming worse.

1. Examine the aluminium extrusions on masts and booms regularly for corrosion. Rinse booms and masts thoroughly with fresh water, before laying them up for the winter. Oil all the stainless-steel details with paraffin oil. Change any corroding screws, bolts, or fittings.

2. Watch out for broken wire strands and for corrosion on standing and running rigging wires. Don't wait for something to give while you're sailing, but change faulty wiring in good time.

3. Sail seams must be checked regularly. If you find any stitches that have worked loose or broken, fix them immediately. The same goes for small holes in the sail cloth. These must be patched immediately (see page 116).

4. Keep the gel coat clean. Don't allow dirt, oil, and so on to become engrained in the gel coat. In waters which are particularly dirty or which otherwise attack the gel coat, the hull sides need to be cleaned and wax-polished several times each season.

5. Watch out for any indications of blistering, especially at and just under the water line. Don't allow wet ropes and anchor chains to lie in their boxes directly against the inside of the hull.

6. Oil and/or soot on the transom indicates poor sealing in the cylinder block or wrong setting of the diesel engine's injection system. Get a professional mechanic to look at the engine, but clean off the soot marks immediately before the chemicals in the soot etch themselves into the gel coat. Chromium polish often does the trick.

7. If the hull has an external ballast keel, the join between the glassfibre hull and the keel should be sealed with a sealant that can be painted over. This prevents water from forcing its way into the glassfibre.

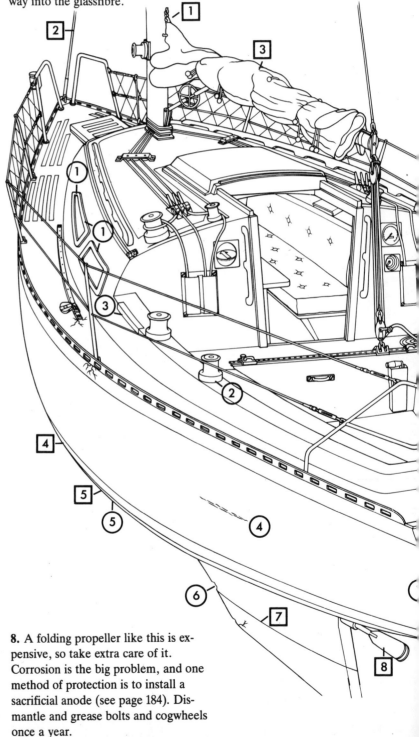

8. A folding propeller like this is expensive, so take extra care of it. Corrosion is the big problem, and one method of protection is to install a sacrificial anode (see page 184). Dismantle and grease bolts and cogwheels once a year.

Damage, leaks, and repairs

Glassfibre is a tough material but if it is repeatedly exposed to stress and wear-and-tear, there will be scratches, cracks, contusions, as well as dulling and crackling of the gel coat. A new boat should always be examined closely from this point of view. Try to establish the boat's weak points and take preventive measures before it is too late. These measures are numbered in circles on the illustration.

The materials from which the glassfibre boat is made are flexible. The hull moves under pressure from the waves and fittings under stress from sheets, etc. Some inferior sealant materials may dry out after a time, which leads to leaking.

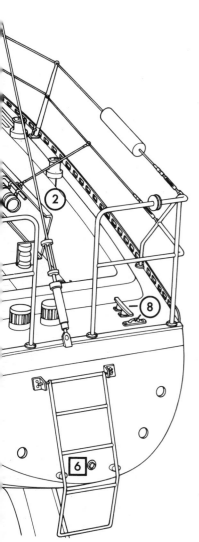

1. Window frames often spring leaks. The only way to seal them again effectively is to remove the whole window and frame and to apply a new sealant (see page 75). Don't harden the screws down too tightly when you mount the frame in position again. Acrylic glass splits easily and stress cracks can also appear in the glassfibre.

2. Stress cracks easily occur around the base of fittings which are subjected to too much stress or which have been mounted with screws with a diametre greater than the holes drilled in the glassfibre. Strengthen the fastening area with a reinforcing plate (see pages 66–69), as soon as signs of stress cracks appear, or do it before, if you suspect that there is any danger of stress cracks occurring just there.

3. A genoa sheet that lies against a glassfibre coaming between the winch and a fairlead soon chafes through the gel coat. Fit a protective covering of aluminium or stainless steel (see page 62).

4. Minor scratches can be wax-polished; deeper ones must be sanded, cleaned, and filled with gel coat (see page 54).

5. Blistering at or below the waterline should always be attended to as soon as it is discovered. Puncture the blisters, sand down, allow to dry properly, and treat, as suggested on pages 51–52.

6. Underwater damage from grounding. Your boat's speed depends very much on a smooth underwater surface. Contusions resulting from this kind of damage allow water to seep into the laminate. Damage to an iron keel can quickly lead to rust. Always take the boat up directly after such an incident and repair the damage.

7. The bow and the join-line (usually sharp-angled) between the hull and the transom are particularly liable to damage from running into jetties and suchlike.

8. Examine each fitting and its fastening—especially those that will be the subject of a lot of stress. Change or re-fasten with better reinforcement plates underneath (see pages 66–69).

BOAT SURVEY: THE MOTOR CRUISER

Although doing a proper survey of a motor cruiser is a job for the expert, you will find, as a boat owner, that it pays to keep a constant check on your boat's condition. Inspect the engine before you go out to sea and, more important, when you return, looking especially for leaks. Keep an eye on all the fittings and fixtures on the boat—leaks, wear-and-tear, and cracking are clues that will indicate that something is going wrong. It is important to catch things before they get serious and go wrong out at sea, which could land you in big trouble and with expensive repair bills once you get ashore.

Many of the defects that you find will not need urgent attention. Note them down so that you can deal with them at the annual refit. In this way, you will already have the nucleus of a list of work when you come to get the boat back into good condition for the new season. With the boat out of the water, you can then carry out a thorough check and add to the list, so as to ensure that all the necessary work gets done.

Although you do not have the expertise of a surveyor, you should be able to spot most of the problems during a methodical inspection, just as the surveyor does. He checks out every part of the boat, looking for clues that might indicate trouble. You can see the same clues, if you know what to look for, but you may have to call in expert help if you cannot readily identify the cause. Write down each problem as you find it, because it is very easy to forget when the time comes to do the work, and you can tick off the items on the list as they are done. Be methodical, and then you won't overlook anything. Divide the boat into sections, and work through these as follows.

Outside hull

Don't just give the hull a casual glance. Place your eye close to the surface and look along it. Any irregularities in the surface will then be obvious.

1. Now inspect every square centimetre of the surface, rubbing your fingers over it as you go along. In this way, blisters or chips will be quickly found. Mark each one as you find it, for later attention. These defects need

Hull inside

Here, you are mainly looking for signs of leaking, which is usually indicated by staining.

5. Look particularly around the hull and deck joints, around portholes, skin fittings, and stern-gear fittings, but check through as much of the inside of the hull as possible (see page 180). While plastic laminate is immune from rot, the timber used in interior construction is not, and any staining might spell trouble, unless treated in the early stages.

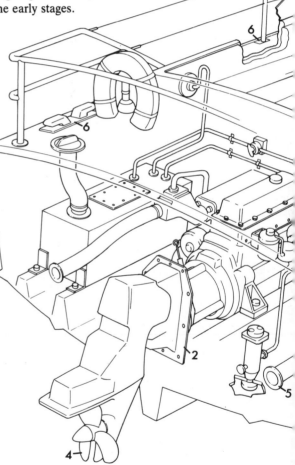

to be treated as on pages 51–52, but first of all you should find out what has caused them. The cause of chipping is fairly obvious, but blistering means that water is getting under the gel coat. Here, you may need expert help. Examine the hull with a magnifying glass, to see if it is pitted. It is not

always easy to examine the underwater surfaces when these are covered in antifouling, so remove the paint from any doubtful-looking areas and examine more closely. Check particularly well around skin fittings, looking for gel-coat cracks and loose bolts.

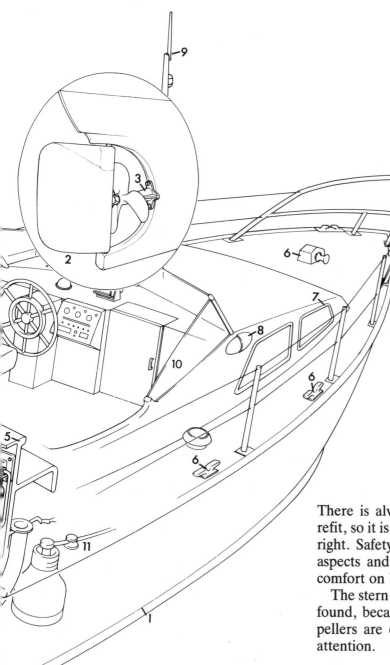

Deck and superstructure

6. Just as on the deck and superstructure of the sailing boat, the places where you are likely to find stress cracks in the gel coat are around the bases of stanchions, cleats, mooring posts, the windlass, fairleads, and mast-attachment points. Again, it is important to identify the cause of the problem before fitting a reinforcement pad under the deck (see page 25).

7. Hatches and windows should be hosed down, to make sure that they seal properly. Look inside for any signs of leaking (see pages 74–75).

8. Open the navigation lights and check for signs of corrosion. The same goes for any other electric fittings.

9. Check that the fastenings of electronic antennae are tight.

10. Check canvas hoods and covers for wear and tear.

11. Check any gas installations visually to see if the pipes are corroded. Check the joints with soapy water for leaks.

Stern gear

There is always plenty to do during the annual refit, so it is important that you get your priorities right. Safety must come first, so attend to these aspects and then look at how you can improve comfort on board.

The stern gear is the area where most trouble is found, because the rudder and propeller or propellers are expected to work all season without attention.

3. The propeller shaft should be lifted up and down in the same way as above, to check it for wear. If the stern tube is water-lubricated, make sure that the water channels are free from marine growth, so that the bearings get an adequate supply of water.

4. Check the propeller blades for chips or cracks, which will have a negative effect on performance. Small ones can be removed by very gentle tapping or by touching up with a file.

. Check the rudder bearing by lifting he rudder up and down, then push the udder post sideways and fore and aft. ny play found in the rudder bearing hould be attended to—this kind of roblem will not get better on its own.
  With a stern drive, you must check he condition of the bellows and the ecuring clips.

Corrosion can affect all metal fittings in this area and is indicated by pitting. If you find any evidence of corrosion, check on the condition of the sacrificial anodes (see page 182). With stern drives or outboards, inspect the whole unit for corrosion, and check the steering for play.

Machinery

This is where you must be particularly vigilant. Rust- or salt-staining will show up any water leaks.

1. Inspect all the seacocks for easy operation. (See page 77 for fitting a larger skin fitting.) Check that hose clips are tight and not corroded. (This applies to toilet and sink fittings as well as to engines.)

2. The exhaust system should be given the same treatment, as a leak here will fill the boat with fumes and water, and can start fires.

3. Oil and fuel leaks are also dangerous and should be fixed, because they will not get better on their own. Follow the pipes in the fuel system back to the tank to make sure that they are well secured and don't chafe against anything.

4. Check that the fuel tanks are well secured.

Examine all hosing and piping. Problems there can stop water getting into and out of the boat.

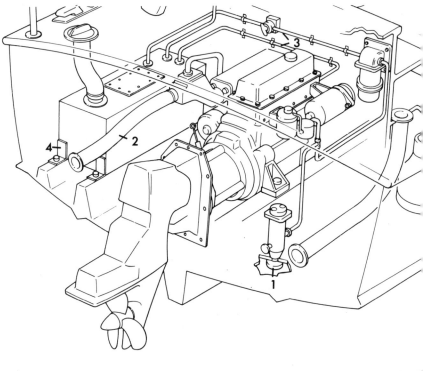

General survey

Is there excessive play in the steering? If the system is hydraulic, check for leaks. If it is mechanical, it should operate smoothly, with no tight spots.

Check the expiry dates on the safety equipment and arrange for any necessary maintenance.

This tour of inspection should take no more than an afternoon, and you will be much more confident in your boat once it is done. When you are driving the boat, look for anything that you might find irritating. What changes can you make to improve the situation? For instance, throttles are often badly placed. It is a simple job to fit a tapered block of wood under the throttle box, thus bringing the levers closer towards you in the important "ahead" position. However, make sure that you still retain full astern movement.

Replacing a fixed helmsman's seat with an adjustable one can make life more comfortable. Ideally, the seat should slide fore and aft, so that you can stand or sit at the wheel, but a height adjustment can also add to comfort.

Often you need a chart at the steering position. A hinged seat of rigid plastic can make a good chart cover, but it is better if it is raised on wooden strips, so that you can slide the chart under. Fasten the sheet down with clips to avoid it blowing away.

If you usually use your boat singlehanded, you need to be agile when mooring. Fit a couple of jam cleats alongside the wheelhouse, to hold the bow and stern lines ready when you are alongside. Don't leave the lines there when you are at sea, as you may end up with them round the propeller.

Anchors are often stowed in a bow locker when not in use. Here they move around when the boat is at sea and cause damage, so they need to be secured. A proper screw clamp is best, but make sure that it can be released quickly, because you may need your anchor in a hurry.

The view astern on a motor cruiser may not be so good, and you can be unpleasantly surprised by being suddenly overtaken by faster boats. If you can't see clearly astern, fit rear-view mirrors, like wing mirrors on a car. Truck mirrors are the best size but make sure that they don't block the side decks.

CHAPTER 2

Working
with
Glassfibre

The previous chapter has described the general building methods used in constructing glassfibre boats in order to show the boat owner how his boat was made, so that he will know what to expect when he is working on any of the glassfibre details on the boat. This chapter covers the tools and methods necessary for working with glassfibre, and the tools that are needed for working on modern masts and spars, which will be covered in a later chapter.

Repairs, maintenance, and improvements to the glassfibre—whether of solid-laminate or sandwich construction—can be carried out by any reasonably handy boat owner. Working with glassfibre is not difficult, if you prepare the work properly, follow the directions closely, keep all materials clean, and be pedantic about working all the air bubbles out of the lamination during lay-up.

On pages 42–43, we show how you may build a simple storage box in glassfibre, but the same methods can be used to make any detail that you want to alter or, perhaps, add to your boat.

THE TOOL BOX

Always buy top-quality tools. It pays in the long run, as inferior products will break easily, and edged tools of poor-quality steel soon lose their cutting edge. Your work will be so much easier if you have the right tools for the job in hand and if they are of good quality.

Good tools are an investment and should be stored safely when kept ashore. A selection must be carried on board when you are at sea, and these must be protected from water, so that they don't rust. They should be dried thoroughly before storing and then kept in some kind of airtight plastic container.

If possible, buy compactly designed tools, as these are more easily handled in the confined spaces on board a boat.

The following is a comprehensive list of all the tools that you will need for boatyard work and for work aboard your boat while at sea.

Marking-out tools

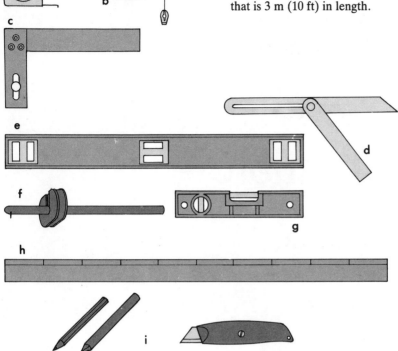

(a) Steel tape with dual marking (metric and inches). Choose one that is 3 m (10 ft) in length.

(b) Plumb bob and line. Always make sure that the boat is upright before building in a fitting, especially when the boat is on land where it may easily be out of true.

(c) Try square (set square). The 150-mm (6″) model is suitable for most cabinet work aboard.

(d) Sliding bevel gauge, for marking mitres and building odd-angled fitments.

(e) Level. Made from aluminium and about 500 mm (2 ft) long.

(f) Mortise gauge, for marking out mortise joints.

(g) Short spirit level.

(h) Straight edge. A piece of Dexion Angle aluminium is fine, provided you check that it is straight and that it does not get knocked out true.

(i) Supply of sharpened pencils and universal knife with renewable blades.

Holding tools

For major construction work, you are going to need a heavy bench with a built-on woodworking vice. For lighter work, a good portable bench can be handy, but often, temporary work has to be carried out using the cockpit and any available spaces in the accommodation. For any major construction jobs, such as renewing wooden rubbing strakes, re-laying deck planking, and so on, a good supply of G-cramps is valuable.

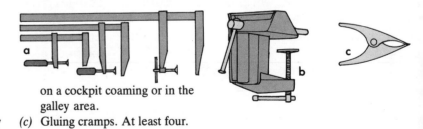

(a) Adjustable cramps, 150 mm (6″), 200 mm (8″), and 250 mm (10″). Excellent for one-handed operation and versatile, because they can accommodate many thicknesses of wood.

(b) A light aluminium vice, for light-duty work. It can be secured easily on a cockpit coaming or in the galley area.

(c) Gluing cramps. At least four.

Abrasive finishing papers

Although bits of glass paper are often used folded in the hand to get into small corners, a proper cork-faced sanding block is the only way to get good surface finish to wood, unless a power sander is used. Sticky-backed abrasive papers are available in rolls for use on special blocks.

The table here refers to silicone carbide abrasive papers (wet and dry) and their applications. To prevent clogging, wet the paper and surface well with water that has a little washing-up liquid in it. When you have finished smoothing the surface with the abrasive paper and the surface has dried

Abrasive finishing papers

Grit-size holes	Applications
30—70	Extremely coarse and only used for roughest joinery to remove splinters from wood.
80—120	For coarse cutting along the direction of the grain. Used for heavy stock removal, and final removal of old burnt-off paint.
180—220	First sanding of new wood surfaces before final finish sanding. Too coarse for paint surface that only needs a cosmetic finish, or for surfaces to be varnished.
240—280	For final rubbing down of old paint prior to undercoating. 280 is suitable for wood to be varnished and for rubbing down undercoating.
320	For finer surface to varnish work after first coats.
400	Used for rubbing down new coat of enamel prior to finishing coat.
500—600	For paint-blemish removing prior to burnishing.

take a one-grade finer paper and use it, dry, on the surface to give a good paint key. Unfinished wood is best sanded with *dry* glass paper of equivalent grade.

Safety

Dust from sanding can be dangerous. Use a safety breathing mask and eye protection.

Planes

If you are planning to do a lot of carpentry, a power plane can soon save cost, as it can prepare rough-sawn timber as well as give a fine finish. (Rough-sawn timber is less expensive than finished, planed planks.) Otherwise, a good hand plane of the combination type, together with a spokeshave and a cabinet scraper, will handle all your planing needs.

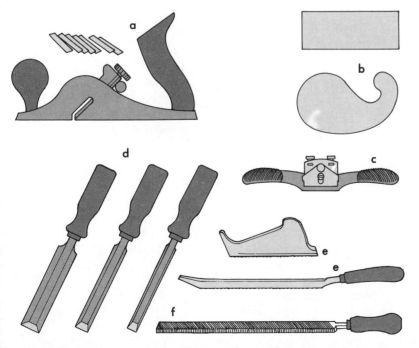

(a) Combination plane.
(b) Cabinet scrapers.
(c) Spokeshave. This should have an adjustable blade, for coarse or fine cut. The rounded bottom type is, perhaps, more useful than the flat, because you can round on internal curves as well as on external.
(d) A set of chisels.
(e) The Surform round file, plane, and block planer are excellent for shaping plastics, laminates, and, of course, wood.
(f) Wood rasp file. This gives a coarse cut that removes stock quickly. Care is needed when finishing, to remove all traces of the rough cut.

Saws

For the reduction of large planks to workable timber sizes, a power saw (circular saw) is invaluable, but where power is not available you need hand saws. Ease of use and final accuracy is dependent on the choice of the proper saw, on, for instance the number of teeth per inch and on the maintenance of the correct set and sharpness.

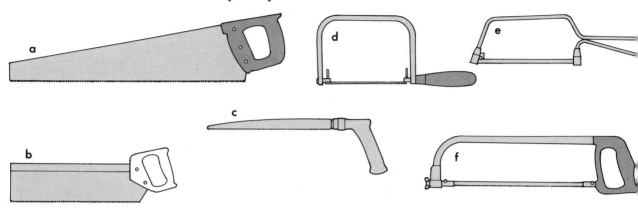

(a) Hand saw. The length can be from about 500 mm (20″) to about 660 mm (26″), with 5–9 teeth per inch (25 mm). Have one rip saw and one cross-cut saw (for coarse cutting along the grain and across the grain, respectively), and one panel saw, for fine cutting.

(b) Back saw. For fine cabinet work. Choose one with a brass back. For a fine finish, the saw should have about 14 teeth per inch (25 mm).

(c) General-purpose saw with adjustable handle and tapered blade. Cuts both wood and metal. Ideal for working in confined spaces or where old cabinet work might contain nails or screws that would ruin any other saw blade.

(d) Coping saw for cutting small curves and removing waste between dovetails.

(e) Light hacksaw. For cutting metal and plastic. Useful in confined spaces.

(f) Hacksaw. Choose a selection of blades with from 14 to 32 teeth per inch (25 mm). Buy flexible blades, until you are proficient with the hacksaw, as these are less easily broken than high-speed steel hardened blades. At least three consecutive teeth must be in contact with the material, so narrow material should be sawn with a blade with plenty of teeth per inch.

Screws and screwdrivers

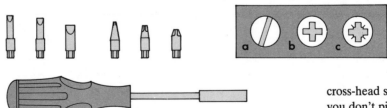

(a) Slot-head screws are still the most common type of fastener head. They demand that the blade of the screwdriver used fits the whole *width* of the slot. If you use the wrong type or size of screwdriver, it will "cam out" and cause serious damage to the screw head, possibly to your fingers, and almost certainly to the surface in which you are screwing. Dirt or paint in the slot can also cause the screwdriver to cam out.

A good tool kit demands a wide selection of screwdriver types and sizes. It is a good idea to have one colour on all your slot-head screwdrivers and another on your cross-head screwdrivers, so that you don't pick up the wrong screwdriver when you are concentrating on the work in hand. An alternative is to have a bits, or multi, screwdriver with a selection of bits, as illustrated.

(b) Phillips head. Prone to cam out due to paint or dirt in slot.

(c) Pozidriv head. This type is obsolete but is still found on older constructions and equipment.

Hammers and pliers

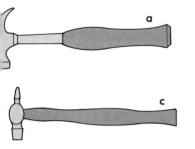
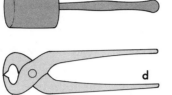
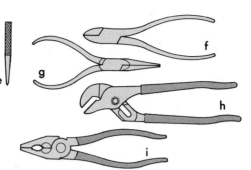

Only use hammers for striking or withdrawing nails. A hammer with a dented or uneven striking surface is useless.

a) Heavy claw hammer. Will withdraw as well as drive nails.

b) Pin hammer. A light one is essential for driving brass pins, which are easily bent.

(c) A round wooden mallet is still best for hitting chisels, even the modern plastic-handled ones.

(d) Pincers. Good for removing small nails and pins.

(e) Nail and pin punch. Match the diameter to the fastener being driven.

(f) Diagonal cutting nippers.

(g) Flatnose pliers.

(h) Water-pump pliers.

(i) Combination pliers.

Hole making

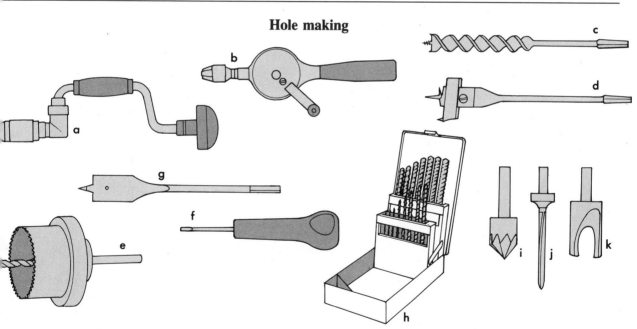

a) Brace with a short swing.

b) Double-pinion hand drill. Don't buy a single-pinion drill, even if it is cheaper.

c) Auger bits, for drilling wood from 5 mm (3/16″) to 40 mm (1 1/2″). Use the right nose type for the job in hand.

d) Expansive bit. Recommended for soft woods only.

e) Hole saws for use in a power drill. These are by far the best tool for use on hardwood, marine-grade plywood, and glassfibre laminate. Glassfibre can still be wicked by cutting edges of any type, but a good-quality hole saw copes well.

(f) Bradawl. Essential hole-maker for starting holes for soft brass pins in cabinet work and in material where any kind of nailing that will be visible is carried out.

(g) Flat bits are used for drilling a wide range of materials. Buy a set for 5 mm (3/16″) to 40 mm (1 1/2″).

(h) Twist drills. For both hand and powered drills. Specialized tips are available for work in extra hard materials. Range from 1.5 mm (1/16″) to 10 mm (3/8″).

(i) Countersink bits to ensure that exposed screw heads sit flush with the surface.

(j) A single-operation drill and countersink saves time.

(k) A wood plug cutter for cutting plugs to conceal screws.

Mechanics tools

The engineering industry throughout the world seems to have gone out of its way to make life awkward for the boat owner by its creation of irreconcilable standards. The American engineering industry sticks to A/F threads, while much of Europe has metric sizes. On top of these are new threads, such as the Isometric threads, which are *supposed* to be universal, as well as many of the old threads, such as the BA sizes and, dare I say it, the Whitworth threads, which are supposed to have gone out of existence years ago. The boat owner needs to have a comprehensive set of tools to cope with this unfortunate variety of fastener sizes.

The scope of the tool kit will be in proportion to the enthusiasm of the boat owner, but because even the unenthusiastic owner may have to cope with mechanical emergencies and undertake some maintenance, a basic kit of good-quality tools is a must. The tool box is best made from plastic, with ventilation holes, but a metal one can be used if it is lined with corrosion-inhibiting paper.

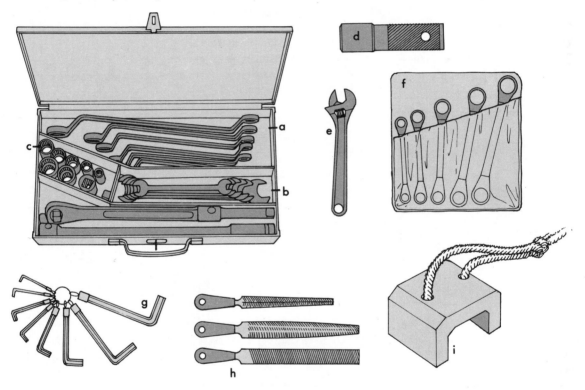

(a) Ring spanners.

(b) Open-ended spanners.

(c) Sockets and drives. An assortment that suits the main thread type used on the engine.

(d) Sparking-plug spanner. All petrol engines need this at one time or the other.

(e) An adjustable wrench will fit the odd awkward-size bolt or nut heads, but even a quality model is no substitute for a correctly fitting spanner or socket.

(f) Electrical items, such as generators and starters, use BA or metric, so a matching set of small ring spanners is needed.

(g) Allen keys.

(h) Files. ALWAYS use a handle on a file, as an open tang can cause serious injury to the wrist. The basic file shapes are flat, half-round, square, and three square. The basic file cuts are: rough cut (very coarse, for soft metals, bakelite, and plastics), bastard cut (standard cut for shaping and dressing steels), second cut (for hard metals), smooth cut and dead-smooth cut (for fine finishing), and single cut (used mainly on saw-sharpening files).

(i) A magnet on a line is a wonderful gadget for retrieving metal tools from bilges or shallow water. Keep it away from the compass!

Power tools

ower tools save a great deal of time and energy, nd make it possible for the boat owner to carry ut major maintenance and rebuilding jobs. Below a list of power tools that are especially useful on e modern glassfibre boat with aluminium masts nd spars.

Electricity can kill, and especially around boats, where a tool dropped in water can be lethal. Power tools are also dangerous if they come in contact with damp or rain. So *always protect the power line with a safety circuit breaker*. Never pick up a live tool that has been dropped in the water, even if you think that the fuse has blown.

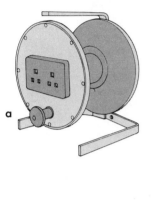

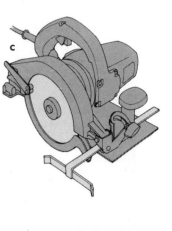

) A cable drum connected via a circuit breaker to the mains or the generator allows safe operation in any situation.

) A variable-speed drill with both mechanical and electronic control is excellent for selecting the right drilling speed for different materials. Some even have hammer-drill capacity. Select the most compact model with the highest watt-rated motor. This will handle buffing, rasping, drilling, wire wheel de-rusting, and flap-wheel finishing easily.

Drills are sometimes sold as a universal tool with lots of attachments. This is not such a good idea, because a lot of time is wasted in changing attachments and because of the danger of burning out motors that are usually rated for running short rather than prolonged periods.

(c) A circular saw is a great moneysaver. You can buy rough timber cheaply, especially if you buy in quantity. The timber can then be reduced to usable dimensions when you need it.

Teflon-coated saw blades tipped with tungsten carbide last very much longer than ordinary blades and are especially good if you are rip-cutting a tough timber like teak. A useful saw-blade diameter is 184 mm (7¼″), with a 58-mm (2¼″) depth of cut.

Remember that it is *vital* to support the length that will fall free when the blade cuts through. Otherwise, the sawn-off length can knock the saw onto the user.

(d) A jig saw is excellent for cross-cutting and for shaping.

(e) A power planer should be small enough to use in one hand yet give a 75-mm (3″) depth of fine-finish cut.

(f) An oscillating sander saves effort and produces an even surface. A circular disc sander (not shown) will save enormous effort when large areas need sanding down, but you have to be careful not to leave circular score marks on glassfibre surfaces, which would then have to be filled in with epoxy filler and sanded smooth, a time-consuming process.

REPAIRING DAMAGE

We have already described the methods and materials used by professional boatbuilders when they build boats in glassfibre. The amateur can, of course, build an entire boat from glassfibre himself, using the methods we described, but in the main, the person who owns a glassfibre boat today has bought it as a fully finished boat or as a shell, which he then finishes, designing the interior to suit his own requirements.

Sooner or later, the boat owner, no matter how careful he has been handling and maintaining his boat, is going to have to carry out some repairs to the glassfibre laminate. No repair or fitting-out job can be successfully carried out without the proper tools and working conditions, so the first thing you should do is to make sure that you have all the necessary tools and material at hand, and that the working conditions are acceptable.

Tools for working with glassfibre

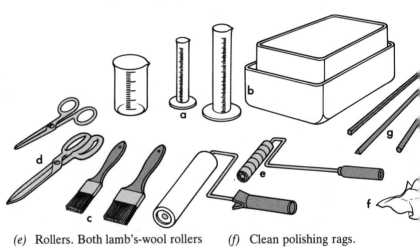

(a) Set of graduated glass cylinders for measuring catalysts, resins, etc. in exact amounts. Have two sets at hand—one that will measure larger amounts and one for small amounts that you may need for small repairs, etc.

(b) Containers for mixing resins. These can range from small paper cups to larger containers. They must be kept scrupulously clean.

(c) Brushes. Buy several cheap paint brushes, with fairly stiff, short bristles, and of varying widths, say 12 to 25 mm (1/2″ to 1″).

(d) Heavy-duty scissors, medium and large.

(e) Rollers. Both lamb's-wool rollers and metal rollers grooved lengthwise.

(f) Clean polishing rags.

(g) Sticks for stirring and mixing.

On the work table

(a) To further ensure that the material is kept clean, keep the rolls of glassfibre cloth, woven roving, or mat on spindles. This means that you can draw off the required lengths without damaging or dirtying the remainder of the roll. If the spindles can be fitted at one end of a work table, then so much the better. The glassfibre material can be pulled out in suitable lengths onto the table and cut off easily. Resist the temptation to pull out and cut off the material in too great lengths—they are awkward to handle and, individually, may take too long to wet-out thoroughly and consolidate on the job. Use progressively smaller pieces of material where the mould presents rapid changes of shape.

Make sure that the glassfibre material and the resins are kept clean all the time. If they are not required immediately, store them close to the mould, where temperature and humidity will be uniform. Don't be tempted to recover material from the floor and apply it to the job even if it appears to be perfectly clean.

(b) Scissors.

(c) Set square.

(d) Tape measure.

(e) Metal ruler.

(f) Supply of strong razor blades with sturdy handle.

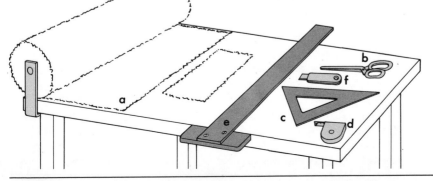

It is essential that both resins and glass materials are handled very carefully to ensure that they are kept clean and totally free of impurities, such as dirt and dust that can be picked up from the floor. Therefore, it is extremely important that, wherever you carry out the work, the working area is clean. This may mean that you are going to have to give your garage or basement workshop a thorough cleaning before you start, but it is well worth it in the end. Your work will not be ruined, and it was about time you cleaned the garage out anyway.

If the first rule of successful glassing is the old cliché, "Cleanliness is next to godliness", the second rule is "No air bubbles". Again and again, the glassfibre material, drenched with resin, must be worked with rollers, first a lamb's-wool roller and then a metal roller, to expel all entrapped air and to ensure that each and every filament of glass is thoroughly wetted-out with resin. (This is the goal, but in practice it is impossible to reach. However, if you work with glassfibre and want good results, you must work towards this goal conscientiously.) Corners and angles have to be attacked with stubborn thoroughness, and a short, stiff-bristled brush must be used to stipple these difficult spots, so that the best possible job is done.

REPAIRING A SMALL HOLE IN THE HULL

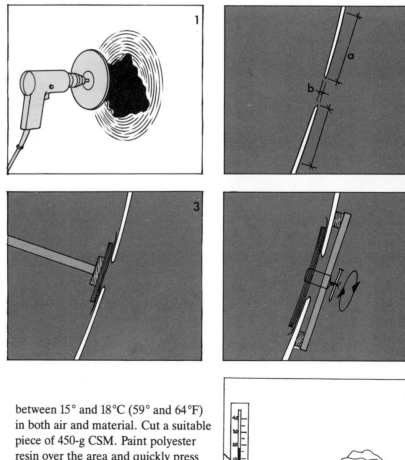

1. Clean up the jagged edges of the hole with a sander. You can also do it with a sharp chisel, but do it carefully, cutting in towards the centre of the hole.

2. A large area around the hole must be covered. The length (*a*) must be 20 times the thickness of the hull (*b*).

If the damage to the glassfibre has occurred at the iron keel, the glassfibre must be sanded down flush to the keel. Vacuum-clean the area but do not wash down in solvent.

3. Apply a piece of sturdy cardboard or plywood as backing to the inside of the hull. Place a piece of polythene plastic sheeting between, so that the glassfibre does not fasten on the backing.

4. If you can't get at the hole from the inside to apply the backing, do it from outside using copper wire through holes in the backing and a narrow piece of wood raised on wooden blocks to allow you to work underneath.

5. You need: preaccelerated polyester resin, catalyst, glass graduate, letter scales, and solvent. Keep the roller and dabbler moist in the solvent. Working temperature must be kept between 15° and 18°C (59° and 64°F) in both air and material. Cut a suitable piece of 450-g CSM. Paint polyester resin over the area and quickly press on the mat. Roll it until it is wet through with resin (it will be transparent then). Now put on another piece of CSM in the same way. After 24 hours, you can sand the area and after a week it can be painted.

MOULDING A STORAGE BOX

Extra storage possibilities are always welcome, and glassfibre boxes can be moulded in any shape and size to fit neatly into an appropriate space, for instance in the bilges.

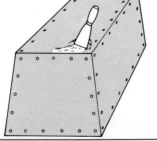

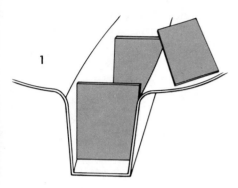

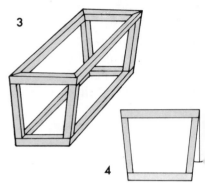

1. First of all, make a template of cardboard, and make sure that it fits easily into the space available. Check that it can be withdrawn easily too. Are you going to have a lid on the box? Is there room to raise the lid in the space in which you intend to have the box?

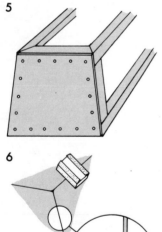

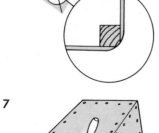

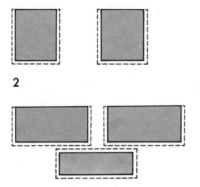

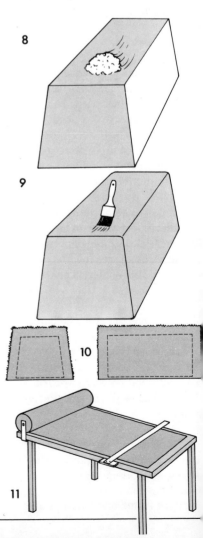

2. Now make a male mould in masonite, with the shiny side out. When cutting the pieces of masonite, remember to take into account the thickness of the laminate and cut them slightly smaller all round than the template.

5. Glue, nail, or screw the masonite pieces to the carcase. Countersink nails or screws.

6. Smooth the edges with abrasive paper and a sanding block. The corners should have radii of at least 6 mm (3/16″).

7. Fill the holes and edges with filler. Sand smooth.

8. Wax the outside of the mould and polish the waxed surface thoroughly. Allow to dry for a couple of hours and repeat the procedure three or four times until the mould has a highly polished surface. Allow to dry for at least 24 hours.

9. Paint an even coat of releasing agent on the polished surface. Allow to stand for a couple of hours.

10. Cut out the first piece of CSM (the solid line). Plan the pieces for the whole layer so that no joins will occur at the corners of the box.

11. Cutting is easiest on a proper working table. Use razor blades in a sturdy handle.

3. Construct a carcase from thin battens for the mould.

4. Make sure that there is a splay of about 2 degrees, to allow the box to be released easily.

Important! Always read the manufacturer's instructions on the various packs, and follow them scrupulously.

Alternatively, you can buy the accelerator and the polyester pre-mixed, which makes things easier.

Mix the catalyst paste with the accelerated resin. *Note!* Never mix accelerator and catalyst directly.

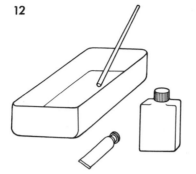

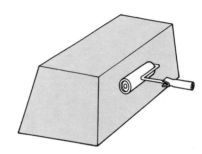

12. Measure the accelerator and the polyester resin in exact amounts (see the manufacturer's instructions) and mix them well.

13. Paint the resin thickly on the mould.

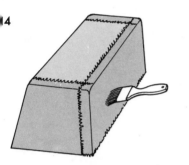

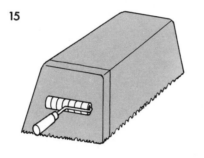

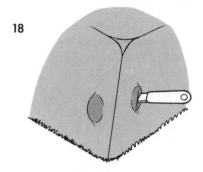

14. Lay-up the first piece of CSM. Press it firmly onto the mould with your hands (wear rubber gloves!) or with a paint brush (wear gloves anyway, so you don't get splatters). Wet the material through.

Cut and lay on the adjacent piece, overlapping by about 50 mm (2″). Leave it for at least two minutes to soak up the resin. Continue until the first layer of material lies snugly all round the mould. Pay special attention to the corners, where the material must fit neatly. There must be no gaps between the mould and the glassfibre layer.

15. Brush on a new layer of resin and work it into the mat with a lamb's-wool roller. Both brush and roller should be worked quickly but carefully, to discourage aeration of the resin in the initial stages of the operation.

16. Having thoroughly wetted-out the material, it is best consolidated in position with a metal-disc roller. Used carefully, this will press the filaments of the section being worked on firmly onto the mould, thus improving the degree of wetting-out and encouraging trapped air bubbles to work their way up to the surface.

Allow the first layer to cure for a couple of hours, before continuing with the second layer (which should be woven roving) and following layers (if there are to be more). The following layers can be applied without waiting for the previous layer to begin to cure.

17. Remember to stagger the joins between the layers, to avoid weak spots.

18. If air bubbles occur that no amount of rolling or stippling will get rid of, cut the cloth with your razor blade to release the air, and then coat with more resin and roll again.

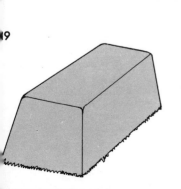

19. Finish with a layer of surfacing tissue and a layer of gel coat, to give the box a water-resistant as well as attractive finish.

20. Leave the laminated box to cure for about 24 hours. Then prise off the box from the mould. Saw off unwanted edges.

The lid, if there is one, is made in the same way.

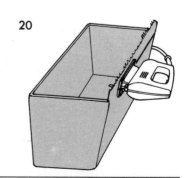

FASTENING WOOD TO LAMINATE

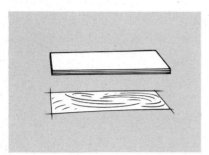

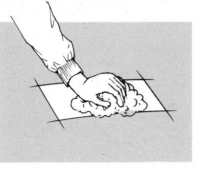

A support for a fixture on the boat can be provided by laminating a wooden batten to the hull laminate.

1. Roughen the area in which the batten is to be fastened. Use a circular sander.

2. Wash with degreasing agent to get rid of all grease and dirt. Then wash with fresh water and allow to dry.

3. Cut a suitable piece of marine plywood as the support batten.

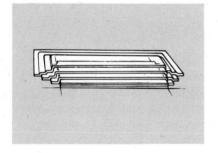

4. Apply epoxy resin to the roughened area on the hull.

5. Bed the batten in the resin and brush it over with epoxy resin. Apply the first layer of CSM. Work it into the resin as previously, especially at the angles between the batten and the hull.

6. Continue the laminating with a layer of woven roving, then with CSM and so on until you are satisfied with the strength of the laminate. Remember to stagger the edges of the cloth pieces and to round their corners.

CHAPTER 3

The Underwater Hull

Neglect of the keel and underwater hull (the wetted surface) is a common problem that perhaps arises from the fact that this part of the boat is not visible to the sailor during the major part of the boating season.

The underwater part of the hull is prey to attacks by marine organisms, and if the antifouling system has not been properly applied or is ineffective for any reason, the boat's speed will be affected, and in the long run, the hull laminate will be attacked.

Blistering is a major problem that is found in varying degrees on as many as twenty-five per cent of all glassfibre-built boats that are five years old. Much research has been carried out in recent years to establish an effective method of providing the glassfibre underwater body with an effective seal against the attack of water. A tar-epoxy system,

painted on under the antifouling system, is considered excellent by many sailors who have tried it, but, as its name suggests, it is black, and this tends to show up under light-coloured antifouling as a stain. Those who want to have a light-coloured antifouling should use a clear epoxy-resin system to seal the glassfibre surface before applying the antifouling.

Acetone is regularly used as a degreasing agent when glassfibre is being cleaned, but nowadays, experts warn against it, as it is considered to be too aggressive and will, in the long run, increase the chances of osmosis, which is the major cause of blistering. There are several proprietary degreasing agents on the market that should be used instead. Ask your local marine-paint supplier to recommend one.

IRON KEELS

Rust is the greatest enemy of the iron keel. Where you find rust, you will inevitably find that the paint is old or has been badly applied.

Sometimes, however, rust will "bleed" through even the most carefully applied coats of epoxy iron primer and antifouling, and this kind of problem requires careful treatment.

Before any paintwork can be effectively repaired, all rust and millscale must be completely removed. The best way to do this is by gritblasting, a process through which small particles of sharp grit are sprayed over the area under high pressure. This is a specialist job requiring specialized equipment. The only alternative open to the ordinary boat owner is elbow grease. Just follow the instructions given here.

Epoxy fillers

Of the many fillers available, epoxy is the most suitable and most widely used. Its main advantage is that it can be applied to most surfaces and finishes, and it is the only type of filler suitable for underwater areas.

Epoxy fillers come in three general types: general-purpose filler, heavy-duty putty-type filler, and surfacing filler. They are used to fill a pitted surface so that it can be faired.

The filler is a two-component (two-pack) product, one component being the hardener, or curing agent. Always read the manufacturer's instructions and follow them carefully.

WARNING! Avoid skin contact with epoxy and its hardeners. Sensitive skin can contract dermatitis.

Treating a rusty iron keel

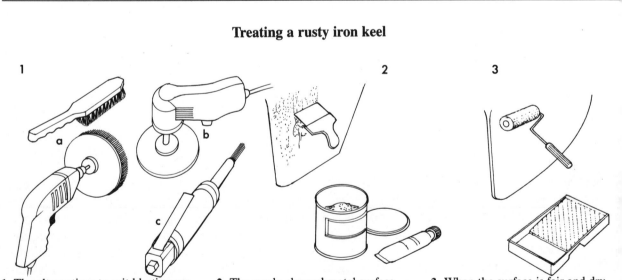

1. The alternatives to grit blasting are wirebrushing *(a)*, using a disc sander *(b)*, and chipping, either manually or with a needle-gun *(c)*. When the area to be painted has been cleaned completely of rust, it must first be brushed free of all dust.

2. The newly cleaned metal surface must be given a rust-neutralizing system, usually based on phosphoric acid, immediately, to prevent new rust from beginning to form. Then apply one coat of thinned (10–15%) epoxy-resin composition. Tar epoxy may also be used. When it has dried, follow with a full, unthinned coat. The surface is now ready for an application of surfacing filler, if required. The filler is applied with a large putty knife.

3. When the surface is fair and dry, finish the paint job with two coats of metallic primer, allowing 24 hours between coats, and top it all with the antifouling system.

Fairing an iron keel with a pocked surface

Where a keel has a large area of pock-marked or otherwise uneven surface, the original fairness can be restored by the application of an epoxy filler applied with a fairing batten.

For best results, keep the edges of the fairing batten clean and sharp, and draw it over the area with a steady, even pressure. Avoid putting too much epoxy filler on at the one time. A thickness of 5 mm (3/16″) is the maximum. If you need to build up the surface, then apply a second coat.

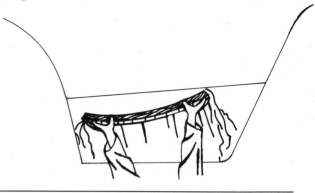

LEAD KEELS

Although they are more expensive, lead keels are preferable to iron. They are easier to repair and easier to maintain. Furthermore, because of the high specific gravity of lead, a keel made of lead provides greater stability than an iron keel of the same weight, as its weight can be concentrated lower down in the keel.

Coating and painting lead keels

First of all, wire brush and sand down the surface. Apply one coat of self-etching primer. Then follow two coats of epoxy primer. When these are dry, fill in all scores and hollows by skimming with epoxy filler. When dry, sand smooth.

Apply two further coats of epoxy primer and finish off with a compatible antifouling system, as per the manufacturer's instructions.

Repairing a lead keel

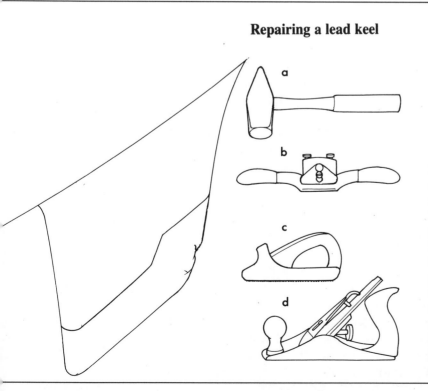

Lead is soft and, therefore, can be easily deformed. The leading and trailing edges as well as the bottom of the lead keel are the parts that most often get damaged. A dented lead keel may be dressed into shape with a planishing hammer *(a)*. Unfair and protruding pieces of lead can be planed off with a metal woodworking plane *(b)* or a spokeshave *(c)*. Another useful tool is a surform *(d)*. Once all protrusions have been removed, scores and hollows can be filled with epoxy filler and sanded smooth.

Keel bolts

The keel bolt is a long stainless-steel bolt, threaded at one end to take a washer and nut. The keel end of the bolt is usually permanently bedded in the keel and cannot be removed for inspection. On a glassfibre boat, inspection is not as important as it is on wooden-hulled boats, as the danger of rusting is minimal. The boat owner may rely on simply checking the nuts every season to ensure that they are bolted down and well bedded in sealant. When buying a second-hand boat, however, it is wise to have the keel x-rayed, to ensure that the bolts have not been damaged during its previous ownership by, for example, striking an underwater obstruction or grounding.

On earlier glassfibre constructions the keel itself was often an integral part of the hull moulding, with a hollow being left in the keel part. This hollow was then filled with lead or iron and laminated over. Serious rusting problems could arise if the laminate around the iron keel got damaged, allowing water to get in. Moreover, if the water froze, the laminate could be badly damaged. In modern constructions, the ballast keel is always bolted to the glassfibre keel or to the hull.

Stud bolts

Stud bolts are the most common method of connecting iron or lead keels. The top of the keel is pre-tapped and the stud bolt is secured from inside. The more extreme the keel shape, and therefore the less the area of contact between the hull and the keel, the greater are the stresses exerted on the join between the hull and the keel. And stresses like this can lead to leakage. Therefore, you must spread a thick layer of sealant between the hull and the washer, and this needs to be checked annually and renewed if necessary.

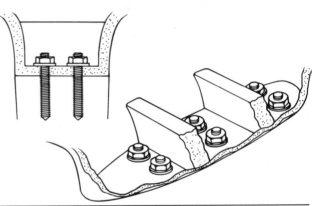

ANTIFOULING

If you didn't use antifouling, your boat's hull would, within just a few weeks of launching, become a home for all manner of weeds, barnacles, and suchlike. This would cause considerable loss of speed and, in the long run, would result in damage to the gel coat.

When choosing an antifouling system for your hull, it is important that you choose the right products to suit your boat and the waters in which it will sail.

It is not uncommon that boats are delivered from the manufacturer with a complete antifouling system. When placing the order for such a boat, you should find out exactly what kind of system is used as a standard, so that you can be certain that the system is suitable for the waters in which you intend to sail. If you are not satisfied with the system used, it is as well to remove it and apply a proven system. This is especially important as regards the primers used, as wrong or badly applied primers sooner or later lead to blistering. Unless you're convinced about the quality of the delivered system, you should do the job yourself, if you have the possibility and the time. Then you will be certain of what kind of antifouling your boat has, and when you want to renew it, you can use the same or a compatible system.

An antifouling system has recently appeared that is based on Teflon. It is a thin liquid and can be sprayed or rolled on, leaving a smooth, thin surface that, depending on the waters sailed in, only needs to be renewed every second year. There are several other new systems on the market that likewise reduce the amount of time and labour that must be spent applying the more traditional systems, and which are, at the same time, more gentle with the marine environment.

How much paint or antifouling to use

When working out how much paint and antifouling you need for your hull, a few simple calculations will take the guesswork out of it.

First of all, refer to Table 1 (below) and select the boat type that is most similar to yours. Work out the area of the hull bottom.

Now refer to Table 2 and select the type of material (antifouling, primer, finish, etc.) and the size of can that you want. Divide the corresponding figure into the figure you have taken from the first chart; this will give you the number of cans you need. For instance, if you have a straight, long-keeled yacht with 8.85 m length of waterline, 3.2 m maximum beam, and 1.22 m draught, the area of the bottom will be $8.85 \times (3.2 + 1.22) = 39.12$ sq m. Say you want to buy enough antifouling for two coats, and you want to buy it in litre cans; then you divide 39.12 by 7.5, to give you 5.22 litres per coat.

So if you want two coats, buy eleven 1-litre cans, and you will have a little over to use as a touch-up prior to launching.

Area to be painted	Formula
Bottoms	*Full-bodied craft such as motor yachts, shallow-draft yachts and straight long-keeled yachts:* LWL × (B + D) = area in square metres
	Medium-draft sailing cruisers with rounded bows: 0.75 × LWL × (B + D) = area in square metres
	Deep-keeled racing craft, cut away forward with short keels: 0.50 × LWL × (B + D)= area in square metres
Topsides	(LOA + B) × (2 × Average Freeboard) = area in square metres
Decks	(LOA + B) × 0.75 = area in square metres *Note: The area taken up by coachroof, cockpit, etc., will have to be subtracted in many cases.*

Calculate the underwater area of the boat's bottom in square metres by using this formula:
  LWL × (B + D)
  where LWL = waterline length, B = maximum beam, D = draft.

  Example: Long-keel motorsailer measuring 29ft × 10ft × 4ft. Convert measurements to metres and apply formula:
  $8.85 \times (3.2 + 1.22) = 39.12m^2$

INTERNATIONAL PAINTS.

TABLE 2

Material type	Covering rate *Square metres per litre can*
Copolymer (polishing) antifouling	7.5
Hard antifouling	8.5–9.0
Primers, undercoats and finishes	10.0–12.0
2-component polyurethane	11.0–12.0

How to apply antifouling to an untreated hull

1. Wash the hull carefully with a suitable cleaning solvent to remove any grease and releasing agent.

2. Matt the surface with fine abrasive paper. DON'T use a circular sander as this can too easily leave deep scores that will damage the gel coat. Use an orbital sander, or better still, wet-sand it by hand, so that you are quite sure that the whole underbody has been done. Some makes of etching primer are supposed to make matting unnecessary, but for safety's sake, it is best to matt the underbody.

3. Wash the underbody with water and leave to dry. If the weather is damp and rainy, as it often is at the end of the sailing season, it might be impossible to get the underbody properly dry, but a good solution to this problem is to wash the underbody in methylated spirits, which evaporate quickly, leaving a dry surface.

4. Apply at least two protective coats of tar epoxy or a clear epoxy-resin system with a brush or roller. Check the manufacturer's instructions to see if you need to smooth down in be-tween coats. The final coat must be as smooth and even as you can possibly make it.

This is not there to provide better adhesion for the coming coat of antifouling, but is intended to prevent water from seeping in through minor imperfections in the gel coat, which would result in blistering developing.

5. Apply the antifouling. Remember that the smoothness of the final surface will affect the speed of the boat.

Preparing the surface of a treated hull

Old antifouling has to be checked carefully, to see if it needs replacing. If the old antifouling is sound but needs a new coat, check first that the new product is compatible with the old. If there is no information on the old antifouling, then for safety's sake, start by priming the old antifouling with a barrier coat of tar epoxy or a clear epoxy-resin system and leave it to harden for seven days before applying the new antifouling.

If the old antifouling is crusty, thick, and peeling, then you have to remove it completely, and start as for a new boat.

Antifouling is poisonous. Never burn it off. If you sand it down, don't use dry abrasive paper—wet paper will bind the poisonous dust. Always protect your eyes, nose, and mouth when working with antifouling. Ideally, use a liquid stripper compatible with glassfibre and a steel scraper.

Antifouling Selector Chart

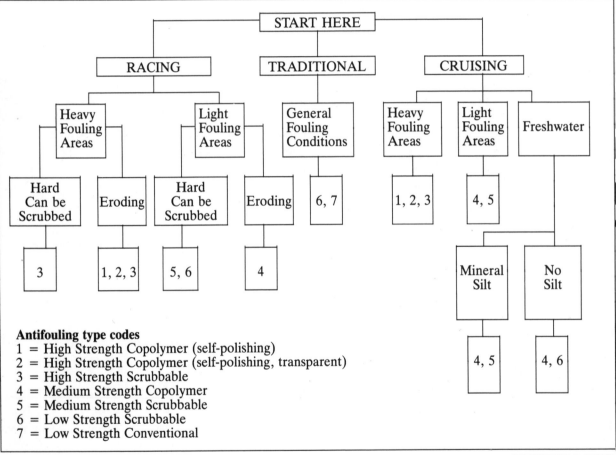

Antifouling type codes
1 = High Strength Copolymer (self-polishing)
2 = High Strength Copolymer (self-polishing, transparent)
3 = High Strength Scrubbable
4 = Medium Strength Copolymer
5 = Medium Strength Scrubbable
6 = Low Strength Scrubbable
7 = Low Strength Conventional

INTERNATIONAL PAINTS.

Water intrusion between ballast keel and hull

The join between the ballast keel and the hull is always sealed with a special sealant, so that water cannot seep in. A new coat of this sealant needs to be applied after a few seasons. Paint it over the join according to the manufacturer's instructions.

BLISTERING

Blistering of the underbody of the yacht (the wetted surface) is a major problem on many glassfibre boats. The resins used for gel coats and for laminating are not impermeable. Water will—slowly—make its way through the gel coat and into the laminate. There are two main causes of water absorption: wicking and osmosis.

Wicking occurs when water, soaking eventually through the laminate, comes in contact with a bundle of glassfibre strands that, however consciously the wetting-out was done, have not been wetted-out. They become soaked with the water, which is drawn along them by capillary action. The bundle swells and causes a blister in the actual laminate.

Osmosis occurs when tiny air bubbles, left after the wetting-out, entrap resin-curing agents and binder to form a mixture of fluids that is more dense than the water in which the yacht floats. The gel coat acts as a semipermeable membrane and the less dense fluid (water) passes through it into the more dense. This causes blisters in the laminate and can even cause the gel coat to "lift" from the nearest layer of glassfibre laminate.

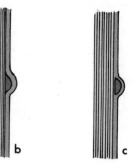

Three kinds of damage caused by blistering.
(a) Delamination caused by wicking.
(b) A blister causes the gel coat to lift, together with the first layer of laminate.
(c) Tiny blisters in the gel coat are often the first indications of trouble. Note them and check regularly to see if they are growing or spreading.

How to prevent blistering

Blister resistance begins at the shipbuilders, when the gel coat is being applied. A gel coat that is between 0.4 and 0.7 mm (1/64″ and 1/32″) is vital to keep the water out. The wise boat owner will, after receiving delivery of his new boat, add three to four coats of tar epoxy to the underbody, thus dramatically improving the water-repellent qualities of the underbody. Tar epoxy is a recent arrival on the marine paint scene, and is recommended if the antifouling is a dark colour. Otherwise, use a clear epoxy-resin system. An antifouling system on top of this completes the underbody protection.

Repairing blistering

If the blistering is little more than cosmetic, that is, occurs sparingly in the gel coat, remove all previous paint by sanding, open the blisters by sanding or spiking them, wash the surface with freshwater from a high-pressure hose, and allow to dry thoroughly. At least six to eight weeks are needed, so it is preferable to do this at the end of the season and to let the hull dry out during the lay-up. A final rinse of all the pits and the whole repair area with methylated spirits (for quick drying-out, as meths evaporates quickly) is a good idea. Fill the pits with epoxy filler, prior to sanding and overpainting. Paint a first coat of tar epoxy or of an epoxy-resin system with a brush. Then apply a minimum of five coats with a roller or a spray gun.

Repairing serious blistering

1. The yacht is hauled and the gel coat over the whole bottom is removed with a grit-blasting machine. This is a job for a professional operator with the necessary equipment. If the blistering is confined to a limited area or scattered in pockets over a wider area then an amateur can do the job with a disc sander or an angle grinder.

2. When all the gel coat is removed, the surface is steam-cleaned or hosed with high-pressure fresh water several times during a period of about a week. After this, the hull must be left to dry thoroughly, which can take up to four months.

3. The drying time can be shortened by covering the entire boat with a polythene cover and using a dehumidifier, but this is expensive. A cheaper alternative is to use a radiator, also inside a polythene cover. During the drying period, it is important that the inside of the boat be kept opened up and as dry and warm as possible, but do not set the dehumidifier at exaggeratedly high temperatures.

4. Once the hull is fully dried, the abraded area is resurfaced with an epoxy filler paste. The whole is then faired and a fully epoxy-resin paint system applied to rebuild the surface to a thickness equal to that of the gel coat which it replaces.

An antifouling system is then added on top of this.

If the blistering has caused very deep pits down into the laminate, then it may call for the application of glassfibre cloth, as illustrated, before being faired and painted.

Remember to use epoxy laminating resin to achieve the best bond between glassfibre cloth and the cleaned and dried surface, and to make the new surface as resistant as possible to water absorption.

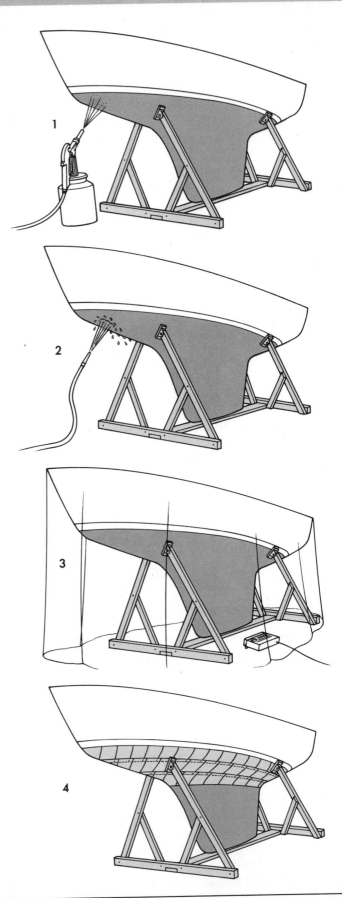

CHAPTER 4

The Hull

Although the underwater hull and the divide between the underwater hull and the topsides are the parts of the hull that require most care, it is the topsides that are visible to the sailor and to everyone in the marina when the boat lies in the water. Therefore, most sailors put an extra bit of effort into getting the topsides into A-1 condition. The gel coat is waxed and polished each spring and autumn, waterlines are marked up and painted with great care, a boot top is painted in an attractive colour, and perhaps the boat's name and port of registration are added.

REPAIRING MINOR DAMAGE TO THE GEL COAT

As we have said before, manufacturer's instructions should always be followed, whatever you are working with—paints, fillers, resins, etc. Check the information on the paint tins concerning working temperature, solvent, and drying times.

Remember that glassfibre provides a cold surface upon which moisture condenses, and this means that dew will spoil any top coats applied in the early morning or late evening, unless the air is particularly dry.

Most sailors tend to retouch paintwork during the spring or autumn maintenance sessions, but this is often the wrong time of year, as it is too cold and there is usually a lot of mist then.

Dust particles in the air are a problem when you are painting, so you should not paint when the wind is blowing, swirling dust up around the boat. A good practice is to hose the ground around the boat with water. This binds up any dust on the ground and diminishes the risk of dust getting into the paint.

Filling a scratch with gel coat

If the damage is superficial, say, a scratch that has not got through to the laminate, you can repaint it quite simply.

1. Wash the surface with fresh water and leave to dry. (Rinsing with methylated spirits will speed up the drying operation.) A fan will help, especially if the boat is indoors.

2. Use a sharp chisel blade or suchlike to scrape the scratch clean. Brush off or vacuum any dust from the area when it has dried.

3. It should be possible to buy gel coat in the boat's original colour. Mix it with hardener in the exact proportions. You only need a tiny amount to repair a scratch.

4. Apply the gel coat to the scratch with a fine brush or even a match. Cover the repair with tape, which presses the gel coat into the scratch at the same time as it provides a smooth surface.

When the gel coat has hardened (have patience!) grind it down smooth with a very fine abrasive paper. Then polish the surface with rubbing compound and then wax it.

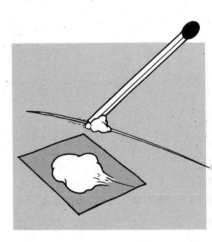

Repainting a larger area with gel coat

1. If the area to be repainted is larger than above, but still the laminate has not been penetrated, sand it down with wet and dry abrasive paper.

2. Wash the sanded area with fresh water and leave to dry. Again, rinsing with methylated spirits will speed up the drying operation.

3. Brush or vacuum any dust from the area when it has dried.

4. Paint with a matching coat of gel. Use a short stiff-haired brush for the first coat, to work the paint into the sanded surface. Then use a fine-haired brush or a painting pad for the other coats.

If you notice that the paint is hard to spread, thin it with a little solvent.

Finish by polishing the surface with rubbing compound and then with boat's wax.

MARKING UP A NEW WATERLINE OR BOOT TOP

There are three reasons for repainting the water line and boot top. Firstly, the gel coat at the waterline may have become faded or discoloured, something which can occur after a few years. See pages 56–57 for how the waterline is repainted.

Secondly, you may need to renew the antifouling; if, for instance, the boat is lying too low in the water and the waterline has been submersed, then it will be necessary to paint a new boot top at the higher level and to paint the intervening area with antifouling. You can use a clear, one-part antifouling which will not affect the gel coat. But if you do this, you must matt the underlying gelcoat, which would otherwise cause the antifouling lacquer to become dull after only a season's sailing and you would then have to renew the antifouling lacquer at the waterline every season.

A better alternative is to go to the pains of moving the boot top well above the waterline, so that the regular antifouling can be painted up to 1 cm (3/8") above the waterline. The method of marking waterline and boot top are given below.

The third reason for having an incorrectly marked waterline and boot top may be that they have not corresponded to the actual waterline from the start (this is sometimes the case with the first few boats from a new series), or that subsequent trimming has made the boat settle more at one end than the other.

Marking your waterline

Often, you discover that your waterline is wrongly placed when you take the boat up at the end of the season and find that the real waterline, now marked by a stained line of debris, oil, etc., does not correspond with the painted one. Mark the stain line with masking tape before you wash off the dirt. You now have the actual waterline.

If you want to raise the waterline and/or boot top by the same distance all around, the simplest method is to take a piece of string equal to the distance, attach a felt-tipped pen to it, and simply mark the new line at close intervals. This will work satisfactorily as long as the distance you want to move the line is not too great—say, 10 mm (3/8"). The method works well, too, if you want to raise the waterline slightly at one end, due to the fact that the fore-and-aft trim has been changed.

If the distance you want to move the line is greater, however, or if there is no boot top and you want to add one to improve the appearance of your boat, then one of the illustrated methods will give a completely acceptable result.

Method 1

This method of marking the waterline is simple and effective. You need a piece of clear plastic hose (a) which you fill with coloured water.

Hold one end of the hose so that the water level at that end is level with the waterline of the boat at the midships point. Move the other end out from that point towards the stern, say 100 mm (4 in), and mark the hull at the level of the water in that end of the hose. Now move the hose along the hull in this fashion, until you have a line of marks all around the hull, showing the waterline.

Decide on the distance between the waterline and the bottom of the boot top, and mark this in the same way. Then decide on the width of the boot top and mark again. You now have

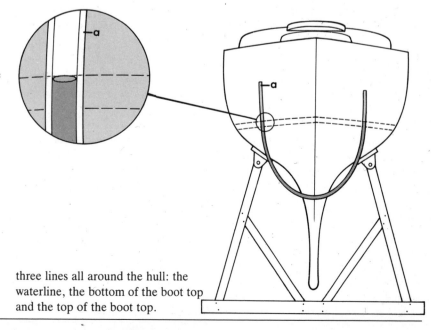

three lines all around the hull: the waterline, the bottom of the boot top and the top of the boot top.

Method 2

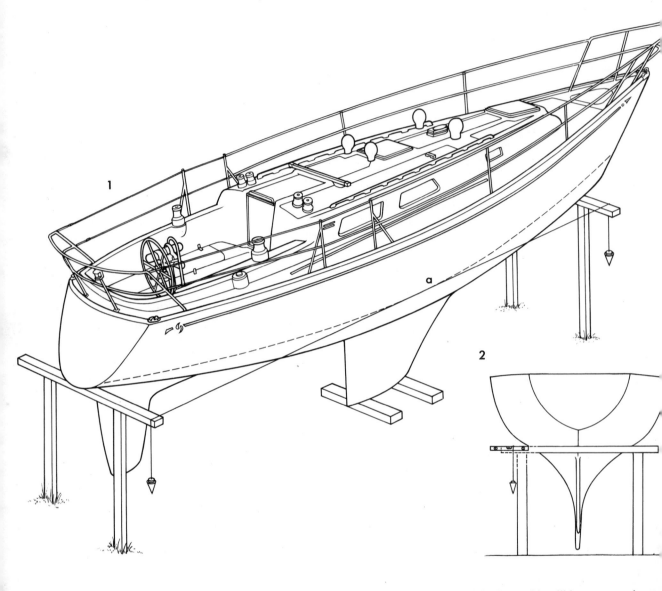

1. With the boat on land and absolutely level (use the spirit level and bobline), mark up the waterline at the fore, aft, and midships points. If the actual waterline cannot be ascertained by the stain method, you must refer to the boat's plans. You can also take the measurements from an identical boat, if there is one convenient in the boatyard.

Build a frame of battens so that the upper edge of the top batten aligns with the waterline mark at the fore and aft ends of the boat. Hang a string, weighted down at each end, over the fore and aft frames, so that the string

touches the waterline amidships (*a*). Mark the waterline there and at close intervals forward and aft.

2. When the curve of the hull becomes so great that you cannot reach the surface with the pen resting on the string, make an extension for the pen, with a thin batten, to which you have attached a small spirit level. This will ensure that the marks you make are absolutely horizontal.

Now decide how far above the waterline you want to have the boot top. At midships, it should be about 50 mm (2″). Depending on the design

of the boat, this will increase to about 100 mm (4″) at the bow and maybe 90 mm (3 1/2″) at the stern.

Adjust the frames at the bow and stern, so that the string now marks the bottom of the boot top. Mark up the line, as above. Then decide on how wide you want the boot top to be and mark the top line of the boot top.

Mask the top and bottom of the boot top with tape and paint it with a two-component lacquer.

PAINTING THE BOOT TOP

On the previous two pages, we have shown how the boot top is marked up. To paint the boot top, it is always advisable to work from the top downwards.

This reduces the possibility of drips spoiling paint already applied.

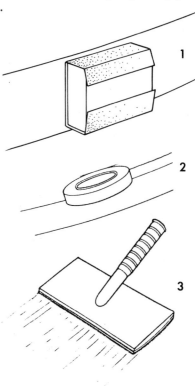

1. To get a good ground for the paint, the area to be painted must be cut back, by sanding down with abrasive paper until you have a smooth, dust-free surface. Before you start, protect the bordering gel coat with wide masking tape, so that you don't sand down gel coat that is not going to be painted. Brush or vacuum the dust off.

2. Mask off the bottom of the boot top with masking tape, making sure that you get good adhesion at the edge of the tape which is going to be painted over. Don't press the other edge against the hull. This will make it easier to remove the masking tape, when the job is finished. Remove the masking tape as soon as you are finished painting, as sunlight can bond it to the surface, and it will be extremely difficult to remove without damaging what you have done.

3. If you have sanded down to the bare laminate, you must apply a coat of recommended primer (to provide adhesion for the following coats of paint).

If you want to change the colour of the boot top, you will need to apply an undercoat. When this has dried, you can apply the top coats, as above.

Note: the drying times will vary and you may find that you have to remove the masking tape in between. This is a time-consuming job but is preferable to having masking tape that is stuck fast to the hull.

A new type of plastic masking tape is now becoming generally available, and this is much better than the old paper tape, as it does not bond to the surface so quickly, but can be pulled off more easily, even after some time in place.

GEL WASHING THE BILGE

The main reason that the bilge of a glassfibre boat is often left unused is the almost invisible spikes and splinters of glassfibre left protruding by the manufacturers. This is easily remedied by giving the whole area a gel wash, which leaves a smooth, clean, and washable surface. Do this after the boat is delivered new, when the bilges are clean.

If the boat is second-hand, then you need to wash the bilges clean and leave to dry properly, before applying the wash.

You need gel coat, a suitable resin, wax additive solution, and catalyst. Use proprietary cleaning solvent, a large brush, and a plastic bucket in which to mix the wash.

As usual when working with fibreglass, the temperature should be no less than 20° C (65° F), and work in well-ventilated conditions.

The mix is very important. To the gel, which you buy in the colour required, you add one-sixth of its volume in resin and 4 cc per kg (0.65 fl oz per lb) of the wax additive solution. Mix the contents thoroughly.

Just before applying, add the catalyst, which is usually 8 cc per kg at 20° C (65° F) or follow the manufacturer's instructions. Mix well and brush on immediately, with pressure on the brush and laying off in both directions. Cover the area with a generous layer of the wash. The resin content will help the gel to flow to a smooth coat. Don't fiddle about by going back over the job. Apply a good coat and then leave it alone!

REPAINTING THE HULL

After about ten years, depending on climate, sailing waters, wear-and-tear, and how well it has been maintained, the finish on a glassfibre boat begins to look dull and tired. It can then be worth considering a complete spray job with two-pot paint system.

It must be pointed out at once that this is no easy undertaking for an amateur. It is tough, painstaking work, and in order to get a top-class result,

which will make your boat look like new again, you are going to have to work with scrupulous precision and to have all the prerequisites, such as your workplace and equipment, in top trim. It is safer to let a professional shipyard do the job, but that is so expensive that it is tempting to try it yourself. If you do, you can count on spending a well-planned forty-eight hours at it.

You need: proprietary degreasing agent; coarse, medium, and fine abrasive paper; a wooden sanding block like that shown helps you to exert an even pressure over the abrasive paper; an oscillating sander, preferably with

dust-suction bag (this is expensive and can often be hired); if you don't have a dust-suction bag, then you'll need a face mask; a rotating sander; rags and a tack cloth (most effective when cleaning up dust from the sanding);

two-pot (two-pack) lacquer; a power spraygun (can often be hired); strong rubber gloves, protective goggles, and a face mask.

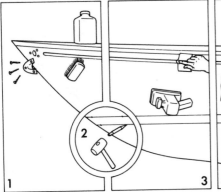
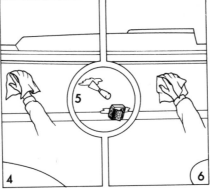
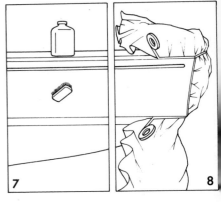

1. Remove all fittings that are going to be in the way. If the superstructure is going to be painted, remove all ventilator flanges and suchlike.

Wash the hull very thoroughly with degreasing agent, so that all old releasing agent, wax, and polish are removed. Wash all surfaces twice. Wear rubber gloves, goggles, and face mask!

2. If the waterline is painted into the gel coat, it too must be repainted. Mark its edge(s) by making small, shallow holes with an awl at regular intervals along it.

3. Sand the surface well, first with coarse abrasive paper and then with fine. When you can't get at it with the sander, do it by hand, for instance the edging trim around the portholes and even in the score for the boot top.

4. Wipe off ALL the sanded dust from the hull with rags or (much better) the tack cloth.

5. Repair any minor scratches in the hull's surface and sand smooth.

6. Wipe off the hull again with the tack cloth.

7. Wash the entire hull with degreasing agent again. Then wash the hull with fresh water.

8. Following the tiny awl marks, cover the waterline with masking tape. Any area that is not to be sprayed must be covered over with plastic, taped into position.

If you reckon on needing two days to spray the entire hull, do only one side per day, and mask off the prow and the stern.

Do not begin spraying if the temperature is under 20°C (68°F). If you are working outdoors, then there should be absolutely no wind.

Mix the two components together in a separate container, according to the instructions on the paint can. As the lacquer hardens quickly, you should only mix enough for, say, two or three coats at a time. Fill the spray gun with the lacquer and start spraying.

All in all, you must spray on 8–10 coats of lacquer. Allow twenty minutes between each coat. This means that if you begin at the prow and work your way back to the stern, you can immediately start the next coat at the prow, because it will take you that long to spray the one side of the hull.

Ideally, you should work indoors. If you're lucky, you can find a shipyard that will let you have a boat shed for a humane rent during the summer months. Otherwise, you can build a covered work platform outdoors by covering a skeleton of wood or aluminium poles with tarpaulin. Give yourself a lot of working space around the boat. Remember that you must work in as dust-free an atmosphere as possible and the temperature should not be lower than 20°C (68°F).

You need to have a sturdy work platform all around the boat, or at least along one side.

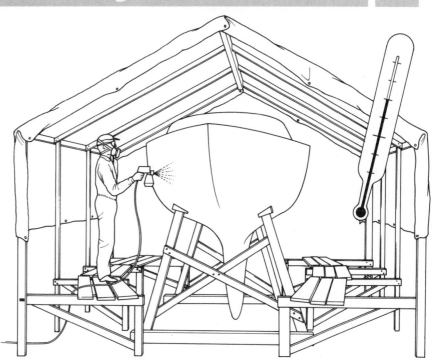

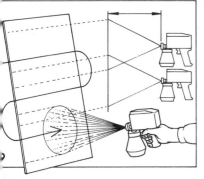

9. Before you start on the actual hull, try your painting technique on the shiny side of an upright sheet of hardboard. The spray nozzle should be held about 500 mm (18″) away from the surface to be painted. Start spraying in the air a little to the left of the left-hand edge of the hardboard and then move the spraygun in a fluid movement along the board, parallel to the ground. Continue a little to the right of the right-hand edge and then return to the surface in the track below where you have painted.

10. Now go over the hull and start spraying in the "starting zone", a little in front of the prow. Move the gun slowly and firmly, parallel to the deck line, from the prow edge back towards the stern.

11. Normally, however, it is safer to do it section by section, the length of each section depending on how far you can reach without changing the angle of the nozzle. Start at the gunwale and work down to the waterline. When you come to the end of a section, release the trigger and continue your movement a little. When you start the return movement, press the trigger again. Otherwise, you will spray two coats on when you turn back, and the paint will start to run.

Each new swathe of paint should overlap the previous one a little, and each section should overlap the previous one a little, so that the thinner coat at the end of each section will receive as much paint as the rest of the section.

Continue in this way until one side of the hull is completely painted. Check and refill your paint supply regularly.

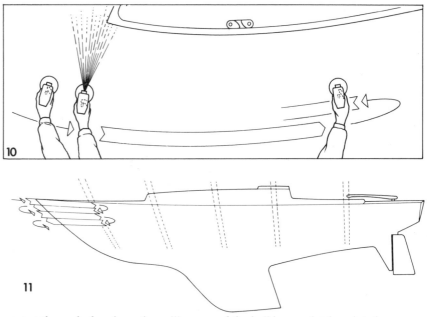

The proper paint for your boat

If you repaint your hull—or any part of your boat for that matter—as described on the previous pages, remember to consult your paint supplier about the choice of paint. This is a major project, and paint is expensive, so if you are not certain that your supplier knows enough about the subject, contact the paint manufacturers. Most reputable marine-paint manufacturers have advisory services that you can call to discuss your specific requirements, or at least they have booklets telling you how to use their products. Another good idea is to talk to other boat owners—either members of your sailing club or those who have their boats laid up for the winter in the same boatyard. Their experience can be extremely valuable, especially when it comes to local conditions, such as the marine environment in the waters where you normally sail.

Compatibility between the paints used is vital.

That is why it is a good idea to use paints—primer, undercoat, and topcoat—from the same manufacturer. Always keep a record of the paints applied and keep it in a place where you can find it, so that next time you are going to paint, you know what to buy.

Nowadays, marine-paint manufacturers offer a wide choice of colours, and it is tempting to try out some new shade. Always think of the complete colour scheme before trying anything too startling, and remember the feelings of your fellow yachtsmen, most of whom will stick to the traditional white.

White reflects the rays of the sun, which means that the paint does not get too hot in direct sunlight. Dark colours absorb heat and, strangely enough, it is more difficult to scrub them clean of stains.

CHAPTER 5

Deck
and
Superstructure

Very often, poor deck layout or badly designed fittings will lead to damage to the deck (and crew!). These faults can be remedied before damage occurs, if the boat owner is aware what can go wrong, so that action can be taken at an early stage, or even when the boat is delivered. Shown on the following pages are a number of the typical things that go wrong on deck.

DECK HARDWARE SURVEY

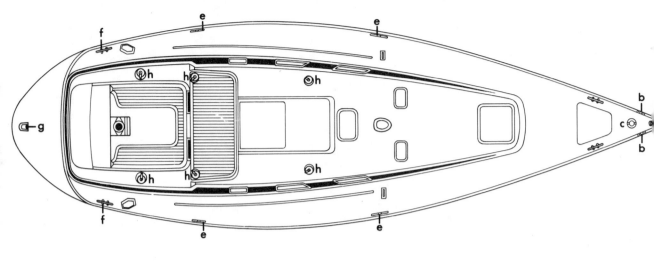

Assess your boat's deck hardware and look at the way it is fastened through the deck. Check for stress cracks both in fittings and in deck.

(a) Stemhead fitting and/or bow roller.
(b) Fairleads that may lead a rope over a glassfibre moulding, causing chafing.
(c) Mooring bollard.
(d) Through-deck forestay fitting.
(e) Fender cleats.
(f) Aft mooring/towing bollards.
(g) Backstay fitting.
(h) Winches.

Poor fittings

The bow roller is, perhaps, inadequate or has not been fitted at all. This means that the anchor chain can easily jump out and saw through the bow. Many modern yachts have no provision for safe handling of the anchor chain, having only a stem-head fitting to take the forestay. The bow roller must be dimensioned to take the anchor chain and should have a locking pin to stop the chain jumping out.

Chafe

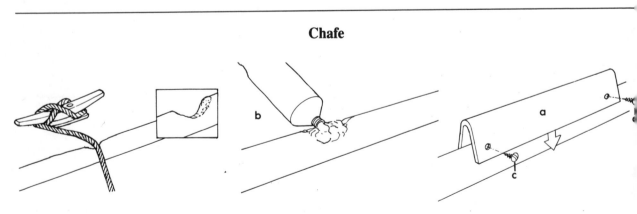

Some deck-hull joins in glassfibre are unprotected by cappings and are easily damaged by fender ropes and mooring lines cutting through the gel coat and getting into the glassfibre laminate.

To repair chafing damage of this kind, you must fit stainless-steel anti-chafe plates (a) over the glassfibre sections that are most vulnerable to damage. Make sure that the length of the plate is generous, that is, in excess of the maximum area that the rope, in any lead, is likely to lie on.

First of all, repair the damaged gel coat with epoxy filler (b) if the damage is not deep. If it is, then you must build up the space with glassfibre cloth and epoxy resin, finished with a coat of gel coat.

Do not use adhesive under the plate, as you may need to replace it. Use a silicone-rubber sealant and self tapping screws (c) to hold it in position. (The screws are not subjected to any direct strain.)

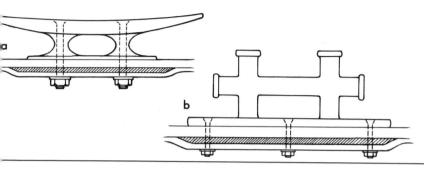

Wrong fittings

A light, "toy" cleat can easily get ripped out of the deck. Such a cleat is no substitute for a heavy-duty double-footed cleat *(a)* or a sturdy crosshead bollard *(b)*, which is through-bolted to the glassfibre deck where there is a wide stress-distributing reinforcement which was built in during lamination or added at a later stage.

STANCHIONS AND LIFELINES

Stanchion bases

Damage to stanchion bases may be due to overloading by human force (some weakminded person swinging off the stanchion), or collision, especially catching onto other boats' rigging or bowsprits. The type of damage depends on the type of stanchion base. The best designs are those that "fail" slowly rather than break rapidly. Two common types are illustrated.

Stress cracks are due to one of two things, overload and incorrrect through-going fitting. Look for hairline cracks around deck fittings, like stanchions and cleats, and get down below and examine the methods (or lack of them) used to reinforce the fittings below deck.

Examine the metal in the fittings for signs of stress, such as cracking, especially if you suspect that the fitting might have been grossly overloaded in a recent emergency. If you see any sign of metal fatigue, there is nothing for it but to change the fitting.

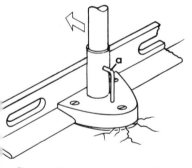

Stress damage to stanchion type 1

The stanchion base is fastened inside the alloy toe rail and overlaps its inboard base, through which two bolts are fastened. Overload in the direction of the arrow causes the bolts through the toe rail to bend and the inside bolt to be ripped through, or, at best, causes stress cracks in, the deck laminate. The light angle iron *(a)* that supports the stanchion holder often snaps off.

. Remove the alloy toe rail and the broken stanchion base.

2. Repair the damaged glassfibre laminate (see page 41). Reinforce the area below the stress-cracked part with a minimum of four laminations of CSM drenched in epoxy resin. Allow to cure.

3. Apply a new cosmetic coat of gel. Allow to cure.

4. Put a new alloy toe rail in place, bedding it in polysulphide sealant. Drill it for the bolts that will go through the stanchion base.

5. Replace the stanchion base, bedding it in polysulphide sealant, and secure it with bolts.

Stress damage to stanchion type 2

This stanchion base is mounted on top of a raised glassfibre toe rail. This is a better design than type 1, because, generally, it fails slowly, the plate *(a)* that supports the stanchion holder

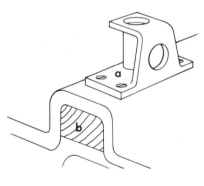

bending rather than snapping under strain. Fatigue cracks in the angles of the toe rail will usually result from this kind of pressure. These will require repair and the area will need reinforcing.

The hollow section in the toe rail should have been filled with a shaped wooden batten *(b)* to at least 100 mm (4″) on each side of the bolted fitting. In addition, reinforcing CSM should be glassed in on the underside to spread the load over a larger area of the deck.

Check-list for stanchions and lifelines

(a) Lifelines should always be plastic-coated.

(b) Anti-chafe ferrules should be fitted where the lifelines pass through the stanchion holes.

(c) Stanchion holes should be rounded off or bushed.

(d) Check for corrosion where the stanchion is in contact with the top of the stanchion holder.

(e) Check also the holding pin, which may be wasted.

(f) Look for metal fatigue at all welded points—where the stanchion holder is connected to its base and the eyes on the pulpit where the lifelines are attached. Hairline cracks indicate metal fatigue.

(g) The tensioning screws should have Monel wire stops bent into place to prevent the screw from undoing.

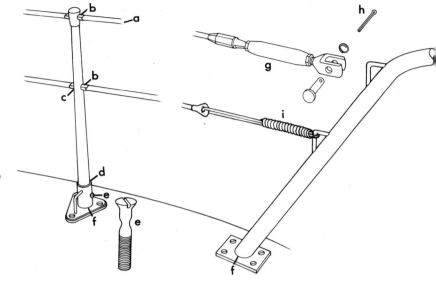

(h) The split pin that secures the clevis pin must be bent back only once. Always replace it after you have straightened it out. Remember to tape over all split pins, to prevent someone cutting a hand on one.

(i) Attach the lower lifeline to the pulpit with a short rope splice, which can be cut quickly in a man-overboard situation, when you have to haul someone aboard.

When fitting or replacing stanchions

(a) Fit the stanchions so that they angle slightly inwards, keeping clear of obstructions such as vertical piles in marinas.

(b) The distance between stanchions should be maximum 2 m (7 ft). On smaller craft, closer spacing (1.25 to 1.5 m, or 4 to 5 ft) is aesthetically pleasing.

(c) Avoid pulpit overhangs that can catch other craft, such as that on the illustrated boat. Likewise, think about that stern fixture for your dinghy or tender. You pay more at your marine berth for this extra length!

(d) Position the pelican hook-and-eye entrance at the lowest point along the shear, to give easy access to the cockpit.

(e) If a radio is carried aboard, the lifeline must have an insulator break (which is *not* tensioned) to prevent causing radio interference.

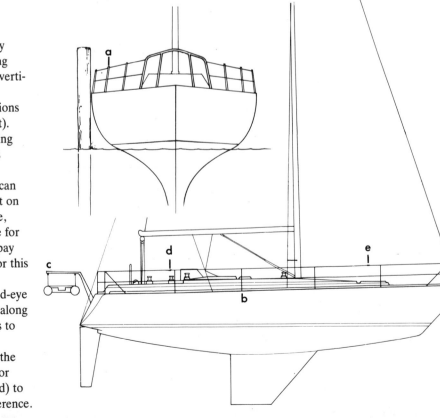

Make your own terminal ends on lifelines

You can buy stainless steel terminals and fit them on the lifelines quite easily. (Courtesy Norseman)

1. Insert the wire through the terminal body and prise back the outer wires from the core.

2. Fit the cone onto the core, so that the core protrudes approximately the diametre of the lifeline.

3. Bend the outer wires back to the core, tapering the ends over the top of the cone.

4. Start mating threads, using the terminal end or a special starter that comes with the terminals.

5. Apply Loctite thread sealant to both threads, and screw the terminal end into the body. Tighten.

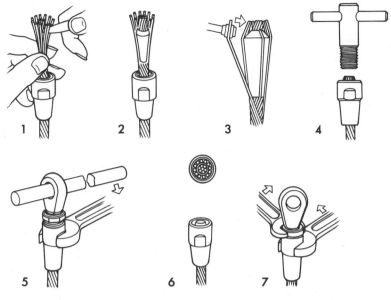

6. Unscrew to inspect and ensure that the wires are evenly spaced and neatly closed over the cone.

7. Apply marine sealant to the blind hole in the terminal end and reassemble. Repeat this until sealant oozes from the body end. Tighten the assembly and locknut.

Lifeline netting

Make your own lifeline netting forward, or buy a suitable piece. This prevents the foresail from blowing overboard during a change. A simple shock-cord (a), fastened at one end to an eye in the deck and with a carbine hook at the other, will hold a changed sail securely in place against the netting until you have more time to stow it properly. Excellent for short-handed crews.

Make the lifelines comfortable

The helmsman and crew can lounge comfortably against the lifelines along the cockpit if the lifelines are replaced by webbing (a) or if the upper lifeline is fitted with a fender (b) that fits snugly under the armpit. Sailing should be as comfortable as you can make it!

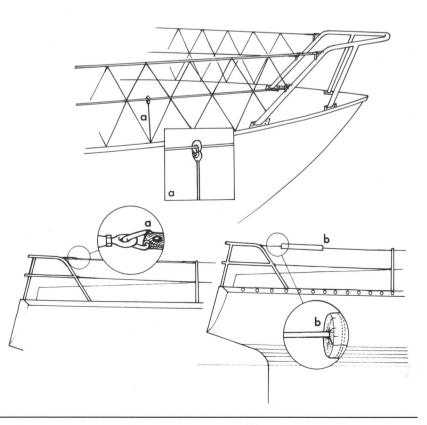

FASTENING HEAVY FITTINGS TO SANDWICH

Fittings that have to be fastened through a sandwich construction with a porous filling are, depending on their function, subjected to different degrees of strain. The porous filling, sandwiched between the two layers of glassfibre laminate, is not strong and hard enough to prevent the throughgoing bolts or screws from working a little loose. The resulting leakage can occur even if watertight silicone-rubber sealant has been used in the boltholes. The laminate can also crack from the strain, eventually loosening the fitting.

(*Right*) The drawing shows some typical fittings that must be fastened with through bolts and support plates, and one, a handed fairlead, that is wrongly mounted. The washers between the bolt and the inner laminate of glassfibre are far too small to spread the strain, and the result is that the material has been squeezed together, allowing enough space for water to seep through.

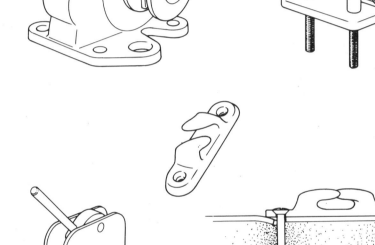

Light-pressure fittings

Below, we show the correct way to fasten a fitting that will have to take a certain amount of strain.

Begin by making a cardboard template of the fitting and mark up and cut out the screw holes. Then fix the template in position and use a pencil or, better, a punch to mark up the holes to be drilled. (Instead of making a template, you can temporarily fix the fitting in position with tape and mark up where the holes are to be drilled).

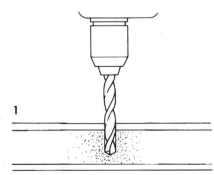

1. Select a drill that is 1 mm (1/32″) narrower than the bolt to be used and drill holes through both layers of laminate.

2. Now go below deck and, using the drilled holes as centre for your hole saw, cut out circular holes five to six times the diameter of the bolt hole.

3. Saw the holes only in the below-deck layer of laminate and the porous filling.
DON'T CUT THROUGH THE TOP-SIDE LAYER!

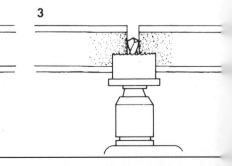

FASTENING LIGHTER FITTINGS TO SANDWICH

A stopper like this is often used to hold halliards that are under heavy pressure, and therefore it needs more than just large washers and through-going bolts and nuts to ensure firm holding. A metal support plate, or base plate, as it is also known, that will spread the strain over a large area of the glassfibre laminate is necessary.

Mark up the holes and drill them through the deck, strengthening them with polymer or epoxy-resin filler, as shown points 1–6, below.

Cut out an aluminium or stainless-steel support plate (*a*) that is about 10 mm (½″) wider all around than the base of the fitting. Sometimes, this support plate is supplied with the fitting.

Make sure the topdeck laminate is clean and dry. Apply watertight silicone-rubber sealant to the area that will be covered by the fitting. Put some sealant into the drilled holes and allow it to harden a little (see the times given on the tube). Then mount the fitting in position and secure it from the topside with the bolts and from belowdeck with the support plate, washers, and nuts. Tighten the nuts and bolts before the sealant has hardened completely.

Secure the nuts with double nuts or lock-nuts. Another way to do this is to crush the threads on the "free" side of the nuts, but this is the poorest alternative and should be done only if you don't have double nuts or lock-nuts.

If the nuts are visible from belowdeck, say in the cabin ceiling, you may want to conceal them by either using attractive-looking domed nuts (*b*) or by covering them with a cut-to measure piece of mahogany or teak (*c*), first drilling out enough wood to allow the piece to be fitted flush. This wooden cover can be fixed in position with a couple of countersunk copper nails or screws.

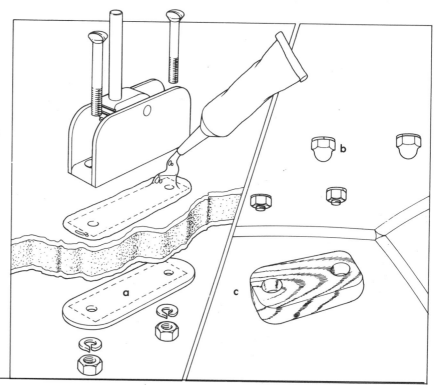

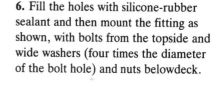

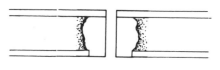

4. Dig out the porous filling with a knife or an old screwdriver. Now fill the hole with a two-component polymer or epoxy-resin filler. Smooth off the belowdeck surface flush with the laminate before the filler hardens.

5. When the filler has set hard, drill through it from above, with the first drill. You now have through holes that will be strong and withstand a lot of strain.

5

6. Fill the holes with silicone-rubber sealant and then mount the fitting as shown, with bolts from the topside and wide washers (four times the diameter of the bolt hole) and nuts belowdeck.

6

Always use marine-grade stainless-steel nuts, bolts, and washers.

FASTENING LIGHT FITTINGS TO SANDWICH

When you cannot get at a fitting from belowdeck to secure it in position, it is possible to fasten the fitting from the topside only, using the method shown and stainless-steel metal bolts that screw into threaded sockets, known as molly nuts. This works both with sandwich construction and with homogenous glassfibre laminate.

Molly nuts are excellent for fastening a fitting that you will mount and demount regularly, for instance spray-hood frames.

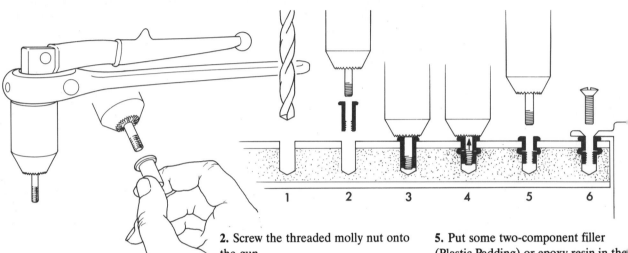

1. Drill shallow holes of the same diametre as the molly nuts. Make sure that the drill does not penetrate the inner laminate. Fill the hole with silicone-rubber sealant.

2. Screw the threaded molly nut onto the gun.

3. Insert the molly nut into the drilled hole, as shown.

4. "Fire" the gun. This compresses the material above the threads without crushing them. The nut is now firmly lodged in the hole.

5. Put some two-component filler (Plastic Padding) or epoxy resin in the nut and on the surface where the fitting will be bedded.

6. Screw on the fitting but do not tighten it immediately, as this would press out all the filler or resin. When the filler has hardened a little, you can screw the fitting fully in.

Using metal screws

Screws should not be used to fasten any kind of fitting that is going to have to withstand pressure, but a light-weight fitting like this small lantern can be fastened in position with metal screws (which are threaded all along the shaft).

Begin by marking up and drilling the holes.

1. Coat the area to be covered by the fitting with watertight silicone-rubber sealant or epoxy resin. Squeeze some sealant onto the screws and into the screw holes. When the sealant has hardened a little, screw the fitting in position but do not tighten fully.

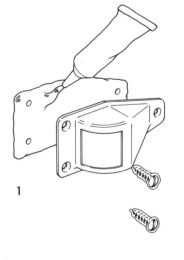

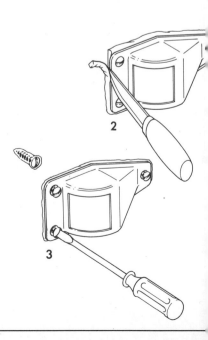

2. Cut away excess sealant.

3. Now tighten the screws fully.

Right) How to fasten a through fitting that will not have to take strain, for instance, mountings for instruments, plexiglass covers, hatch coamings, and so on.

Follow the procedures described opposite for marking up the holes. Simply drill through holes and mount the fitting with bolts, washers, and nuts.

. Mark up the hole with a template or dividers.

. Use a power jig to saw out the hole, about 3 mm (⅛″) inside the marked circle.

. Use a half-round file to file the circle to the required diameter. Do it from the inside if the hole is going to be visible from the inside cabin. Then seal the edges with polymer or epoxy-

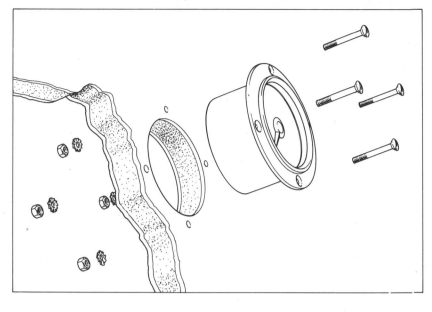

resin filling to prevent water from entering the laminate.

FASTENING FITTINGS TO LAMINATE

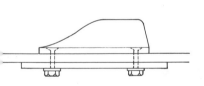

Fitting load-spreading plates to single-thickness GRP hulls
A 4-mm (3/16″) plate of aluminium or a 9-mm (3/8″) piece of marine plywood of an area considerably wider than the fitting, will spread stress loads effectively beyond the base of the fitting.

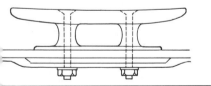

Heavy-duty fittings
A load-spreading plate that backs a fitting that could be exposed to very heavy loading, such as a winch base or an anchor or towing bollard, can be glassed in with layers of glassfibre cloth and resin. Do not glass in the bolts, as you may need to remove the fitting.

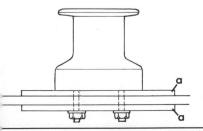

Spreading the load for a heavily loaded fitting
Marine-grade light-alloy plates *(a)* are fastened between the fitting's base plate and the deck, and, on the underside, between the locking nuts and the deck. Nuts and bolts must be of stainless steel, which is compatible with the aluminium. Polysulphide sealant is spread on the bolt threads before fastening, and the topside plate is bedded in it. This method of fastening is suitable for davits, anchor-chain and towing bollards, winches, and anchor windlasses.

NON-SKID SURFACES

When a glassfibre deck is smooth moulded, or when it has a moulded patterned finish, it is dangerous to work on, especially when wet. There are three ways you might improve the situation. To begin with, all you need to consider is the plan of your deck.

Laying down stick-on deck covering

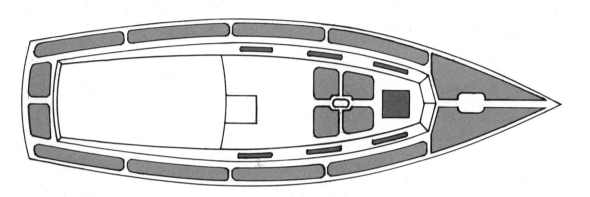

1. Cut out paper templates (patterns) of all the areas to receive the deck covering.

2. Find out the sizes in which sheets of the material are available and, laying out the templates in the most economical way, work out the number of sheets you require.

3. Cut out the sheet material according to the templates.

4. Read the manufacturer's instructions and use only the recommended adhesive. Lay down the material in the way specified by the manufacturer.

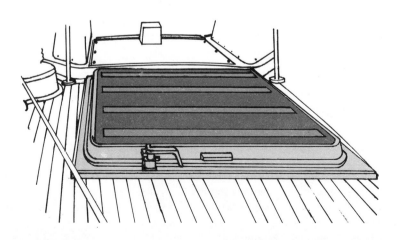

Non-skid strips
Hatches of acrylic glass are very slippery when wet, so strips of non-skid material should be stuck on to them. Another area that should be treated with non-skid material is the forehead where you very often go on board.

LAYING TEAK

A teak deck on a glassfibre boat not only makes the boat more attractive, it also raises the value of the boat and provides a hard-wearing surface that is practically non-skid and maintenance-free. Teak is an extremely hard wood that is oily, and thus well suited to the rigours of the marine climate. An annual dosing of teak oil will keep the surface looking good, although many prefer to allow the wood to adopt a natural weathered look.

To lay teak on a glassfibre deck, you do not have to have a completely even surface. Even if the deck is strongly patterned with anti-skid material, you can still achieve an excellent result.

You need: teak planks, say 12×35 mm (1/2″× 1/2″), stainless-steel screws, and the correct adhesive/sealant.

The teak planks should be profiled on one edge and straight on the other, so that when they are fitted together, a gap of about 5 mm (3/16″) wide and about 6 mm (1/4″) deep remains between them. This gap will be filled with a sealant, to keep out water and form the attractive-looking black seam that one associates with teak decks.

Seam profile is important from the point of view of keeping out the water. A square-sided profile is more effective than the "V" shaped profile that is sometimes found on prefabricated teak planking, and the depth of the gap should be not less than 6 mm (1/4″) for a 35-mm (1 1/2″) wide teak plank.

The choice of the adhesive/sealant is vital, because the structural glassfibre laminate and the teak cladding are likely to have different movements, the former under the influence of the waves and the latter under the influence of the weather (from cold and rain to hot sunshine). A polyurethane-based sealant is the best bet here, as it adheres extremely well both to teak and to glassfibre laminate. The same sealant can be used for the seam, but a two-part polysulphide resin is recommended instead, if only because this has had the opportunity of standing the test of time longer.

1. Make a drawing of the area that you want to cover in teak, so that you know how much wood you need (buy more than you need, to allow for waste), and so that you see where problems may arise, such as when the planking will come up against a hatch or the superstructure. Obstacles like these must be framed with teak, to provide a neat, attractive finish for the deck planking that will butt against them.

2. Clear the deck of all fittings, such as bollards, cleats, stanchions, etc.

(continued on next page)

3. Make templates of the king planks. Transfer the shape onto suitable teak planks and saw out the king planks. Then rout out a rebate, 6 mm (1/4″) deep and 5 mm (3/16″) wide, all around the king planks, to take the snapes of the deck planks.

4. Spread a thick even coat of the polyurethane-based sealant where the king planks are to be fitted. Put them in place and drill countersunk holes through the plank and into the laminate. The drill should go through the teak, through the laminate, and stop just as it has pierced the inside of the laminate and entered a part of the sandwich filling. Never drill through the inside layer of laminate. Tighten down each screw. Note how deep the screw should go into a sandwich construction (detail).

5. Take the first plank and cut its end so that it fits neatly into the appropriate snape in the king plank. Before laying the first plank, cover the edge of the deck (where the deck meets the hull) with a layer of sealant. Lay the plank in this, with the profiled edge pointing towards the midships. As you are going to fill a space between the toe rail or coaming and the first teak plank with the polysulphide sealant, you must establish this space by inserting some small pieces of wood (*a*), the width of the seam, between the toe rail and the plank, until the plank is securely fastened in place. Then you can remove the spacing pieces with a chisel.

Cramp the plank in position while you are drilling and fastening it.

6. Countersink screw holes at 500-mm (10″) intervals with a suitably stoppered countersink drill.

7. Continue now by cutting the end of the second plank to fit its snape in the king plank. Then spread more sealant, in which to bed the plank, the straight edge of which is to butt against the profile of the first plank. Drill and screw as before.

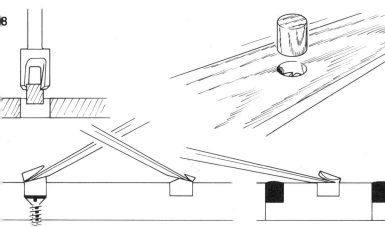

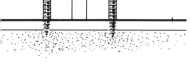

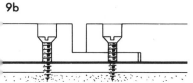

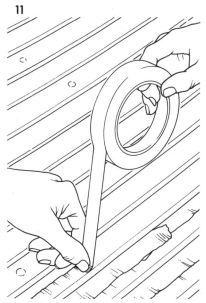

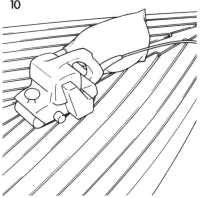

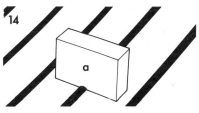

8. Cut wooden plugs to fill the countersunk holes. Turn the grain of each plug in the same direction as that of the plank, and glue the plugs with epoxy resin.

Trim each plug flush with the deck with a sharp chisel, using three cuts, as shown.

9. Each strip is fitted neatly *(a)* end-to-end to the next, with about 5 mm (3/16″) between them for the sealant. An alternative is to lap joint them *(b)*, again leaving a gap for sealant. Fasten the planks about 5 mm (3/16″) in from the end of each strip.

10. When all the planks have been plugged, the deck is sanded down, preferably with a sanding machine. Remove all the dust, using a vacuum cleaner.

11. Mask the seams with masking tape. Many deck sealants require that the teak be primed to ensure maximum adhesion. Check the manufacturer's instructions, and prime the seam gaps, if necessary. Then mix the sealant thoroughly, and only a gun-full at a time. Pourable grades of sealant are available, but the skeleton gun makes things easier. However, there are those who insist on using pourable sealant which they press in with a trowel or a putty knife, as there is a chance that sealant from the gun may contain air bubbles.

12. Fill the plastic cartridge with the mixed sealant, and insert it into the skeleton gun.

Overfill the joints slightly, to allow for final trimming.

13. When the sealant has fully cured, excess is removed with a sharp chisel. Fine deck finish can be achieved with some makes of sealant that allow both sanding and planing after cure.

14. An alternative finish is to increase the non-skid quality of the teak deck by moulding the excess sealant into a raised profile with a wooden template *(a)*.

RECAULKING A LAID TEAK DECK

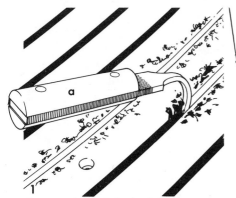

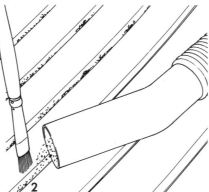

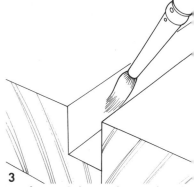

Prepare the deck in the following way.

1. Rake out all the old marine glue or sealant. Use a seam rake *(a)* that you make yourself from an old file, onto which you put a comfortable handle.

2. Brush or, even better, vacuum out the seam and degrease any oily areas.

3. Many deck sealants require seams to be primed to ensure maximum adhesion to the teak. Check the

manufacturer's instructions and apply the primer accordingly.

Then continue as on the previous page, steps 11–13.

REPLACING A DAMAGED TEAK PLANK

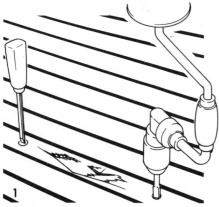

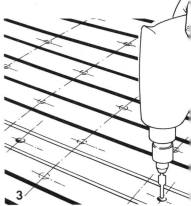

A heavy object, especially if it has sharp edges, can damage a plank beyond repair, and it must then be replaced.

1. First, you must remove the damaged plank. Use a chisel to break up the dowels covering the countersunk screws. Use a fine chisel, slightly smaller in width than the diametre of the dowel. Remove the screws. They

will probably be difficult to remove, so use a brace and bit and tighten them further slightly before winding them up.
Remove the sealant. Prise up the damaged plank carefully. If the deck is relatively new, you can probably buy a standard-dimensioned replacement plank. Otherwise, you must buy a rough plank of suitable dimensions and trim and plane it to size.

2. Apply a new bedding of deck sealant and lay in the new plank.

3. Remember that when you drill new holes in the replacement plank you must not use the old holes drilled in the laminate underneath. Position the holes so that new holes are drilled in the laminate.
Finish by renewing the seam sealant as described on the previous page.

WINDOWS AND PORTLIGHTS

Windows and portlights are a potential source of leaks. Rubber sealants crack with age, or the wrong sealant can have been used from the beginning. Fatigue cracks appearing in the framing or in the glazing material are another cause of leaking, while yet another is bad bonding between the outer and inner lamination skins. The final problem can be difficult to trace to its source, as the water may enter the laminate quite some distance away from where it leaks into the boat.

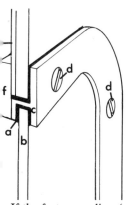

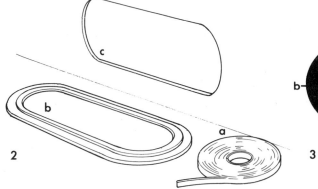

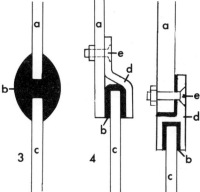

1. If the factory sealing (a) between the glazing material (b) and the extrusion (c) has failed, it must be replaced. Remove the glazing, take away the old sealing, clean the join area, and fill the area with epoxy resin putty before applying new sealant and replacing the extrusion and the glazing. The best sealant for use above the waterline is silicone-rubber sealant, which cures slowly, thus giving you time to install the window and to clean up before it sets. Always coat the screws (d) with sealant, when replacing them. Note the way in which the cabin lining (e) is fitted under the window's inside beading (f).

2. Marine-grade double-sided sticky sealing strip (a) is more expensive than silicone-rubber sealant but is quicker and cleaner to use and fills irregularities between the two surfaces well. (b) Window. (c) Cabin wall.

3. If this type of window seal leaks, it may be possible to inject sealant under the rubber. Otherwise, you're going to need a new sealant.
(a) Coachroof of glassfibre laminate.
(b) Rubber seal.
(c) Glazing.

4. Two different aluminium-extrusion frames. Leaks may arise either around the rubber seal or through the bolts. Remove the glazing by undoing the bolts, fit a new rubber seal around the glazing, apply silicone-rubber sealant to the outside surface of the laminate, particularly around the bolt holes. Insert bolts and tighten.
(a) Coachroof laminate.
(b) Rubber seal.
(c) Glazing.
(d) Aluminium frame.
(e) Nut and bolt.

Fitting double-profile seals

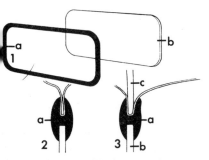

1. Fit the inner profile (a) onto the glazing (b).

2. Insert two turns of thin string inside the outer profile, which will fit onto the coachroof laminate(c).

3. Coat the laminate with liquid detergent. Hold the window with the attached seal in position so that the lips of the outer profile are pressed against the edge of the laminate. Pulling on the string will bend back the lip of the seal to allow it to be pressed home onto the laminate.

Fitting a window seal to a framed window

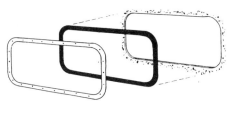

Clean the laminate surface. Apply silicone-rubber sealant around the edges of the laminate. Fit the rubber seal onto the glazing. Position the window and press it home with the frame. Screw the frame in position with screws covered in silicone-rubber sealant.

Fitting a seal to a divided-frame window

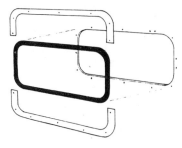

Apply the rubber seal to the glazing. Slide the two halves of the frame around the glazing and seal, using liquid detergent as lubrication. Bolt the frame to the window opening.

THE COCKPIT

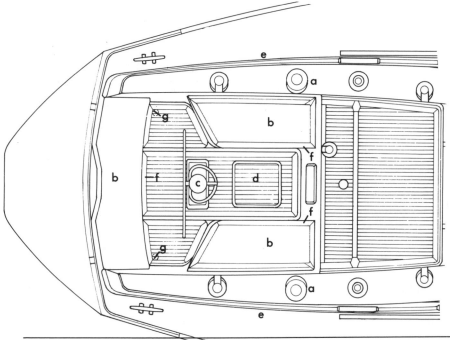

Cockpit problems

(a) Stress cracks where the winches are fastened will lead to leaking.

(b) Seating. Are the surfaces worn? Is the drainage satisfactory?

(c) Steering pedestal. Fix gratings around it. See pages 78–79.

(d) Engine access hatch. Does it leak? See below. Is the sound insulation acceptable?

(e) Coamings. Are the edges uncomfortably sharp? Have they been chipped or marked by feet?

(f) Lockers. Check the drainage. Are the items in the lockers easily accessible, or are they packed on top of each other?

(g) Cockpit drains. Are they adequate? They should be covered by gratings. Do they have valves?

Repairing glassfibre at|a winch base

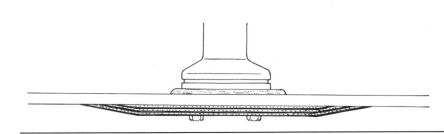

Remove the winch, reinforce the coaming from below with layers of CSM and epoxy resin. Apply a new coat of gel. Fit a teak pad beneath the winch base to take some of the bolt compression. Be sparing with sealant, as this can block drains in the base of some winches.

Engine-room hatch improvement

A hatch lying flush with the cockpit floor can be improved as shown. A wooden batten (a) is bonded to the hatch upstand (b) with layers of CSM and resin, to form a wide land. A 25-mm (1″) single-sided sticky, preformed sealant strip (c) is fitted all around to exclude water and to block engine noise. A drainage pipe (d) will carry off the water that gets into the waterway.

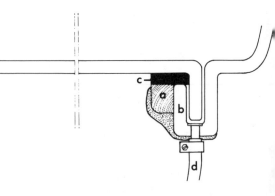

Repairing a coaming

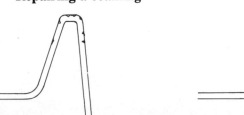

This coaming gives too narrow a grip and can be easily damaged by feet. Improve it by adding a teak capping profile, which covers the damage and provides a better handhold. It is, of course, even better if you add that capping profile when you buy the boat, thus preventing any damage from occurring.

COCKPIT DRAINAGE

Free water surfaces inside a boat seriously affect stability, and it is often found that a boat's drainage system is totally inadequate to remove any quantity of water speedily. Remember that the cockpit of even a small cruiser has at least three times the volume of your bath. Check how long it takes your 35-mm (1 1/2") bath outlet to empty your bath, and then look at the dimensions of your cockpit's drain pipes. Boats using sheltered waters may need only two drains, while boats for open-water cruising should have four.

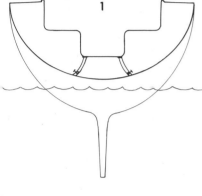

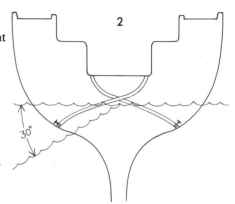

1. Cross-section of a light-displacement boat, with straight, "same side" drainage pipes draining the cockpit above the waterline.

2. Cross-section of a heavy-displacement boat which uses "cross over" drainage pipes draining the cockpit through seacocks below the waterline.

Cockpit seating

Seats can fill with water when the boat heels, or when it rains heavily. Drain this onto the cockpit floor or through the hull above the waterline via a 10-mm (3/8") plastic pipe *(a)* fastened by hose clips *(b)* to a copper-headed tube *(c)* countersunk in the seat and bedded in sealant. If the seat has a locker *(d)*, the waterway *(e)* should also be fitted with a drainage pipe *(f)* at the aft end.

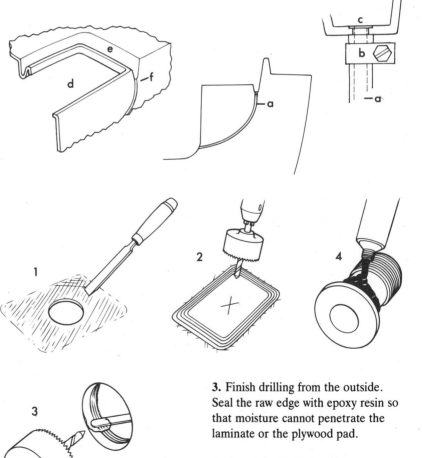

Upgrading a drainage system with no valves

In this case, the hull was made of solid laminate and the drainage pipe and outlet were under-dimensioned.

1. Remove the existing skin fitting. Clean off the glassfibre surface where a reinforcing plate is to be fitted. Score the laminate with a chisel corner to give the bonding material a better grip.

2. Cut a generous piece of marine-grade plywood and bevel the edges. Glue it into position with a bedding of epoxy resin glue. Start a hole, sawing from the inside until the drill point breaks through.

3. Finish drilling from the outside. Seal the raw edge with epoxy resin so that moisture cannot penetrate the laminate or the plywood pad.

4. Coat the skin fitting with polysulphide sealant before tightening home from inside the hull.

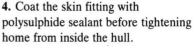

Gratings for cockpits with steering pedestals

1. When making cockpit gratings, you are going to need to make a full-size plan of the grating frame. Use ordinary brown parcel paper—it's cheaper.

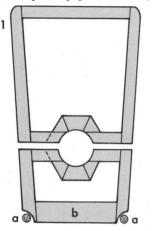

Measure the angles of the cockpit corners with a sliding bevel and transfer these angles onto the drawing. You need to have a two-piece grating if you have a steering pedestal in the middle.

Remember that self-draining cockpit outlets must not to be covered by grating, so you need to cut out a notch for these (a). Use a wider piece of wood (b) at the aft end of the cockpit, so that you will have plenty of timber to form lands for the halving joints in those corners.

Mark off lengths of timber from the plan. Plane them if you have rough timber and then saw them to length.

The final pieces should be about 50 × 20 mm (2″ × 3/4″), if the grating strips are 25 mm × 20 (1″ × 3/4″).

2. The "smart" way to join the frame is to use halving joints (a) for the two sternmost joints (over the draining holes) and mortise-and-tenon joints for the rest. However, modern adhesives provide such a strong join that the amateur ship's carpenter can use halving joints and adhesive all around.

Make halving joints for all the corner joins and for the pedestal frames (b). Lay out all the pieces on a flat surface and assemble them, without gluing, to ensure that they are going to lie flat when joined together.

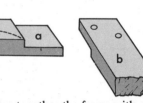

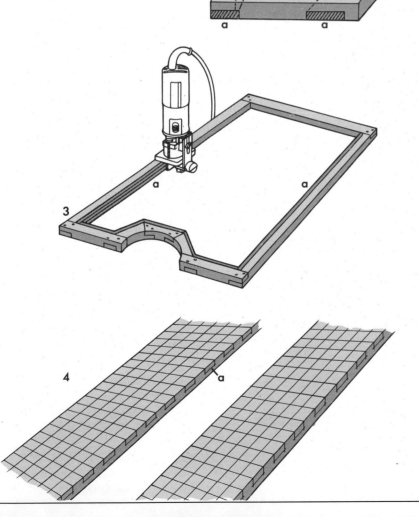

3. Glue together the frame with a phenolic resin glue. Use cramps to hold the joins together while the glue is hardening. Some people like to strengthen the joins further by drilling holes through them and plugging them with suitable pieces of wood dowelling, covered in glue.

When the glue has hardened, saw out the shape of the steering pedestal in the frame. Saw out semicircular notches in the frame where it covers the self-draining outlets. Smooth off these edges with sanding block and abrasive paper.

Make a rebate (a) to take the grating strips, using a router with a rebating cutter. If you don't have one, use a circular saw before gluing the frame together, and cut out the corners with a sharp chisel.

4. Make the grating strips from a plank that is 125 × 25 mm (5″ × 1″). Cut the plank into pieces about 1″ (25 mm) longer than the frame. Cramp the pieces together and mark up the halving joints (a). These should be 25 mm (1″) wide and about 30 mm (1 1/8″) apart, so that shoes or toes don't get caught in between.

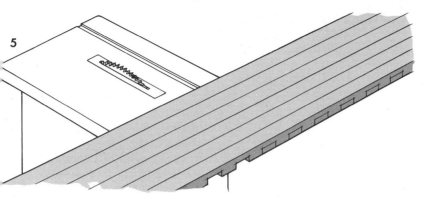

5. Cut the halving joints out with the circular saw, cutting first the outside edges of each joint and then the intermediate waste material, by moving the workpiece a saw blade's width at a time.

6. Then cut the pieces into the correct width (25 mm/1″) and plane their edges smooth, so that the finished strips are 25 × 20 mm (1″ × 3/4″).

7. Fit the crosswise and lengthwise strips together to form a latticework, which you lay on a flat surface. Place the frame on top of it and mark the ends, where you need to cut a lap joint to fit the rebate already cut in the frame. Cut out the lap joint with the circular saw.

8. Turn the latticework upside down, lay the frame over it, and glue and screw the frame to the latticework.

Simple cockpit gratings

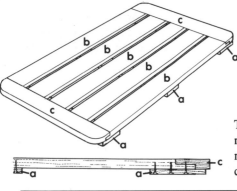

The following is a more simple way of making gratings, especially if there is no steering pedestal to take into account.

The frame is simply a suitable number of planks of marine plywood (*a*) laid crosswise with about 400 mm (16″) in between and screwed and glued from beneath to the lengthwise grating strips (*b*) of, say, teak, sawn and planed to 150 × 12 mm (6″ × 1/2″).

The end pieces (*c*) are of teak and are joined to the lengthwise strips by simple halving joints, as before. When the glue has dried, round the corners.

Grabrails

Choose a sound piece of well-seasoned timber, with straight grain and no knots.

1. Saw and plane the timber into two equal lengths, somewhat longer than the planned grabrail. Spot-glue the two pieces together, with a layer of newspaper in between to ensure that you can separate them afterwards. The glue is to be in the area where you are going to cut the holes.

2. Mark out the cut-outs for the handholds.

3. Secure the workpiece in a vice or in cramps, with cushion pieces of wood between.
   Using a hole saw, drill at the marked points. When the drill point breaks through, stop and turn the piece over. Then finish off from the other side. This prevents splintering.

4. Use a jigsaw to cut out the rest of the handhold. Taper the sides with a plane. Use a wood rasp to shape the round parts, and finish off by smoothing down with abrasive paper. Separate the two grabrails, and smooth off the insides.

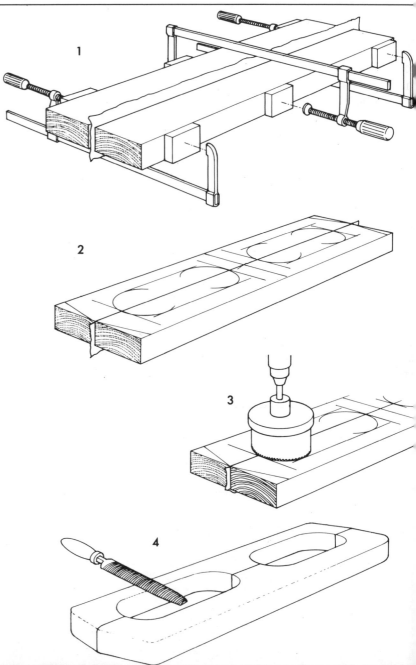

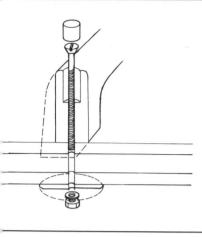

5. When mounting the grabrails, never use screws. Always use stainless steel or aluminium bronze nuts, bolts, and washers. For mounting instructions, see pages 66–67, lower.

6. Sometimes, it is useful to fit twin handrails, one serving belowdeck and one on the topsides. A single bolt, plugged at either end, will secure them through laminate. Reinforcement plates may be necessary.

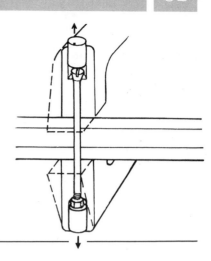

Cockpit seating

If the seating is in need of repair, repaint the cockpit area with two-part polyurethane. Use masking tape to get neat finishes around the areas showing wear. If you cannot match the original colour scheme exactly, it is better to have a contrasting colour rather than a tone that is near the original, as this will show the rest of the surfaces up.

Fitting teak slats for seating

1. Seating slats can be screwed to single-skin laminate by screws from below.

slats or varnishing/oiling the slats is a difficult and fiddling job. The following method is a good solution to this problem.

3. Make the slatted seating in sections and bolt them in place on the cockpit moulding (a), so that they can be easily removed when the laminate must be washed. The slats are screwed and glued to end pieces (b) and joined

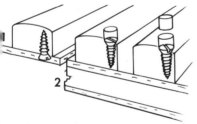

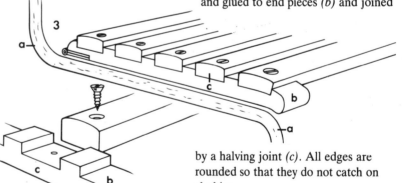

2. Sandwich construction requires screwing from above through countersunk holes that must then be plugged.

The problem with both these methods is that cleaning between the

by a halving joint (c). All edges are rounded so that they do not catch on clothing.

Other tips for the cockpit

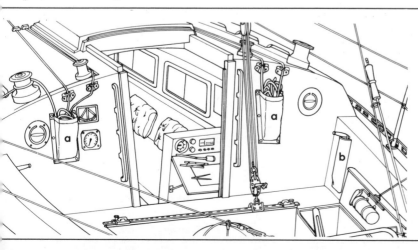

The confined cockpit area must be kept neat, and the illustrated canvas holders (a), with popper fasteners to hold them to the fore wall of the cockpit, are very handy for storing the ends of the halyards.

Another handy item to have attached to the cockpit walls is a winch-handle holder (b). These are available commercially but you can easily make them yourself from canvas.

HEADLININGS

Headlinings: method 1

1. Divide the ceiling into panels; the number of panels depends on the size of the cabin, but two or four is sufficient on a normal boat. The main join between the panels should be along the centre line of the boat, thus making it easier to fit the headlinings around holes for the mast, lights, ventilators, etc.

2. Make a hardboard template of the ceiling area and allow 5 mm (3/16″) extra all around. Place the template on 5-mm (3/16″) plywood and mark out the panels carefully. Mark out any holes for lights, etc. Cut out the panels and necessary holes with a jigsaw. Sand the edges.

Fit and fix the panels into position on the ceiling. The panels are not yet finished, but securing them properly at this stage provides an exact location via the screw holes, when the panels are finally completed. Secure with self-tapping screws into glassfibre or with with wood screws into timber. Keep the outer screws to the very edge of the panels so that they will be covered by beadings when finishing. For screws in the centre of the panels which will not be covered, use chrome raised-head screws in cups.

3. Mark the panel faces to be covered by the fabric or textile. Remove the panels and glue the covering material onto each panel, folding over at the edges and stapling on the reverse side.

4. Prepare beadings to cover the joins between the panels and where the panels meet the cabin sides. Sand, varnish or polish the beadings before fitting. Mitre the corners and fix the beadings neatly into place with chrome raised-head screws.

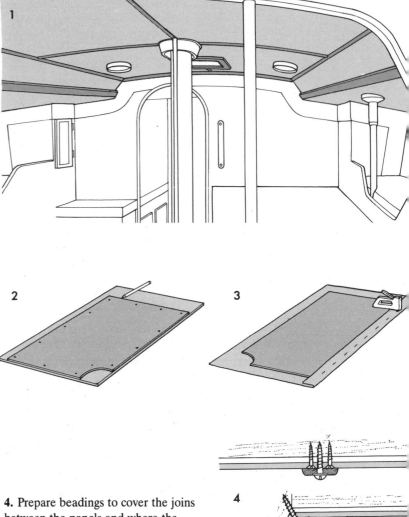

Headlinings: method 2

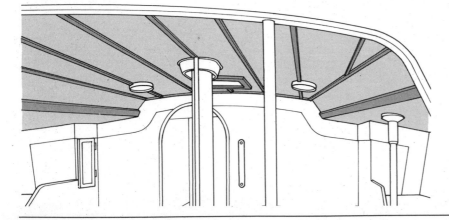

This method of fitting headlinings is simple and the result is attractive. Also, it allows access behind.

The materials required are:
30 × 10 mm (1 3/16″ × 3/8″) softwood battens for groundwork, varnished hardwood beadings, 25 mm (1″), and 250 × 3 mm (10″ × 1/8″) plywood strip covered in the required material.

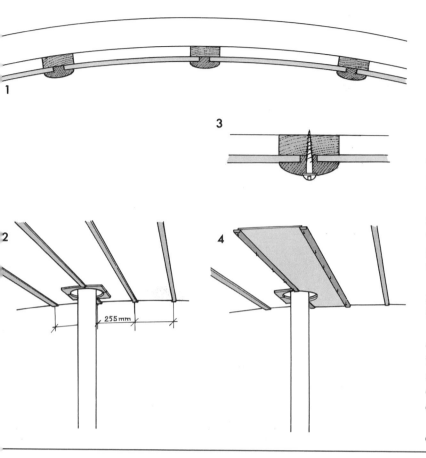

1. If possible, buy beadings that have the illustrated profile. Otherwise, you must use a router to make the rebate necessary. The rebate should have the thickness of the plywood strips plus the covering material.

2. Begin by securing a batten along the centre line with self-tapping screws, if the material underneath is fibreglass laminate, or wood screws if it is timber.

Now attach the rest of the battens at 255 mm (10″) centres, ensuring that they lie fair and in parallel lines. If necessary, pack them slightly to ensure that they are fair.

3. Begin at the centre line; fit a beading onto the batten that is there.

4. Work first to the one side and then to the other, fitting the covered panels and beadings, and trimming the ends of the panels to suit the length of the cabin, as you go.

To finish, fit beading along the edges, as previously described.

Insulating cabin walls

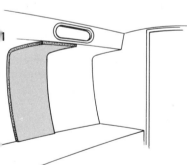

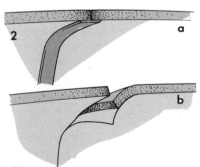

Insulating the cabin walls will make the cabin more comfortable to live in and will improve the atmosphere, making it warmer and drier. Ordinary insulating material won't do, because it is too thick and will decrease the available cabin space. Furthermore, its cells are open and will absorb water, and water-soaked insulation is useless from the point of view of thermal efficiency. Cork sheeting is popular, and thin, flame-retardant insulation matting is best.

1. Insulation material is cut into panels and fastened directly to the cabin walls. It often has self-adhesive backing, but contact glue is better, as it is impossible to adjust self-adhesive material once in place and the self-adhesion often fails after a time.

First make paper templates of the area to be covered. Then cut out the insulation material to measure, cover both wall and material with glue, and press into place.

2. The joins between neighbouring panels can be handled in two ways.
(a) Join the two pieces edge-to-edge and cover the join with a strip of plastic tape. This will stop condensation from seeping through.
(b) Cut a strip of the material from its covering so that the bared covering overlaps the join neatly. Contact glue is needed to fasten the bared covering over the neighbouring piece. The ends of the insulation are then finished off attractively with a varnished wood strip.

Crossover berths

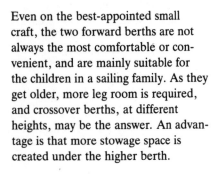

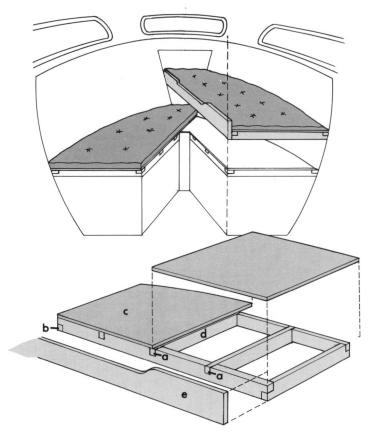

Even on the best-appointed small craft, the two forward berths are not always the most comfortable or convenient, and are mainly suitable for the children in a sailing family. As they get older, more leg room is required, and crossover berths, at different heights, may be the answer. An advantage is that more stowage space is created under the higher berth.

Make an accurate template of the shape of the berth at the required height.

Most of the joinery work can be made ashore, from prepared battens of 40 × 70 mm (1 1/2″ × 3″) softwood. The berth frame is put together with glued and screwed halving joints (a). The corners are joined by corner half laps (b).

The inside of the frame (which lies against the hull) may be scarfed to provide a side frame that bends towards the hull, thus giving several support possibilities, whereby the frame can be held up by sturdy support battens laminated to the inside of the hull.

The support battens can be lipped to provide an even safer hold on the berth.

The frame is supported on the inside by a batten that is bolted to the bulkhead.

The mattress is supported by two panels (c) of 9-mm (3/8″) plywood, series-drilled with 2-mm (1/8″) holes for ventilation. These panels join flush with each other on the frame's central bearer (d).

The final job is to fit leeboards (e). These are made from 150 × 20 mm (6 × 3/4″) hardwood, glued and screwed to the side frame, suitably contoured and with all edges rounded off.

Folding worktop

Many galleys are located next to the forward berths, where an added worktop can be invaluable for cooking or as an extra navigation table. The construction is simple: 12-mm (1/2″) plywood or blockwood, perhaps with a lipping. Simple sliding bolts will keep the table in its folded position. A batten (a) screwed to the galley partition supports one side, while a chain (b) or hinged wing supports the other side.

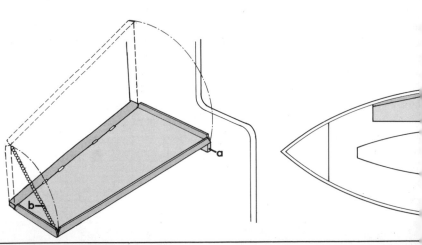

Step locker

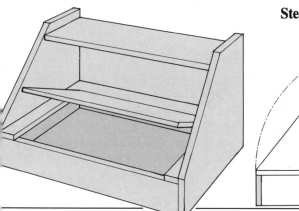

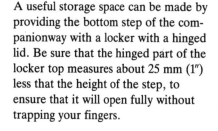

A useful storage space can be made by providing the bottom step of the companionway with a locker with a hinged lid. Be sure that the hinged part of the locker top measures about 25 mm (1″) less that the height of the step, to ensure that it will open fully without trapping your fingers.

Crockery stowage

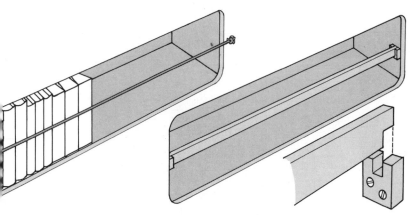

Safe and soundproof crockery stowage is a boon. This customized crockery rack is partitioned to suit the size of the plates, etc. that you use on board.

The box is lined with foam. Cutouts in each section make it easy to lift out the crockery. If there is enough space beneath the side deck and the galley, the ends and back of the rack may be extended downwards to make a further stowage space.

Shelves

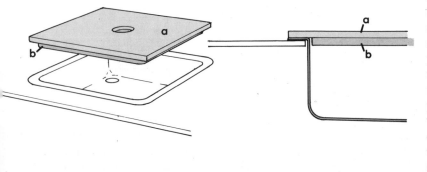

Extra shelf space is usually essential, and here are some ideas. Soft foam rubber at the back of a shelf reduces noise. The front can be secured with a simple bungy or a removable batten. The fiddle rail should be of good size, with open corners so that the shelf can be cleaned easily. See the detail for how to fit the batten so that it can be removed easily.

Extra working surface

Adding a removable worktop over the sink increases the galley's working surface. In most production boats, the sink is fitted on top of the galley, so you need only make a worktop *(a)* that fits over the sink opening, being larger than it by, say, 25 mm (1″). A second piece of wood *(b)*, fastened under the worktop, is slightly less than the area of the sink, so that it fits neatly into the opening, preventing the top from sliding about in heavy weather.

HEATING AND VENTILATION

The "cold wall"

Condensation and humidity in glass-fibre boats can be especially annoying if you have a heater in an insufficiently ventilated cabin, even if the boat itself is well insulated.

In most boats, you can get rid of this fairly easily by dehumidifying the damp inlet air before it gets into the cabin, which means that the air coming in will not be damp, although still cold. What happens is that the damp air is led over a cold surface which turns the dampness into drops of moisture that collect on the cold surface. Normally, the cold surface would

be the bilge or some other part of the hull surface below the waterline, but you can improve this by installing a stainless-steel box *(a)* in the bilge or in the bottom of a stowage in the cockpit. Fit an inlet vent in the cockpit, as low as possible. Connect a 10–15 cm (4–6″) flexible alloy hose between the stainless-steel box and the inlet vent, and another one between the box and the outlet vent into the cabin. The moisture is then collected in the box as the damp air is drawn through it, and drier cold air flows into the cabin at floor level.

The cold air rises towards the ceiling

when it is heated up, and circulation is created in this way. Ventilation vents in the cabin roof aid the circulation.

If you have a heater, locate the inlet vent as close as possible to the bottom of the heater, so that the incoming air is warmed quickly and a cosy, dry and warm cabin is provided.

(a) Inlet vent in cockpit takes in humid air.
(b) Stainless-steel "cold wall" box, with drain plug that leads the gathered moisture into the bilges.
(c) Flexible alloy hose.
(d) Outlet vent.
(e) Heater.

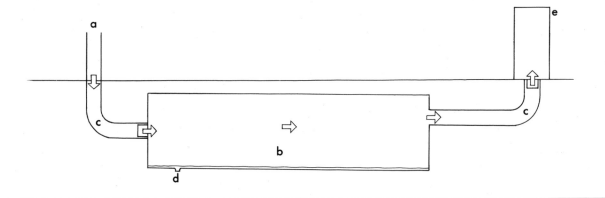

Heating the living areas

Most heating appliances for small boats use combustion to produce heat, and this means that oxygen is used and replaced by poisonous carbon monoxide. It is vital, therefore, that belowdeck ventilation is adequate.

Heaters should be through-bolted to a bulkhead, so that they cannot be knocked loose by someone falling against them in heavy weather.

The heater on the right *(upper)* for boats up to 10 m (30 ft) blows warm air in two directions, so if it is mounted on a bulkhead with a convenient hole, it can heat two adjoining cabins. A damper makes it possible to close off one hot-air outlet so that all heat is concentrated in one cabin. The combusted air is expelled through the through-deck ducting and also draws used air from the cabin, thus making

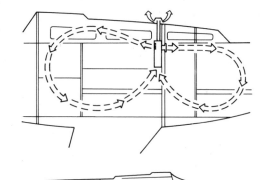

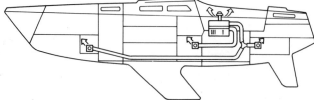

possible a greater exchange of air. A more powerful heater, suitable for boats over 10 m (30 ft), shown *(lower)*,

need not be mounted in a cabin but is fitted with ducts that will lead the heated air to all the cabins on board.

Air intakes for heating

Remember that every heater needs air for effective combustion. An arrangement like the one illustrated *(right, upper)* is simple but effective. A flexible hose *(a)* is led from the anchor box in the fore through the anchor-box bulkhead and under a bunk *(b)*, the foot of which has a vent that leads the air out near the bottom of the heater.

An alternative is also shown *(right, lower)* where the air is led further down, through the galley floor and up under the heater. This provides something of the "cold wall" effect described opposite.

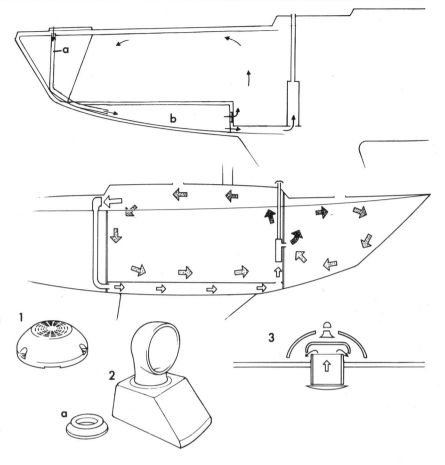

Ventilators

1. This low-profile deck ventilator does not interfere too much with deck working space. This type is not for deep-sea yachts, as it is not easily sealed off.

2. The dorade-type ventilator allows rain and small amounts of sea water to drain without excluding the air. The mushroom vent *(a)* in the base of this one allows complete sealing off in heavy weather. The cowl itself is removable, so that it does not provide

dangerous resistance to green water. A cover plate can substitute for it.

3. The mushroom vent is effective and has the advantage that it can be closed from within.

Louvres

The addition of simple louvre ventilators to washboards and to the doors on cabins, wardrobes, lockers, drawers *(not on toilet doors)* will make for a safer and healthier belowdeck climate. Remember to have louvres at the top and bottom of the doors, to encourage the circulation of the air.

For very heavy weather, you should have a cover for the louvre on the washboard. Take a piece of acrylic sheeting, round the edges, drill suitable holes, and fit it over the louvre on raised edges that have threaded bolts glued in position, so that the cover can be quickly screwed on with nuts, when a heavy storm rises. To protect clothing, use dome-headed nuts.

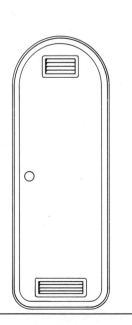

Another way to prevent water getting through the washboard louvre, while at the same time allowing air into the cabin, is shown here. Screw one piece of acrylic sheeting *(a)* on the outside of the washboard *(b)* so that a 25-mm (1") gap is left at the bottom of the louvre. A second piece of acrylic *(c)* is screwed to the inside of the washboard, leaving a similar gap at the top.

PLUMBING

Depending on the degree of comfort that you want to have in your boat, there are many water systems available. We show here a cold-water system, for those of a hardier nature or who sail in warm waters.

(a) Raw-water inlet.
(b) Filter.
(c) Pump.
(d) Water pipe to toilet.
(e) Galley pump (water for rinsing only).
(f) Connection for seawater shower or hose to wash the deck.
(g) Freshwater tank. Do not place it near a source of heat, such as the engine.
(h) Freshwater filler pipe.
(i) Freshwater vent.
(j) Filter.
(k) Pump.
(l) Freshwater galley pump.
(m) Freshwater handbasin pump.

Hot- and cold-water system

(a) Raw-water inlet.
(b) Filter.
(c) Pump.
(d) Water pipe to toilet.
(e) Galley pump water for rinsing only.
(f) Connection for seawater shower or hose to wash the deck.
(g) Freshwater tank. Do not place it near a source of heat, such as the engine.
(h) Freshwater filler pipe.
(i) Freshwater vent.
(j) Filter.
(k) Pump.
(l) Freshwater galley pump.
(m) Freshwater handbasin pump.
(n) T-coupling and pipe to water heater.
(o) Non-return valve.
(p) Water heater.
(q) Heating coil.
(r) Safety pressure valve.
(s) Hot water to galley pump.
(t) Hot water to shower.
(u) Hot water to handbasin.

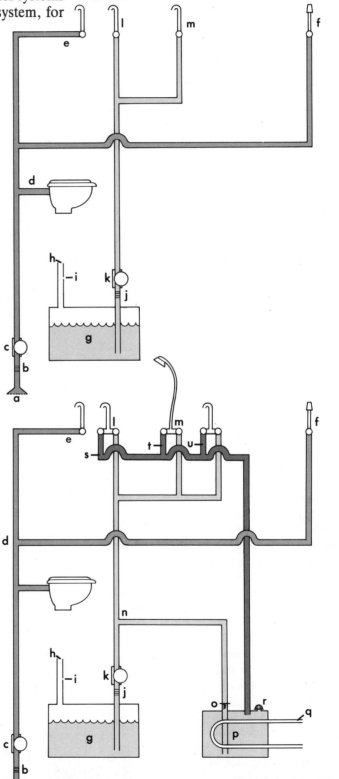

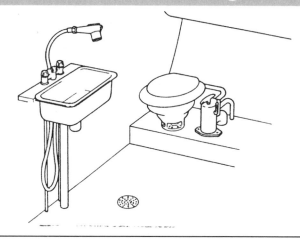

Shower-room and toilet

A combined shower-room and toilet makes the most use of the limited space on board a small boat, but you must see to it that the crew is trained to dry the floor after a shower!

Wasteholding tanks

A waste tank is a sanitary necessity on board any pleasure boat. There are two ways to empty tanks. The first is by suction pumping at a marina or boat harbour, and the second is to pump the waste overboard while far out to sea. The problem with the first method is that this facility is not available everywhere, which can lead to problems if you don't have the second method available. We describe here how you can install a waste tank and pump for the second method.

tank completely or partly under the waterline. In such a case, you need to install a second pump, for pumping the contents of the waste tank into the sea.

The waste tank should be of stainless steel and all packing glands, pipes, and hose clips should be of the highest quality, to avoid breakdowns and unpleasant smells.

Installing a waste tank

The toilet must be of good quality, with a sturdy pump. The waste tank is placed above the waterline, just below the deck, which means that after use the contents of the toilet are pumped up to the tank by the toilet pump. The waste tank can then be emptied by the force of gravity through its skin fitting, which is below the waterline.

An alternative is to place the waste

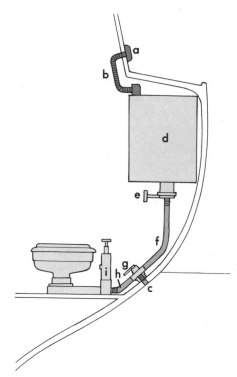

(a) Ventilation valve.
(b) Reinforced plastic tubing.
(c) Seacock (inlet).
(d) Holding tank (capacity about 30 litres/8 gallons) of stainless steel.
(e) Valve.
(f) Reinforced plastic tubing of suitable size, fastened with double hose clips and sealed with silicone-rubber sealant.
(g) T-coupling leading to seacock outlet.
(h) Reinforced plastic tubing, like (f).
(i) Toilet pump.

The bilge pump

A reliable bilge pump is indispensable. All boats gather water in their bilges, and if the water is allowed to lie there, dampness will spread in the boat, causing rust, mildew, and condensation. Furthermore, if the hull is holed, the bilge pump should be able to keep pace with the leak.

We show here a hand-powered diaphragm bilge pump (a) that is

operated from the cockpit. The intake hose (b) is fitted with a strainer (c) to prevent the pump from being clogged. If the pump seems to be working badly, check that the strainer is clear from debris. There should be a convenient hatch available so that you can get at the filter, when necessary. Bilge water is pumped out through a discharge hose (d) that attaches to a skin fitting (e) above the waterline.

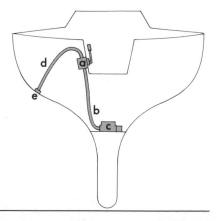

GAS INSTALLATION

Butane and propane are the most usual types of gas used on board boats. Installing gas on board is easy, and because it's easy, there is the temptation to be nonchalant about the safety aspect. Treat all gas with healthy respect and use your common sense when dealing with it.

Normally, two bottles of gas are stowed together, which means that a spare is always available. They must be stowed in a specially built box or an adapted locker in the cockpit. The bottom of the gas-stowage compartment must be above the waterline, because, unlike domestic gas, butane does not disperse quickly. Also, it is heavier than air, so any leakage could cause a hazardous build-up of the gas at the lowest point. For this reason, the gas-stowage compartment must be vented overboard through a skin fitting, well away from engine-exhaust outlets.

Shown are several methods of storing gas.

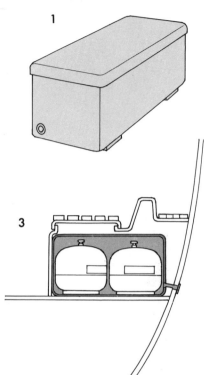

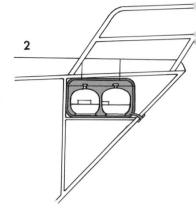

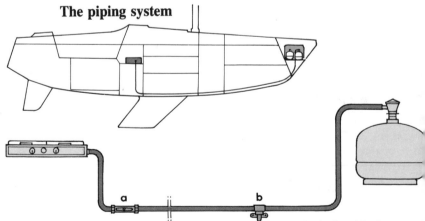

1. The cylinders can also be stored on deck in a box that should be attractively painted to fit in with the general colour scheme.
2. Another place to store gas cylinders is between the hull and a fore-and-aft bulkhead. Make sure that you have some kind of a hatch through which you can have easy access to the cylinders for changing, etc.
3. A specially built glassfibre box that you can make yourself (see pages 42–43). This can be inserted in one of the seat lockers in the cockpit.

The piping system

The regulator should be fitted to a flexible hose, so that you can easily change from one cylinder to the other.

Pipe the gas through seamless copper tubing, which is soft enough to be bent to fit where required, without any special equipment. If you must join two pieces of copper tubing, use compression fittings, which do not require any sealing tape or compound to produce a perfect joint. Note: the nuts on the compression fittings should be tightened securely, but do not overtighten. Secure the pipes about every 100 mm (4″) to prevent them from shaking loose from vibrations.

If the cooker is the only gas appliance in the galley, run the copper feed pipe to a conveniently placed on/off tap. Just inside a galley locker adjacent to the cooker is a convenient spot to choose. From this tap, a flexible, armoured hose completes the run to the cooker. This final piece of flexible hose allows the cooker to be pulled out a little for cleaning.

Extra length is required if the cooker is gimbled. The last connection into the cooker is usually via a tapered thread fitting, secured with PTFE joint-sealing tape or a non-hardening joint sealer.

If there is more than one appliance in the galley that is run on gas, then you must connect the supply to a two-way fitting that is screwed securely to a bulkhead in the galley. Then continue each supply via a copper pipe to an on/off tap. It is very important that each

appliance can be isolated by its own on/off tap.

Once your installation work is complete, with pipes and appliances in place, call in your local gas fitter and get him to test the system. This only takes a moment and is well worth the reassurance and peace of mind that it will give you. If you round off your safety precautions by installing an electronic gas-leak detector, then you can be confident in your gas system.

CHAPTER 6

Rigging

There is something about standing rigging that makes it one of the most neglected areas on board a yacht. Due to the robust nature of standing rigging, it is often taken for granted. The true sailor, however, who has a healthy respect for conditions at sea, will pay a lot of attention to this important part of the yacht's equipment. The rigging and spars are the yacht's powerplant, and they are not subjected to extreme test until it really blows at sea, when you most need to trust them!

"How long will stainless-steel rigging last?" is one of the most common questions asked of manufacturers. A major company in this field has replied that so many variables are involved that it is impossible to answer accurately—but assuming that there are no extremes involved, a guide could be as follows: once around the world in the Whitbread Race; three heavy races, such as transatlantic races; five to eight years of seasonal ocean racing; ten years around the buoys; or twelve to fifteen years of summer cruising.

RIGGING TOOL KIT

The further offshore you sail, the more you may have to cope with, and the more tools you will need. The following are necessary for repair of rigging.

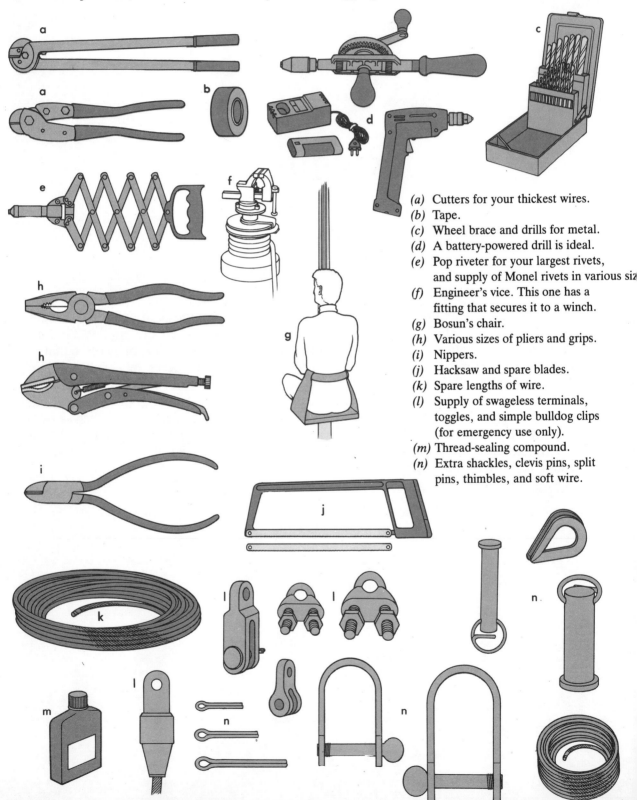

(a) Cutters for your thickest wires.
(b) Tape.
(c) Wheel brace and drills for metal.
(d) A battery-powered drill is ideal.
(e) Pop riveter for your largest rivets, and supply of Monel rivets in various sizes.
(f) Engineer's vice. This one has a fitting that secures it to a winch.
(g) Bosun's chair.
(h) Various sizes of pliers and grips.
(i) Nippers.
(j) Hacksaw and spare blades.
(k) Spare lengths of wire.
(l) Supply of swageless terminals, toggles, and simple bulldog clips (for emergency use only).
(m) Thread-sealing compound.
(n) Extra shackles, clevis pins, split pins, thimbles, and soft wire.

RIGGING TYPES

Masthead rig

The masthead rig has been the dominating rig type for many years. It is typified by having the forestay attached to the top of the mast and large foresails relative to the mainsail. It has quite a low profile and is rather difficult to trim, but is regarded as a sound, steady rig that is, perhaps, the most suitable for ocean-going vessels.

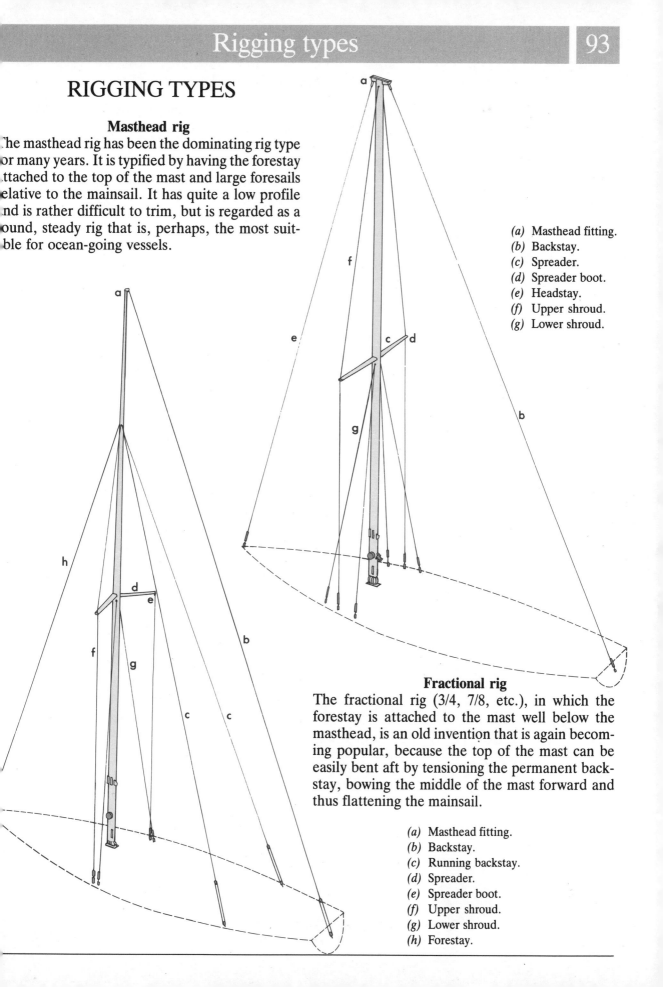

(a) Masthead fitting.
(b) Backstay.
(c) Spreader.
(d) Spreader boot.
(e) Headstay.
(f) Upper shroud.
(g) Lower shroud.

Fractional rig

The fractional rig (3/4, 7/8, etc.), in which the forestay is attached to the mast well below the masthead, is an old invention that is again becoming popular, because the top of the mast can be easily bent aft by tensioning the permanent backstay, bowing the middle of the mast forward and thus flattening the mainsail.

(a) Masthead fitting.
(b) Backstay.
(c) Running backstay.
(d) Spreader.
(e) Spreader boot.
(f) Upper shroud.
(g) Lower shroud.
(h) Forestay.

MASTS AND BOOMS

The control lines must run freely through the mast and masthead. A mainsheet halyard, a spinnaker halyard, a forestay halyard (sometimes two), a spinnaker-boom lift, and a topping lift, as well as a wiring conduit, all have to pass down the centre of a mast, and provision must also be made for an emergency halyard to be reeved.

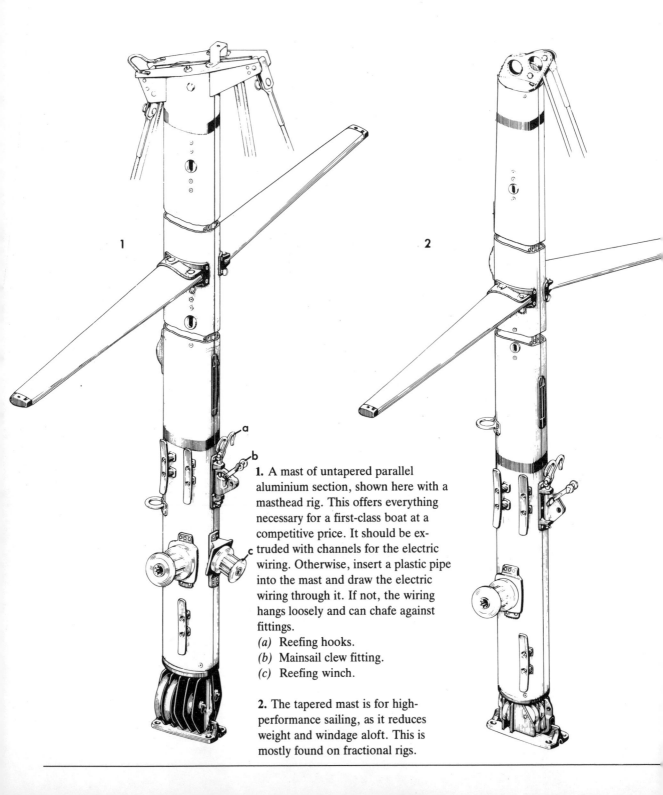

1. A mast of untapered parallel aluminium section, shown here with a masthead rig. This offers everything necessary for a first-class boat at a competitive price. It should be extruded with channels for the electric wiring. Otherwise, insert a plastic pipe into the mast and draw the electric wiring through it. If not, the wiring hangs loosely and can chafe against fittings.
(a) Reefing hooks.
(b) Mainsail clew fitting.
(c) Reefing winch.

2. The tapered mast is for high-performance sailing, as it reduces weight and windage aloft. This is mostly found on fractional rigs.

Mast survey

Modern aluminium masts need only a good wash in fresh water, followed by wax polishing. Remember to give the inside of the mast a good hosing to get rid of the salt. While doing this, inspect the mast for other possible problems.

Check that all sheaves and blocks are undamaged and move freely.

Check all the welds for fatigue cracks. If you find a crack, stop it from growing by drilling a 5-mm (3/16″) hole at the very end of the crack, and then seek expert advice immediately.

Check the tracks, plungers, and slides. Everything should be free and move easily. Spray with silicone anti-friction spray.

Check that the masthead light works and that the lens is not cracked.

Booms

1. A slab-reefing boom, made from lightweight mast extrusions. The reef lines through the leech should lead well aft along the boom, to tighten the foot and flatten the sail (see page 103).

2. To support the boom's weight while the sail is lowered or reefed, a topping lift is normally needed, but instead a rodkick (*a*) can be added to the traditional kicking strap.

SPINNAKER POLES

Modern materials can make spinnaker poles thin-walled and light, yet strong.

1. Dip-pole gybing suits boats over 10 m (30 ft) with large spinnakers. The inner end fits on a cup in a slide on the mast.

2. End-for-end gybing suits a spinnaker of 70 sq m (750 sq ft) or less. These smaller spinnaker poles are fastened to a mast fitting which slides on a track on the mast and is fixed with a spring plunger.

A safe and simple alternative to dip-gybe poles on large spinnakers is two end-for-end spinnaker poles. Extras needed are a lift, downhaul, and mast fitting on the track. This lift could be attached to the standard lift line, just below the sheave when the lift is trimmed to its utmost position.

(a) Spinnaker uplift.
(b) Downhaul.
(c) Release rope for piston lock.

Jockey poles

This short spinnaker boom (1.5 times the boat's breadth) has the usual fitting at one end to attach to the mast, properly just at the level where the spinnaker guy normally passes th mast. The other end has a sheave through which the spinnaker guy (the windward sheet) runs.

FASTENING FITTINGS TO ALLOY SPARS

Fastening a fitting on an extruded aluminium mast or spar can only be done from the outside. We show three methods here: with *pop rivets*, *self-tapping screws* and *machine screws*.

Holes in aluminium must be made with care. The surface is anodized, but the bared metal corrodes unless insulated with epoxy resin or a similar sealant.

Aluminium is easily worked with metal drills, hacksaws, and files—but if you use a drill, prevent it from "wandering" by starting the hole with a fin drill or a handheld punch or mandrel.

Pop-rivetting a winch base plate

This method is effective for fittings that must tak heavy pressure at an angle. For extreme pressure use rivets of stainless steel or Monel (a corrosion resistant alloy of nickel and copper). The rive length should equal the sum of the fitting and mas thicknesses.

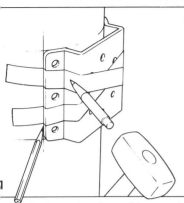

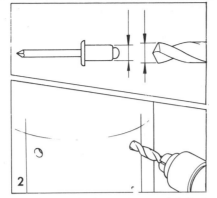

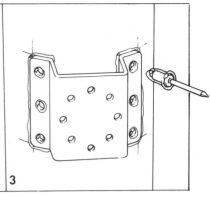

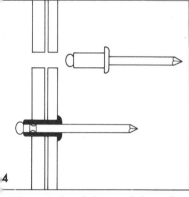

1. Fix the base plate in position on the mast with strong tape. Mark the contour of the base plate on the mast with pencil. Start the holes with a punch.

2. Remove the base plate, and drill the holes with a drill big enough to give a tiny clearance (say, 0.2 mm) around each rivet.

3. Put silicone-rubber sealant on the rivet body, on the back of the base plate, and in the drilled holes.

Let the sealant harden for a few minutes. Align a hole on the plate with its drilled hole and insert the rivet.

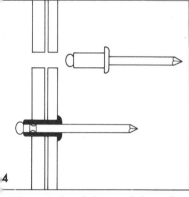

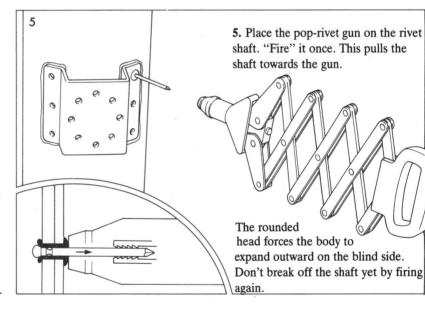

4. The pop rivet is inserted through the matching plate hole and drilled hole. The rivet body, which is relatively soft and will be crushed and spread out under pressure, is shown here and in the next drawings in black.

5. Place the pop-rivet gun on the rivet shaft. "Fire" it once. This pulls the shaft towards the gun.

The rounded head forces the body to expand outward on the blind side. Don't break off the shaft yet by firing again.

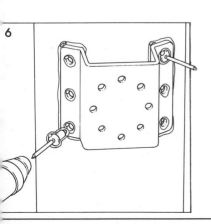

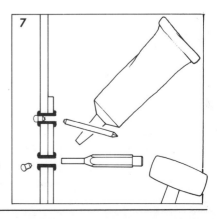

6. Now align the diagonally opposite holes and insert a rivet. Fire twice, breaking off the rivet shaft and fixing the winch base plate in position. Next, break off the first rivet shaft by firing again. Then insert and fire the other rivets. Remove any excess sealant with a wooden spatula, so that the aluminium will not be scratched.

7. Knock out the rivet heads and the pieces of their shafts, as otherwise they may cause corrosion. Fill the holes left by the shafts with sealant.

Self-tapping screws

These are used to fasten fittings that do not take much strain, or to fix a fitting in place temporarily until you can do the job properly. Use screws of the best-quality stainless steel.

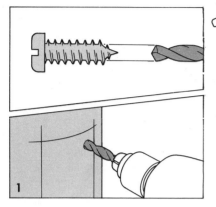

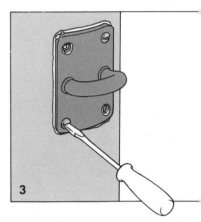

1. Mark the position of the fitting. Start the holes with a punch.

Drill the screw holes. Each hole must be only slightly narrower than the screw plus its thread; otherwise the screws will be very hard to screw in.

2. Use the shortest possible screws. Cut off their points to protect the halyards inside the mast. Apply sealant to the fitting back, screws and drilled holes.

3. After a few minutes, screw on the fitting, starting with diagonally opposite screws. Then scrape away any excess sealant with a wooden spatula.

Thread-tapped machine screws

Due to their design, some fittings—such as plastic cleats and clam cleats—have to be fastened by screws. To ensure that they can withstand pressure, it is necessary to use thread-tapped machine screws.

This is also an especially good method of fastening a fitting that has to be removed now and then for service—such as some types of masthead lights. The machine screws can simply be screwed out when removing the fitting.

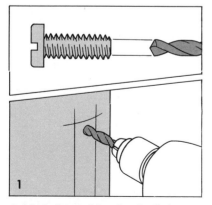

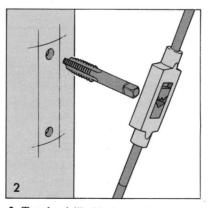

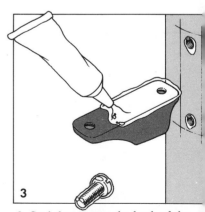

1. Mark the position for the fitting, and start the screw holes with a punch.

Drill holes for thread taps, as wide as a machine screw minus its threads.

2. Tap the drilled holes, using a thread tap of the correct dimension.

3. Seal the screws, the back of the fitting, and the holes with silicone-rubber sealant. After a few minutes, mount the fitting. Scrape away excess sealant with a wooden spatula.

RODS AND WIRE

nspection of standing rigging when giving the rigging its annual wash with fresh water should be sufficient. Pay most attention to where it meets a erminal fitting.

Look for tiny cracks and corrosion in the rigging nd swage terminals, and also tell-tale "needling" which indicates broken wire strands.

Check that no split pins are missing, and that all locking devices, such as split pins, nuts, and soft wire, are properly secured. Never re-use a split pin that has been opened.

Check clevis pins for damage. Check where shrouds pass over spreaders and where wires are subjected to uneven loads.

Stainless-steel wire

Stainless-steel wire is very strong, easy to fit, and most work on it can be done on board. It makes good standing rigging and is in widespread use. The wire is designed to an exact balance, contra-rotating one around the other to give maximum strength with minimum stretch. To maintain the correct relationship to terminals and rigging screws, or turnbuckles, they should be fitted so that the rigging screw shortens when wound in a clockwise direction.

Rod rigging

Solid rod rigging has been used for years on most boats built purely for racing, on many top-quality performance-oriented production boats, and more and more on boats built strictly for offshore cruising/racing. Rod rigging has the advantage of low stretch and good aerodynamic qualities, and it is made up in the factory in the exact lengths required. It is about 20% more expensive than wire of the same diametre.

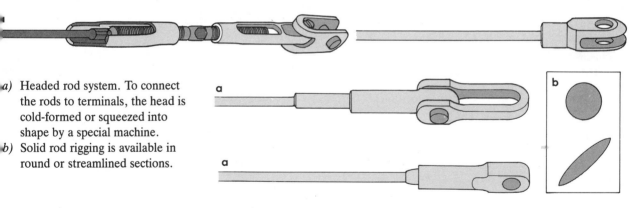

a) Headed rod system. To connect the rods to terminals, the head is cold-formed or squeezed into shape by a special machine.
b) Solid rod rigging is available in round or streamlined sections.

Comparison between stainless-steel wire and stainless-steel rod in standing rigging

wire equivalent 1 × 19 wire diametre (in)	rod diametre (inches)	wire breaking strength (foot/lb)	rod breaking strength (foot/lb)	wire weight per foot (lbs)	rod weight per foot (lbs)
5⁄32 (.166)	.143	2.816	3.300	.053	0.55
3⁄16 (.196)	.172	3.960	4.700	.072	.080
7⁄32 (.229)	.198	5.295	6.300	.101	.106
1⁄4 (.260)	.225	7.084	8.200	.130	.136
9⁄32 (.291)	.250	7.810	10.300	.161	.168
5⁄16 (.323)	.281	10.208	12.500	.209	.213
3⁄8 (.385)	.330	14.476	17.500	.290	.293
7⁄16 (.453)	.375	19.294	22.500	.397	.379
1⁄2 (.515)	.437	25.630	30.000	.533	.515

Rigging screws

The most advanced screws have chrome-bronze bodies or insert threads, as chrome bronze provides better nonjamming performance when used against male threads of stainless steel. Check the width and depth of the throat against your forestay fitting, cha:n plates, etc. Too little depth of throat can damage the clevis pin and to the rigging-screw thread. Fitting a toggle can often prevent this.

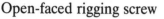

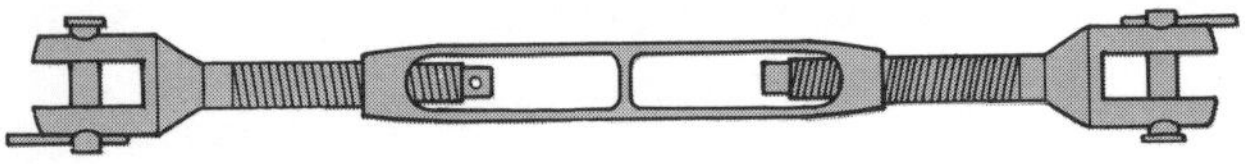

Open-faced rigging screw

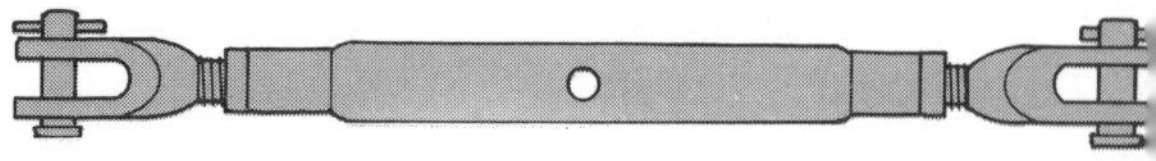

Closed-face rigging screw

Toggles

Rigging can become fatigued if used out of alignment. Rigging is designed to accept a direct in-line loading, and this can be ensured by the correct use of toggles. A toggle is a universally useful item that solves many rigging problems by simply allowing full freedom of movement.

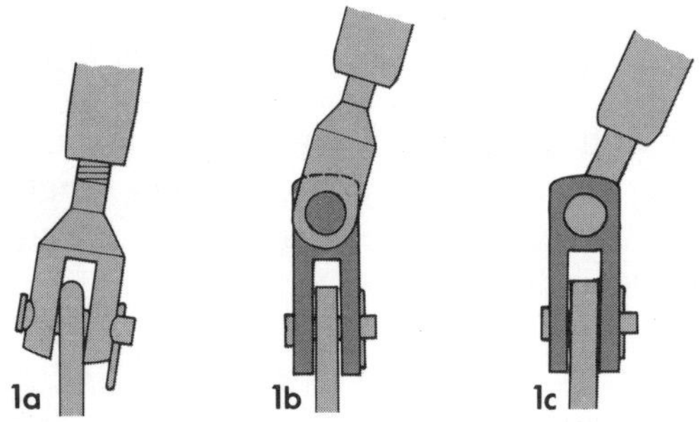

1a   1b   1c

1. Toggles solve non-alignment problems.
(a) The chain plate and rigging screw are badly out of line.
(b) A toggle corrects this.
(c) Some rigging screws are delivered fitted with a toggle screw.

TOGGLE DIMENSIONS

Pin dia and hole dia		Toggle length C/L to C/L of pin		Fork width	
mm	in	mm	in	mm	in
6.3	¼	32	1¼	8.2	21/64
7.9	5/16	38	1½	10.0	25/64
11.1	7/16	52	21/16	13.0	33/64
12.7	½	57	2¼	13.0	33/64
16.0	5/8	65	29/16	16.0	5/8
19.0	¾	79	31/8	19.0	¾
22.0	7/8	95	3¾	22.0	7/8
24.0	1	95	3¾	25.4	1
28.5	1⅛	110	45/16	28.5	1⅛
35.0	1⅜	127	5	35.0	1⅜

Gibbs Marine Fitting

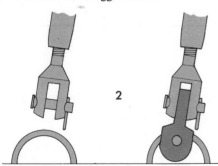

2

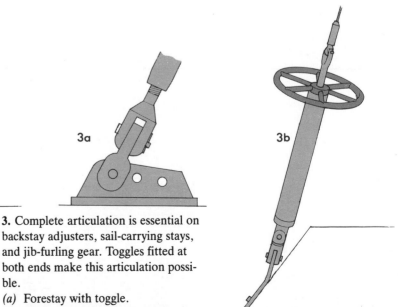

3a   3b

2. If a stay is too short, a suitably sized toggle will do the trick. If the stay is still too short when you have added a toggle, you can add another toggle at the other end.

3. Complete articulation is essential on backstay adjusters, sail-carrying stays, and jib-furling gear. Toggles fitted at both ends make this articulation possible.
(a) Forestay with toggle.
(b) Backstay adjuster with toggle.

SAIL-HANDLING SYSTEMS

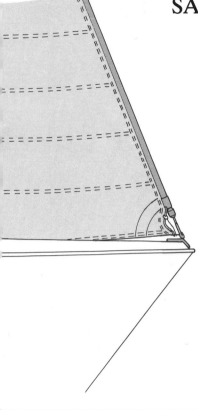

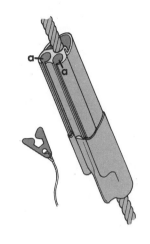

The forestay headfoil

The traditional forestay of wire or rod can be usefully complemented by fitting it with a grooved headfoil or by replacing it entirely with a complete headfoil system. The headfoil presents a straighter and more aerodynamic leech to the wind and makes it easier to change foresails. These are available with one or two grooves *(a)*. The double-grooved headfoil allows you to change foresails quickly, since the new foresail can be fitted and—if you have two foresail halyards—even hoisted, before the other sail is lowered. The leech of the foresail has a plastic beading that is fed via a feeder into the groove.

Headfoils are mainly used on racing boats. The disadvantage is that the lowered sail is difficult to handle on the foredeck in a heavy sea, especially if there is only a limited crew, because, contrary to normal practice, the lowered foresail is only attached to the halyard and can thus easily blow overboard.

Your local sailmaker can easily adapt a conventional foresail to suit the headfoil's groove.

Roller reefing

Many well-appointed cruising yachts from about 8 to 25 m (20 to 80 ft) have self-furling (roller reefing) systems.

All-out racing does not allow roller reefing, so it is a big advantage if you can remove the drum *(a)* for racing, and leave the rest of the assembly in place.

Two dimensions are important when you are choosing a self-furler: the diametre and the length of the forestay, measured between the centres of the masthead and stemhead toggle-pins. Usually the toggles do not come with the device but must be fitted at the top and bottom of the forestay.

Almost any genoa can be adapted to roller reefing with a luff tape which fits into another extruded groove in the roller-reefing stay; but unless the sail is specifically cut for roller furling, the boat cannot give maximum performance when the sail is reefed. A specially designed genoa, as shown here in three reefing stages, is cut to keep the right shape and not belly in any reefed condition.

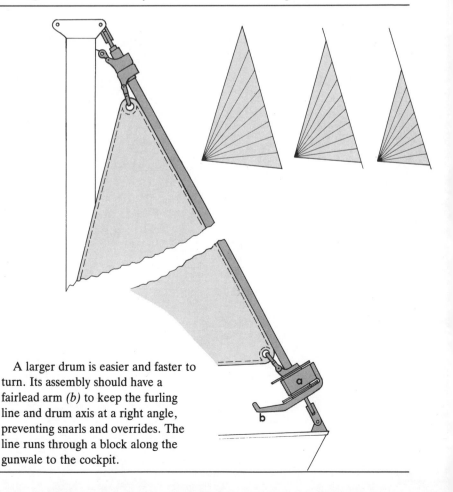

A larger drum is easier and faster to turn. Its assembly should have a fairlead arm *(b)* to keep the furling line and drum axis at a right angle, preventing snarls and overrides. The line runs through a block along the gunwale to the cockpit.

Foresail reefing

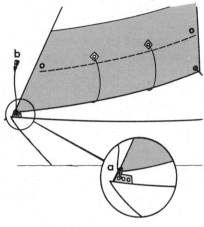

This traditional method is again increasing in popularity and is especially useful when you want to reduce the sail area of a heavy genoa, rather than change it for a smaller jib. A double foresail hook fitting *(a)* at the stemhead or a long wire with a quick-release shackle *(b)* makes it easier to switch the tack of the sail.

Improving the fore triangle

Many yachtsmen complement their roller-reefed foresail with a conventionally hoisted, smaller foresail on an extra forestay just aft of the roller-reefing system. This forestay is used mainly to carry a storm jib, but also for an extra foresail when broad reaching and sailing across the wind.

If this extra forestay is permanently fastened, you cannot easily tack with the roller-reefing genoa, so make the deck end of the extra forestay detachable, so that, when not in use, it is attached to an eye at the base of the mast.

A second stemhead fastening *(a)* must be fitted, through-fastened to the deck with a sturdy reinforcing plate (and preferably with a rodstay through the forepeak and down to the stem). The stemhead fitting has a short wheel-tensioned stay *(b)*, which is attached to the extra forestay via a pelican hook.

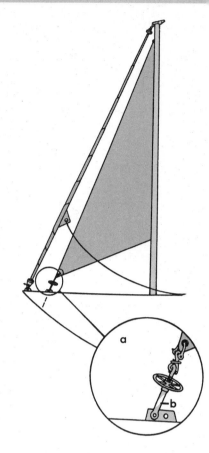

Self-tacking foresail

This system is good for fast, frequent tacking in confined waters.

The system uses a main-sheet traveller track *(a)*, bent with its ends farther forward and higher above the deck than its centre. Its radius should equal that followed by the foresail clew. The track must be angled forward so that the sheet pulls at right angles to the traveller *(b)*, which is of the type used for main sheets and has sturdy bearings.

The track sits on stainless-steel tube *(c)*, 20 mm (3/4″) thick, through-fastened to the deck or cabin sides with reinforcement plates. The track has adjustable end-stoppers, for tuning the outermost positions of the traveller.

A metal strengthening-plate in the clew has several sheet-holes for varying the sheeting angle. The jib sheet leads from the traveller via a block in the spinnaker boom's fixture on the mast and the jibsheet block aft to the cockpit.

Mainsail reefing

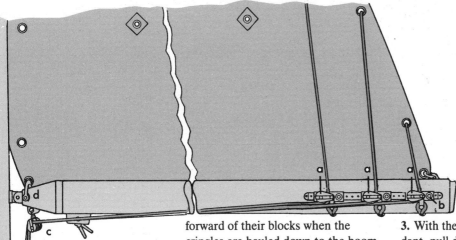

oller reefing has been largely re-
laced by slab reefing, a modern
ariant of the traditional points reef-
g. A properly set-up slab-reefing
ystem is simpler and quicker than
oller reefing, and the reefed sail
erforms better. A roller-reefing boom
annot have its kicking strap set when
he sail is rolled in along it—a clear
isadvantage when running.

Modern boats are usually delivered
ith slab reefing, but if you have roller
eefing, or if your boom is not well
quipped for slab reefing, you can
dapt or improve it as illustrated.

Depending on the number of reefs
ou have in the mainsail (usually two
r three), you use two or three cheek
locks (a), each with a spring-loaded
ocation plunger and an eye. These
locks slide on tracks (b) that are
astened to each side of the aft end of
he boom.

Fit blocks for reef no. 1 and for the
attening reef in one track and the
lock for reef no. 2 in the track on the
ther side. Each reefing line is
astened to the eye in the block, is led
nder the boom and up through the
eefing cringle (grommet) and back
own to the block, which is then
ocked in position so that the reefed
ringles are drawn about 10 cm (4″)

forward of their blocks when the
cringles are hauled down to the boom.
This will flatten the mainsail when part
of it is reefed along the boom.

The reefing lines should be of 8-mm
(5/16″) plaited rope. To reduce the
number of lines along the boom you
can use a reefing pendant (c) with a
shackle at the end. The ends of the
reefing lines are then fitted with an eye
to connect them to the shackle. The
reefing lines (or the reefing pendant if
you are using one) are led via double
stoppers on the boom's underside
through a double block to a winch on
the aft of the mast.

This winch must be mounted on an
angled base so that the angle of pull
from the block is correct. Alternatively, the reefing lines can be led
further aft to a winch on the aft of the
cabin top via a further double block
with becket at the mast foot.

The mast leech, reefing cringles
(grommets) and cunningham hole,
which are also used when flattening
the mainsail, are fastened to hooks on
either side of the gooseneck (d).

How to slab-reef

1. Set the topping lift. Lower the
mainsail halyard until the luff cringle
can be hooked onto the free hook at
the gooseneck.

2. Stretch the luff of the mainsail with
a few turns on the mainsail halyard's
winch.

3. With the help of the reefing pendant, pull down the relevant reef
cringle tightly to the boom with the
reefing winch on the mast or in the
cockpit. Secure the reefing line in the
stopper.

4. Bunt the sail and tie it with reef
points or shock cords through the
eyelets in the sail.

5. Release the topping lift and sheet
home the mainsail.

Mast roller furling
There are specially built masts available which contain a rotatable rod
round which the mainsail can be furled
(below).

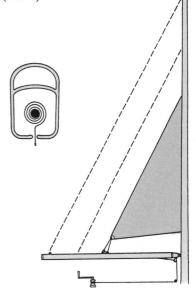

SETTING UP THE MAST

Dressing the mast

1. The boat should lie alongside the jetty. Arrange the mast with its foot facing the forward end of the boat. This will provide a straight lift for the crane and you won't have to turn the mast around in mid-air.

2. Place the mast on trestles, turned to lie on its aft (track) side. Ensure that it is well supported. Use wedges to stop sideways movement, and place padding (such as sacking) between the mast and the wedges and trestle crossbars.

3. Fit the spreaders or crosstrees first. This will help you to keep things in place as you dress the mast.

4. Fit and reeve all the running rigging and make it secure to the base of the mast. Pull each halyard down to the bottom of the mast and secure, each to its own cleat, so that they don't hang free and risk fastening in something when you are lifting the mast on board.

Check that there are stopping knots at the ends of the halyards to prevent them being lost inside the mast.

5. Check that the spreader and masthead lanterns are working properly, and spray them with anti-corrosion spray.

On masts with external halyards, make sure that they are fitted to the correct side of the spreaders: main

halyards aft, jib and spinnaker halyards forward, etc. Leave one forward halyard, say the spinnaker halyard, free to retrieve the lifting strop from the mast, when the mast has been stepped in place and secured

6. Fit the standing rigging on the correct side of the spreaders. Tie it with cord in logical order—the port and starboard shrouds, the forestay, and the backstay—at the base of the mast to hold them in place. Be sure that there is nothing to chafe against where the shrouds pass through the spreaders. Check now that any masthead antenna or wind indicators are in position.

Lifting the mast

Experienced riggers know instinctively where to place the rope lifting-strop on the mast. They always use sacking or some similar material to prevent it from chafing the mast.

The rule of thumb is to position the strop about one-third of the mast length down from the head, with the

point of the lift to the forward. If the strop is too near the top, the mast head will crash against the top of the crane. If it is too low, the mast will swing endwise and risk being damaged at one or both ends.

A line *(a)*, known as a flaker, is attached to the strop and secured to

one of the mast's winches to prevent the strop from riding up out of position.

Note the anti-chafe sacking, the type of strop knot used, and the way in which the standing and running rigging are secured neatly to the mast.

Raise the mast with the crane, sup-

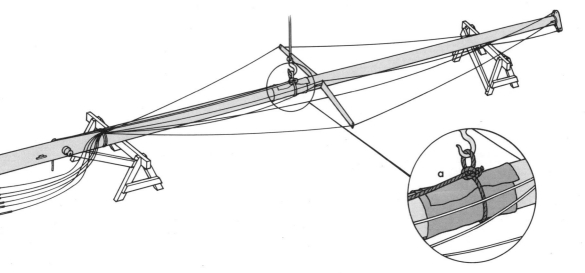

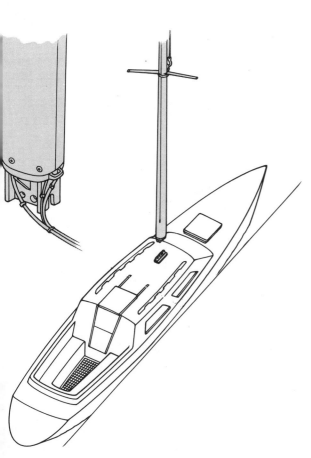

porting and guiding it by holding it at the foot. Position the mast just above the deck fitting or mast hole. Be sure that the cables to the lanterns and to any other instruments in the masthead are clear of the mast foot and the deck or mast hole. Put the mast foot in place and secure it.

Stepping and securing the mast

As soon as the mast foot is in position, secure it in place. With the mast stepped, secure the shrouds to their chainplates and tighten them, hand-tight. Then secure the backstay to its chainplate and the forestay to the stemhead fitting. With the mast secured, you can discharge the crane and remove the strop.

Trimming the mast

Begin by adjusting the shrouds. Start with the lower shrouds and then go on to the cap shrouds, checking as you go that the mast is straight and upright.

All masts should have some rake aft. Find out the exact degree of rake from the boatbuilder and adjust the mast with the backstay. Then tension the forestay accordingly.

A useful tool for checking that the tension on the rigging is correct is now available on the market. Known as a rig-tension meter, it is especially useful for checking that the wire on each side of a shroud has the same tension.

When you have tested the boat's trim on a sailing trip, and made any adjustments that you consider necessary, secure the rigging screws with new clevis pins and tape over them. (Even better than tape is to use a suitably dimensioned piece of plastic tubing that you had threaded over the ends of the shrouds and stays before you attached them to their fittings. Tape leaves sticky glue on the rigging screws).

Trimming the mast on a fractional rig

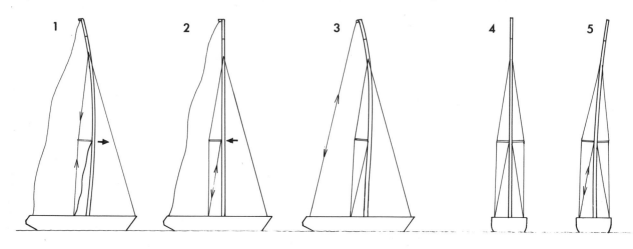

With a 7/8 rig, a curved mast is obtained by tensioning the forestay against the backstay.

1. Tighten the cap shrouds so that the mast is pressed forward where the spreaders are. Then tighten the lower shrouds to pull this part of the mast aft.

2. Tighten the forestay a little.

3. Tighten the backstay. (This mainly affects the upper part of the mast, tensions the forestay, and flattens the mainsail.)

4. Check that the mast is vertical when seen from behind or in front.

5. In this case, the port lowers and the starboard cap shrouds are too tight. A sideways bend in the mast can result.

REPLACING A HALYARD

This is a simple job, if you tackle it in the right order.

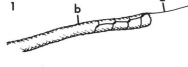

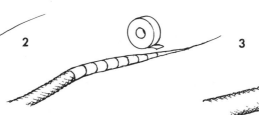

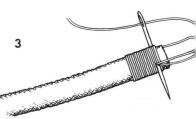

1. Attach a light drawline *(a)* to the end of the old halyard *(b)*, using clove hitches or rolling hitches.

2. Tape the knots over neatly.

3. Alternatively, make a stitched whipping at the end of the old halyard, and form a loop with some of the whipping. Tie on the drawline.

    Remove the old halyard by drawing it up through the mast and out through

the top. Don't let the end of the drawline vanish into the mast! Detach the old halyard and attach the new in the same way and reverse the procedure, drawing the new halyard down through the mast from the top.

Retrieving a lost halyard

If you have lost the end of the halyard inside the mast and out through the top, attach a small weight (such as a nut) to a light draw line twice the length of the mast. Get up to the masthead on the bosun's chair, and feed the weighted draw line down inside the mast. Feel for it with a loop of stiff wire at the base of the mast and draw it out. Attach its other end to the halyard (1–3 above) and draw it down through the mast.

SAILING FROM THE COCKPIT

Most modern boats are now equipped to be sailed from the cockpit, thus alleviating the necessity of working on a dangerous, wet, pitching and rolling deck. The most obvious advantages are that the boat can be sailed singlehanded, or at least short-handed, and this suits the family sailor very well. It also affords the opportunity for the disabled to really sail a boat.

Deck layout and fittings

We show a system for handling the halyards and other control lines which run from the mast foot through blocks *(a)* and on through distributor blocks *(b)*.

Stoppers *(c)* are fitted to obviate the need for a winch for each line. Stoppers constitute the heart of the cockpit-sailing system. Traditional jamming cleats will do the job, but difficulty may be experienced when trying to release ropes under heavy load, because they need to be pulled back before they'll release. The type of stopper illustrated is easy to use. Simply pull the lever on top of the stopper towards you and the sheet will be released, no matter what the load is.

One winch *(d)*, centrally placed, can cope easily with four or five lines. Each line passes through the stopper and can be operated by the winch. To operate the system, you simply winch the rope as tightly as you require. Then lock off the rope in the stopper and release the rope from the winch.

For added security, a secondary cleat may be fitted, aft of the stoppers.

Lines leading down into the cockpit must be coiled down and either hung on hooks or stowed neatly in canvas bags (see page 81).

The control lines can be arranged in the following way:

- *(e)* Main sheet.
- *(f)* Spinnaker sheet.
- *(g)* Genoa sheet.
- *(h)* Spinnaker-pole downhaul.
- *(i)* Spinnaker-pole lift.
- *(j)* Genoa halyard.
- *(k)* Main outhaul.
- *(l)* Kicking-strap.
- *(m)* Cunningham.
- *(n)* Main boom topping lift.
- *(o)* Main halyard.
- *(p)* Spinnaker halyard.
- *(q)* Spinnaker guy.
- *(r)* Flattening reef.
- *(s)* Reef no. 1.
- *(t)* Reef no. 2.
- *(u)* Reefing winch.

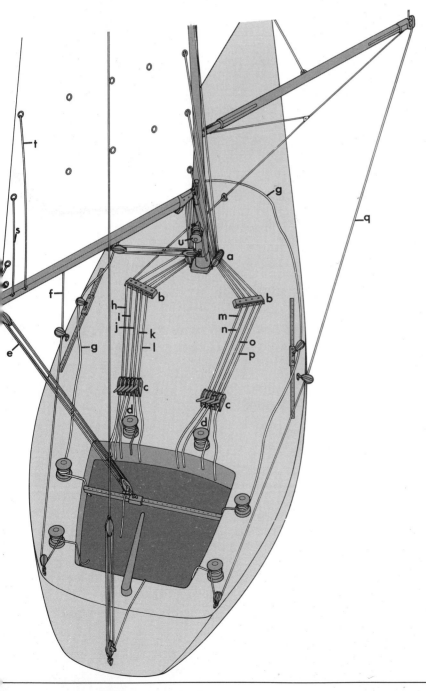

ROPES AND ROPEWORK

The wide variety of ropes available can easily confuse the sailor who wants to buy the correct rope for a certain purpose. Colour-coded ropes are very useful, as the colour indicates what use a rope has. The generally accepted colour code is white for the mainsail, blue for the jib/genoa, and red for the spinnaker. This coding is not completely universal, so there may be regional exceptions. The following is a brief description of the most usual types available.

Nylon

Used for anchoring, mooring, and towing. Tends to become stiff when wet, and sinks.

Polyester

Used for sheets and halyards. Almost as strong as nylon; stretches less. Very flexible, resistant to wear. It sinks.

Polypropylene

A general-purpose rope, often used for mooring. Less strong than Polyester, has medium stretch, and floats.

Kevlar

Used for halyards, sheets, and control ropes, this relatively new material has very high strength with low stretch. It is fireproof and sinks.

Mat nylon

Used for mooring, anchoring, and towing. Not as strong as bright-finished nylon, it has more stretch. Stays soft and flexible when wet, and it sinks.

Sheets and halyards size selector
If your boat is rigged with larger sails than those named below, use the rope size indicated for the sail area.

Overall yacht length m (ft)	6–8 (20–26)	9 (30)	10 (33)	11 (36)	12 (39)
Approx. sail area sq ft (sq m)					
Main	90 (8.4)	144 (13.4)	171 (16)	198 (18.4)	252 (23.4)
Genoa/jib	100 (9.3)	180 (16.8)	270 (25)	360 (33.5)	340 (42)
Spinnaker	405 (37.7)	495 (46)	585 (54)	765 (71)	990 (92)
Sheet size mm (in)					
Main	8 (5/16)	8 (5/16)	8 (5/16)	10 (3/8)	12 (1/2)
Genoa/jib	10 (3/8)	10 (3/8)	12 (1/2)	14 (9/16)	12 (1/2)
Spinnaker	8 (5/16)	10 (3/8)	10 (3/8)	10 (3/8)	12 (1/2)
Spinnaker/ guy	10 (3/8)	10 (3/8)	12 (1/2)	12 (1/2)	12 (1/2)
Halyard size mm (in)					
Main	8 (5/16)	10 (3/8)	10 (3/8)	10 (3/8)	12 (1/2)
Genoa/jib	8 (5/16)	10 (3/8)	10 (3/8)	12 (1/2)	12 (1/2)
Spinnaker	8 (5/16)	8 (5/16)	10 (3/8)	10 (3/8)	12 (1/2)

SPLICING A PLAITED ROPE

We show here three methods of splicing a plaited rope: sew-and-serve, rope-to-wire, and a method used by professionals which leaves no visible sign of the splice. (*Courtesy Marlow Ropes Ltd*)

Sew-and-serve method

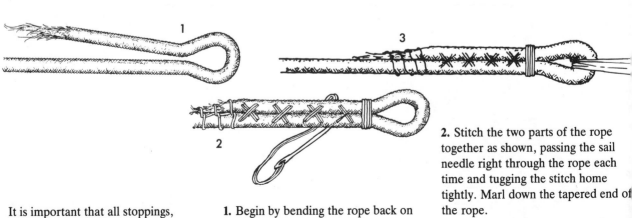

It is important that all stoppings, sewing, and serving are tightly and neatly done, otherwise the eye splice will be loose and weak.

1. Begin by bending the rope back on itself to a distance of about eight times the diametre of the eye you want to form. Taper the end of the rope.

2. Stitch the two parts of the rope together as shown, passing the sail needle right through the rope each time and tugging the stitch home tightly. Marl down the tapered end of the rope.

3. Now set the rope up taut between two posts.

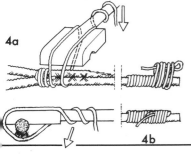

4a

4b

4. Take whipping twine and bind it around the rope at the base of the eye. Take the serving tool, now as a mallet, and wind the whipping twine around it as shown *(a)*, and serve the twine around the rope until the tapered end is well covered.

Remove the mallet and secure the end of the twine by slacking back as shown *(b)*.

Finish off by hauling tight on the end.

Rope-to-wire splice

1

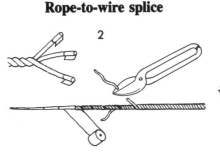

2

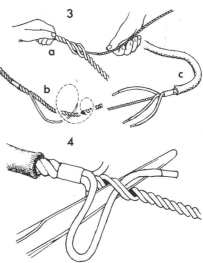

3

4

1. Wire halyards are long-lasting and efficient, but hard on the hands and difficult to make fast. A rope spliced to the wire is the answer. The splice shown here is for 16 Plait Marlow Polyester rope and a wire that is about half the rope's diameter.

2. Tape the ends of the core's strands and the end of the wire (which must be tapered first with a 225-mm (9″) taper.

3. *(a)* Open up the lay about 750 mm (30″) from the core end and insert the wire. Wind tape around the core at this point to hold the wire in place.

(b) Twist the wire into the lay of the rope with a spiralling action so that it is brought into the centre of the core. The wire should be about 200 mm (8″) into the rope. Tape at this point.

(c) Slide the outer cover down over the core to the tape.

4. Splice the three strands of the core into the wire *against* the lay. Pass each strand of rope under two strands of wire, then repeat until three rounds of tucks have been made.

5

6

7

5. Taper the rope strands before making the fourth and fifth tucks. Then cut off the ends.

6. Slide the cover down over the splice and whip tightly. Unlay the remaining part of the cover into separate yarns and divide into three, tapering the ends.

7. Splice the cover into the wire *with* the lay. Make one round of tucks first. Then make sure that on the second round you tuck the same rope strands under the same two wire strands you started with.

8. Five tucks are required. With each round, remove a yarn from the rope to give a tapered appearance. Cut off the ends.

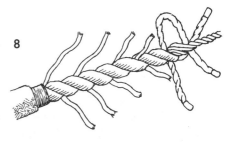

8

The professional's eye splice

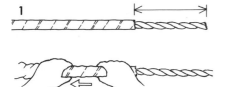

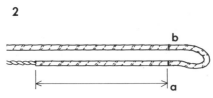

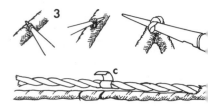

1. Cut off the heatsealed end and push back the outer case, exposing 100 mm (4″) of inner core.

Holding the end of the case to the core, push back the slack for 1 m (39″).

2. Putting a bend in the rope, measure from the end of the case 300 mm (12″) and mark *(a)* and *(b)* to the size of the eye required.

3. With a Swedish fid or marlin spike, open the case at mark *(b)* by lifting the strands, making a small hole through which the inner core can be seen. Insert the fid and hook out the inner core. Pull until it has been removed. The rope appears to have two tails. Pass a piece of rigging tape around the inner core at position *(c)*.

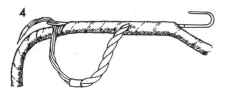

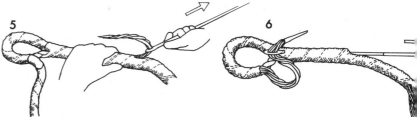

4. Insert the splicing needle at a position 350 mm (14″) from mark *(b)* and, taking care not to ensnare the inner core, push the needle down inside the outer case until it emerges at mark *(a)*. Now thread the tail of the inner core through the eye of the needle. To do this, it is necessary to taper the end of the inner core by cutting out 50% of the yarns at the taped position. It may also help to tape the end.

5. With the inner core tail threaded, pull the splicing needle out of the rope to bring the inner core down through the middle. Keep pulling until the eye has formed and the end of the inner core has merged.

Now push some loose case in the outer cover back towards the eye, ready for the next stage of the splice.

6. The final part of the splice construction is to pull the outer cover tail through the rope in the same fashion. Begin by unpicking and cutting out 6 yarn ends at a position some 50 mm (2″) from the eye end of the outer case tail. Insert the splicing needle 200 mm (8″) from the neck of the eye and thread the outer cover tail and pull this down through the middle of the rope.

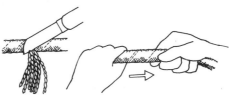

7. The splice should now look like the drawing in this figure with the outer cover tail and inner core tail emerging from different positions (and preferably on different sides) along the rope. Pull everything tight, give the splice a

good snatch to bed the yarns down, and cut off the end with a sharp knife.

Finally, run a hand over the outer cover from the eye end down until the cut-off ends disappear inside the rope.

8. If a thimble is required, then this can be inserted while the eye is being formed and before the ends are pulled tight.

CHAPTER 7

Sails

SAILCLOTH

Modern sailcloth is a high-tech synthetic material which has many advantages over the old woven flax and cotton sails. To understand the exact compositon of some of the materials, you would need to be a chemist, but the trade names—Nylon, Dacron, Terylene, Kevlar and Mylar—are familiar to most sailors.

Cruising sailcloth

Good cruising sailcloth is specifically designed for the job. Although it is economically priced when compared to the cost of racing sailcloth, it is not a cheap version of the same. Cruising sailcloths give top performance over a wide range of conditions. They are strong and durable, with exceptionally long life, yet they are soft and easy to handle and stow.

Racing/cruising sailcloth

This cloth is designed for the cruising man who likes to race, and is ideal for club and class competitions. It is similar to cruising sailcloth but with a finish that makes it behave more like racing cloth. So they give high performance for competitive sailing at the same time as they are suitable for cruising.

Racing sailcloth

The prime consideration of racing sailcloth is performance, and there are many specialized cloths with, for instance, high-density weaves, that have been developed for specific types of racing. Most racing sailcloth is tough and difficult to handle, but when you have lots of willing muscle in your crew, who cares?

Cruising and cruising/racing sailcloth

Boat length	UP TO 21'	22'–26'	27'–31'	32'–36'	37'–42'	43'–49'	50'–55'
Mainsail	6oz 203gm	7oz 237gm	9oz 305gm	10oz 339gm	11oz 373gm	13oz 441gm	14oz 475gm
Light No. 1 genoa	4oz 136gm	4oz 136gm	4oz 136gm	4oz 136gm	5oz 170gm	6oz 203gm	6oz 203gm
No. 1 genoa	6oz 203gm	6oz 203gm	7oz 237gm	7oz 237gm	8oz 271gm	8oz 271gm	10oz 339gm
No. 2 genoa	6oz 203gm	7oz 237gm	7oz 237gm	9oz 305gm	9oz 305gm	10oz 339gm	11oz 373gm
No. 3 genoa	6oz 203gm	7oz 237gm	7oz 237gm	9oz 305gm	10oz 339gm	10oz 339gm	11oz 373gm
No. 4 jib	7oz 237gm	7oz 237gm	9oz 305gm	10oz 339gm	11oz 373gm	11oz 373gm	12oz 407gm
Storm jib	7oz 237gm	8oz 271gm	10oz 339gm	12oz 407gm	13oz 441gm	14oz 475gm	14oz 475gm
Tri sail	7oz 237gm	8oz 271gm	10oz 339gm	12oz 407gm	13oz 441gm	14oz 475gm	14oz 475gm

Racing sailcloth weights

Boat length	¼ Ton 24'–26'	½ Ton 27'–31'	¾ Ton 32'–34'	1 Ton 35'–39'	2 Ton 40' +
High-aspect mainsail	8oz 271gm F	8oz 271gm F	9oz 305gm H/J	11oz 373gm L	8oz 271gm F (2 sails)
Low-aspect mainsail	7oz 237gm D	9oz 305gm G	10oz 339gm K	10oz 339gm K	12oz 407gm
No. 1 light genoa	4oz 136gm A/B	4oz 136gm A	4oz 136gm A	4oz 136 gm A	4oz 136gm A
No. 1 heavy genoa	6oz 203gm C	7oz 237gm D	7oz 237gm D	9oz 305gm G	9oz 305gm G
No. 2 genoa	7oz 237gm D	7oz 237gm D	8oz 271gm E	9oz 305gm J	9oz 305gm J
No. 3 genoa	7oz 237gm D	9oz 305gm G	9oz 305gm J	10oz 339gm K	10oz 339gm K
No. 4 jib			9oz 305gm J	10oz 339gm K	10oz 339gm K
No. 4 heavy jib		99oz 305gm J	10oz 339gm K	10oz 339gm K	12oz 407gm
Storm jib	9oz 305gm G	10oz 339gm K	10oz 339gm K	12oz 407gm	13oz 441gm
Tri sail	9oz 305gm G	10oz 339gm K	10oz 339gm K	12oz 407gm	13oz 441gm

HAYWARDS CLOTH.

Details of racing sailcloth

A Intended for lightweight racing headsails. Successful for both crosscut and mitred light genoas on all sizes of boats.

B Designed for crosscut headsails on racing craft up to ½ ton (maximum usage—light genoas). Also ideal for both mainsails and jibs on small dinghies.

C Balanced headsail cloth for both crosscut and mitred sails, particularly low-aspect genoas. Also recommended for low-aspect dinghy headsails (505, FD, etc.)

D Another balanced high-performance headsail cloth, but also extensively used for low-aspect mainsails.

E Universal headsail cloth of a square construction. Suitable for a very wide range of sails for racing craft of various lengths.

F High-performance mainsail cloth, particularly for high-aspect ratio sails. Also suitable for high-aspect ratio headsails.

G For larger racing craft requiring a strong cloth for crosscut No. 2 and No. 3 genoas and even working jibs. Also suitable for low-aspect mainsails on boats of about ½ ton.

H Designed to meet sailmakers' requirements for heavier racing mainsail cloths, suitable for boats from about ½ ton upwards.

J Very popular because of its high quality combined with economic price. Features a very strong weft for high aspect mainsails on boats of around ¾ ton, and is also very effectively used for working jibs.

K Balanced headsail cloth developed for large, heavy racing applications. It will cope with the heavy loadings imposed by vigorous use of multi-ratio winches. Also suitable for low-aspect mainsails.

L Mainsail fabric for racing craft of around 1 ton. This is designed to give high performance under heavy loading strains, but also to be durable for long life.

Weight conversion table

Yacht sailcloth

U.K. oz	Gram	U.S. oz
3.8	129	3.0
5.0	170	4.0
6.3	215	5.0
7.6	258	6.0
8.9	301	7.0
10.1	344	8.0
11.4	387	9.0
12.6	430	10.0
14.0	473	11.0
15.2	516	12.0

Glossary of terms

USA weight—ozs per yard
The weight in ounces calculated on 1 yard (36 inches) × 28½ inches wide.

UK weight—ozs per square yard
The weight in ounces calculated on 1 yard (36 inches) of cloth × 1 yard (36 inches) wide.

Metric weight—grams per square metre
The weight in grams calculated on 1 metre (39.4 inches) of cloth × 1 metre (39.4 inches) wide.

Conversion factors

USA wt × 1.26 = UK wt
UK wt × 0.79 = USA wt
USA wt × 43.0 = wt in gm/m²
UK wt × 33.9 = wt in gm/m²
Grams ÷ 43 = USA oz
Grams ÷ 33.9 = UK oz
Metres to feet × 3.2808
Feet to metres × 0.3048

SAIL TYPES

Sail technology has become a state-of-the-art science, and as new materials are developed, they open up new possibilities in design.

Mainsail

This is the yacht's main engine, providing the main motive force, even if it is not necessarily the largest sail on board.

Headsail

Traditionally, headsails were always mitre-cut to provide as much stability as possible; but with modern materials, sailcloth design is such that crosscut designs are possible without any sacrifices.

Spinnakers

Weight being the main factor when it comes to spinnakers, nylon is normally favoured.

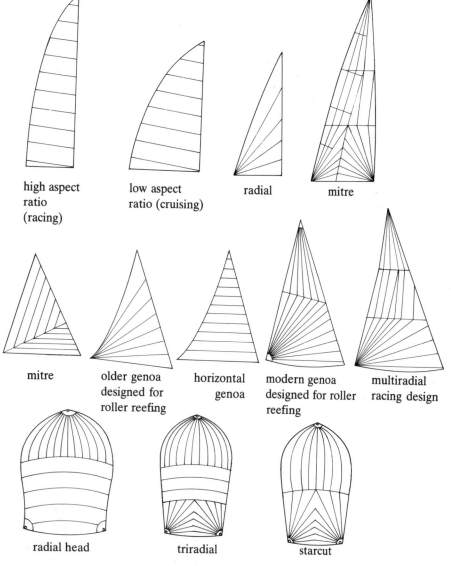

high aspect ratio (racing)

low aspect ratio (cruising)

radial

mitre

mitre

older genoa designed for roller reefing

horizontal genoa

modern genoa designed for roller reefing

multiradial racing design

radial head

triradial

starcut

MAINTAINING SAILS

Although synthetic sailcloth is tough, it should be handled carefully. Sails are expensive, and deserve proper treatment. They will then not only last longer but also give better service.

It is particularly important, with old sails as well as new, to avoid stretching the leech. So when hoisting and lowering the mainsail, always take the weight of the boom on the topping lift. For the same reason, pull headsails down by the luff, not by the leech.

Folding and stowing sails

Polyester and nylon sails deteriorate with long-term exposure to the elements, so they should always be covered when not in use. Those which detach completely should be removed and stowed away properly. Those which roll around the boom or forestay must, when furled, have covers fitted. If you have Mylar or Kevlar sails, which are especially sensitive to the ultra-violet rays of the sun, then you must cover them with sail coats at every opportunity.

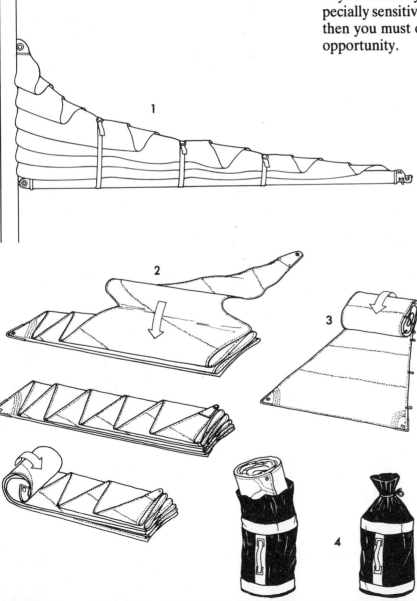

1. If the mainsail does not have roller reefing but stays on the boom, it must be flaked over the boom in a zigzag fashion. Tie the sail loosely before fitting on its sail coat.

2. Mainsails that detach should also be flaked, either from the luff or the foot in widths of 2–3 ft (60–90 cm). Each time you flake the sail, change the flake width a little, to avoid forming permanent creases. After flaking, roll the sail from its widest end and stow it in a sail bag large enough to avoid cramming.

3. Headsails should be rolled down their luff lines from head to tack, then rolled in the other direction towards the clew.

4. If stowing for any length of time, make sure sails are dry before bagging them. Even when bagged, they must be treated with care. Stow them in a dry place where they won't be squashed. In their bags, they are particularly vulnerable to creasing, which lessens their performance.

Cleaning and maintaining sails

All sails should be kept clean. Dirty and salt-stained sails are unattractive, will perform poorly, and need replacing sooner.

With the larger sails, it is probably impractical to wash them at home, so it is better to use the valet service offered by your local sail loft.

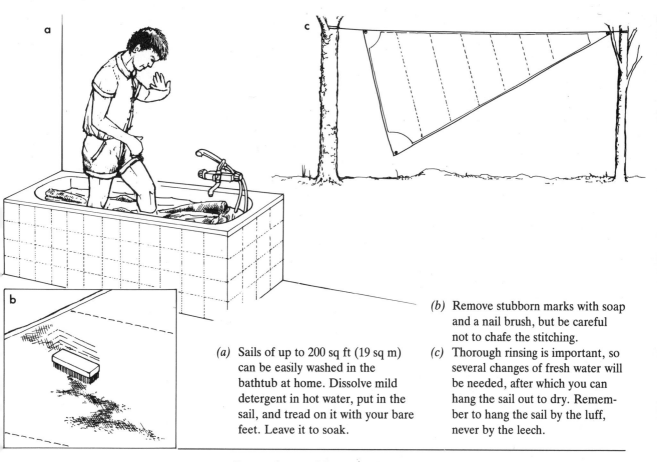

(a) Sails of up to 200 sq ft (19 sq m) can be easily washed in the bathtub at home. Dissolve mild detergent in hot water, put in the sail, and tread on it with your bare feet. Leave it to soak.

(b) Remove stubborn marks with soap and a nail brush, but be careful not to chafe the stitching.

(c) Thorough rinsing is important, so several changes of fresh water will be needed, after which you can hang the sail out to dry. Remember to hang the sail by the luff, never by the leech.

Removing stubborn stains

Stains should be removed as soon as possible after they occur. Don't wait for the annual laundering.

SALT: Rinse with fresh water, paying extra attention to multi-layer areas such as clew, head, and tack.

GREASE, OIL AND TAR: These are the worst stains to remove. If the staining is light, it can often be removed with white spirit followed by hot water and mild detergent. If this does not work, resort to trichloroethylene, but make sure that there is plenty of ventilation, and wash thoroughly with fresh water afterwards.

MILDEW: Wash with mild detergent in warm water, rinse in fresh water, and then give it a quick soak in a solution of household bleach (see the pack for details). Wash out afterwards, rinse and hang up to dry. Wash the sail bags, too.

BLOOD: Wash immediately with cold water. If the blood has dried, you may have to soak the stain in household bleach.

PAINT AND VARNISH: Use white spirit, neat detergent, or trichloroethylene. Do not use alkali-based paint strippers or you will ruin the sailcloth.

RUST: Oxalic acid will often remove this, but great care should be taken. The right solution is 1 oz per pint of water (50 g per litre). Mix it in a plastic container. Wear protective gloves throughout. Immerse the stained area until the rust has dissolved, then wash out with fresh water and detergent. Rinse thoroughly.

EMERGENCY SAIL REPAIRS

Permanent repairs and alterations are the work of the professional sailmaker, but there are times when emergency repairs are necessary, for instance when you don't have a spare sail and need to use the damaged one to get you home. However, emergency repairs are only temporary measures—so get the repair done professionally as soon as possible.

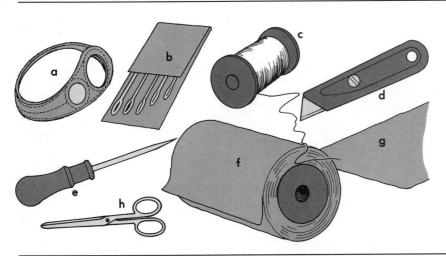

On-board emergency kit
(a) Sewing palm.
(b) A set of sailmaker's needles.
(c) Nylon thread. Thread is quoted in breaking strains, and a good guide is to halve the ounce/weight of the sailcloth and call it pounds. So if your sail is of 8-oz material, then use thread with a 4-lb breaking strain.
(d) Sharp knife.
(e) Brad awl or spike.
(f) Self-adhesive Dacron.
(g) Pieces of sail cloth.
(h) Scissors.

Repairing a tear

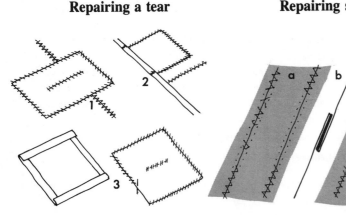

Repairing seams

Reinforcing clews

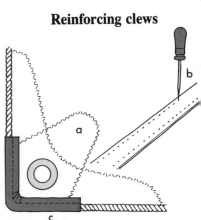

1. Take a piece of sail cloth or self-adhesive Dacron that is larger than the tear. Make sure that the two edges of the tear are pulled together neatly, and secure the repair cloth to both sides of the sail. Stitch around the edges.

2. If the tear is close to a bolt rope or luff wire, the patch should go right around the wire to the other side, and then be stitched.

3. For older sails, a canvas patch may be the remedy. Fold each edge under and stitch securely around each edge.

If seams come adrift at sea, they should be repaired as quickly as possible to prevent the damage spreading.
(a) The damaged seam seen from in front. Remove all traces of damaged stitches.
(b) The seam seen from the side. Secure with double-sided adhesive tape between the layers of sailcloth.
(c) The seam seen from in front, now restitched using straight stitches.

Areas of high chafing can be reinforced with soft leather.
(a) Cut the leather to fit the clew.
(b) Make holes for the stitches with a brad awl.
(c) Take the sewing palm and stitch the leather securely into place, using nylon thread (doubled if necessary).

Tears in spinnakers are repaired with special spinnaker repair tape which is applied to both sides of the sail.

CHAPTER 8

Engines

The diesel engine has gained enormously in popularity with boat owners because it is rugged, reliable, and safe. It works on the principle of compression/ignition. Air is heated to several hundred degrees as it is compressed in the cylinder by the piston. At or near the top of the stroke, a tiny but precise quantity of fuel is injected at enormously high pressure (to overcome that already in the cylinder). The fuel burns, creating even higher pressure to drive the piston down on the power stroke. The diesel engine has to be built ruggedly in order to withstand these pressures, and, as the fuel is not as inflammable as petrol, it is very much safer. A diesel engine tends to be more expensive than a petrol engine because of the precise engineering involved in both the engine and the fuel system. Many modern diesel engines can match the power-to-weight ratio of petrol engines, and can be found as inboard units, as outdrives, and as sail drives. These is even an outboard diesel engine on the market.

Knowing your diesel

Unseen here, because it is on the other side of the engine, is the oil filter.

(a) Air inlet. Keep filter gauzes/elements clean. Blank off for the winter with a plastic bag.

(b) Oil-breather pipe in the rocker box. Ensure that it is clean and well-jointed.

(c) Cooling-water pressure/filler cap (only in freshwater systems). See that it seats well.

(d) Oil-filler cap in top of rocker box. See that it is secured.

(e) Diesel injectors. This is extremely high-pressure precision equipment. Do not interfere with it, except when it fails (see "Fault finding", page 121).

(f) Fuel filter—see opposite.

(g) Gear box/reduction-gear box. Renew any filters once a year. Always drain down old oils and replace before winter. NEVER overfill, as this can cause excess pressures which may blow the oil seals.

(h) Starter motor. Keep dry when draining down the cooling water. Check that the cables to the starter motor are secure.

(i) Drain plug for sump. If you can reach it, you drain the dirty oil down through this. Otherwise, you must use:

(j) Sump pump for emptying dirty oil. For use at winter lay-up time. If not built onto the engine, it can be inserted in the dipstick hole.

(k) Impeller-type pump. See detailed instructions under "Cooling", page 131.

(l) Rubber belt drive. Keep it tightened so that the longest run has about 12–15 mm (1/2″–5/8″) depression. Do not overtighten, as the bearings on the generator, water pumps, and main drive pulley will suffer.

(m) Alternator (old engines use a dynamo), which generates electric power to recharge the batteries. Keep it dry when filling the cooling system.

(n) Freshwater pump. Nearby or under the header tank will be found the thermostat which stabilizes cooling-water temperatures round the engine block on direct and indirect water-cooled engines.

In addition, some inboard diesels have heat exchangers (see page 130) and turbocharging (see page 120).

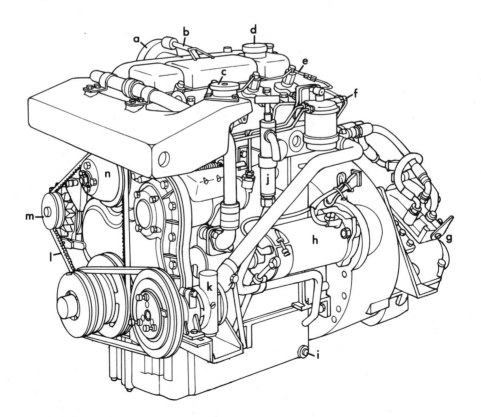

The fuel system

There are two sides to the diesel-pump system: a low-pressure side, from the fuel tank to the injection pump, and a high-pressure side from the injection pump to each injector (there is one injector for each cylinder). It is essential that you read the engine manufacturer's instruction manual and know how to bleed air from the whole length of the fuel system. Air in the system prevents starting and usually occurs after an engine has been allowed to run out of fuel, or when some part of the system has been dismantled for servicing.

(a) Fuel injectors. These should be cleaned, serviced and calibrated by the service depot only. See "Fault finding", page 121, to know what the trouble is.

(b) Bleed-back line to transport excess fuel back to the tank.

(c) Main fuel filter on engine. It has an air-bleed screw in the top. This filter should be renewed annually.

(d) Fuel lift pump. Clean or replace the filter gauze in the top annually. Always carry a spare pump

at sea. When the diaphragm fails, get professional help.

(e) Fuel filter, or agglomerator for removing water from the fuel. Drain down regularly. Renew the filter gauze/element annually.

(f) Injection pump. A distributor-type pump is shown here, but some engines use a piston pump to pressurize the fuel. Professional service will be needed only rarely for calibration, or for replacement of the whole pump with a new or factory-rebuilt unit.

(g) Tank breather pipe. It must be positioned outside the coamings/hull but where no rain or sea water can possibly get into the tank. The flame gauze fitted to the end of the breather pipe should be kept clean of dust.

(h) Filler cap on deck. For refilling the fuel tank. The gasket must be watertight and deck water must not gather around the filler cap.

(i) The double clipping on all flexible sections of the fuel pipe must be checked for tightness. Vibrations can loosen them.

(j) The fuel tank must be firmly seated.

(k) The tank, piping, and filler cap must be bonded electrically to the earth to prevent a static spark from starting a fire or explosion.

(l) Up-take pipe in the fuel tank. The up-take pipe should be 19 mm (3/4″) from the bottom of the tank. Keep the fuel tank full, to prevent condensation. Drain down the tank and clean it every spring by removing the tank top.

(m) Fuel shut-off valves, on the supply and feed-back pipe. Close these in a fire situation, during the winter, or when the boat is left unmanned for long, to prevent syphoning if a fuel line breaks.

(n) A flexible section of the fuel pipe absorbs engine vibration. It should be supported along its length, so that the terminal ends do not take its full weight.

(o) Baffles in the fuel tank prevent excessive fuel movement that could starve the engine or upset the boat's stability in heavy weather.

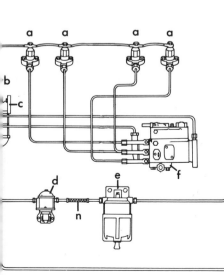

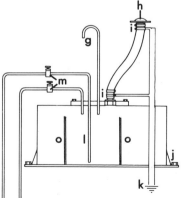

The fuel filter

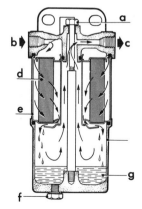

(a) Retaining bolt.
(b) Fuel inlet.
(c) Fuel outlet for filtered fuel.
(d) Filter element.
(e) Steel canister.
(f) Drain plug.
(g) Agglomerated water.

The turbocharger

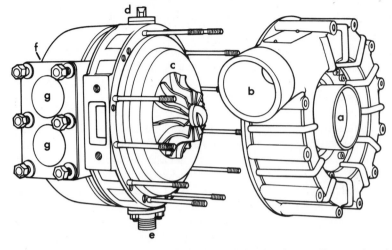

Many diesel and petrol engines now use a turbocharger to increase the power output. This precision unit allows only limited maintenance by the amateur. If anything goes wrong, go to the service depot.

(a) Compressor inlet (from air filter).
(b) Compressor outlet to cylinders, sometimes via intercooler/heat exchanger.
(c) Compressor.
(d) Oil inlet.
(e) Oil outlet.
(f) Exhaust turbine outlet.
(g) Exhaust gas inlets.

The following jobs can be done yourself:

1. Lubrication. First-class lubrication is essential, as the unit spins at 90,000 rpm plus. Pressurized oil, often cooled in a heat exchanger, is usually fed from the clean side of the main engine oil filter. You may also find an extra full-flow filter with no by-pass valve between the main engine filter and the turbocharger to guarantee cleaner oil. Replace the filters at recommended intervals and use premium-grade oil formulated for turbo-charged engines.

2. Cooling. The turbine, compressor and shafting are made to very fine tolerances and need cool conditions. Clean the heat-exchanger and aftercooler tube stacks to make sure that they remain efficient.

Ensure that the air drawn into the compressor is as cool as possible, by having ventilation fans in the engine room or some other cold-air intake arrangement.

3. Air cleaning. The great volume of air entering the compressor must be clean, so check that any rubber connecting hose between the air filter and the compressor inlet is intact. Tiny debris entering the turbocharger at these rpms will wreck it. Learn how to remove the compressor cover and clean debris that builds up on the blades and casing. Use approved liquid cleaners—NO metal tools or screwdrivers.

Turbocharger problems

1. Vibration from the main engine can damage air and lubrication-oil connections. Always check daily for small leaks (and also for water leaks if the turbocharger is water-cooled).
2. Smoke can be caused by
  – choked air cleaner
  – failure of fuel-pump calibration

  – excessive back pressure in the exhaust system, resulting in partial blockage

3. Seizure through lack of oil or excessive end play on shaft, allowing rotating units to hit the casing.

In an emergency, and when no debris has been ingested into the engine, it is possible to run the engine at a very small throttle opening for a short period.

DIESEL-ENGINE FAULT FINDING

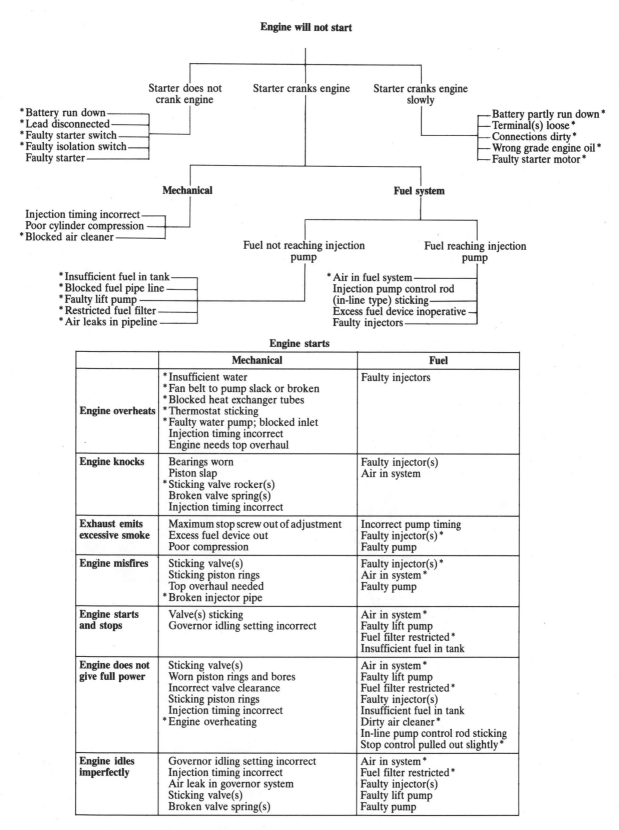

Engine will not start

Starter does not crank engine · Starter cranks engine · Starter cranks engine slowly

* Battery run down
* Lead disconnected
* Faulty starter switch
* Faulty isolation switch
  Faulty starter

— Battery partly run down *
— Terminal(s) loose *
— Connections dirty *
— Wrong grade engine oil *
— Faulty starter motor *

Mechanical

Injection timing incorrect
Poor cylinder compression
* Blocked air cleaner

Fuel system

Fuel not reaching injection pump

* Insufficient fuel in tank
* Blocked fuel pipe line
* Faulty lift pump
* Restricted fuel filter
* Air leaks in pipeline

Fuel reaching injection pump

* Air in fuel system
  Injection pump control rod (in-line type) sticking
  Excess fuel device inoperative
  Faulty injectors

Engine starts

	Mechanical	Fuel
Engine overheats	* Insufficient water * Fan belt to pump slack or broken * Blocked heat exchanger tubes * Thermostat sticking * Faulty water pump; blocked inlet Injection timing incorrect Engine needs top overhaul	Faulty injectors
Engine knocks	Bearings worn Piston slap * Sticking valve rocker(s) Broken valve spring(s) Injection timing incorrect	Faulty injector(s) Air in system
Exhaust emits excessive smoke	Maximum stop screw out of adjustment Excess fuel device out Poor compression	Incorrect pump timing Faulty injector(s) * Faulty pump
Engine misfires	Sticking valve(s) Sticking piston rings Top overhaul needed * Broken injector pipe	Faulty injector(s) * Air in system * Faulty pump
Engine starts and stops	Valve(s) sticking Governor idling setting incorrect	Air in system * Faulty lift pump Fuel filter restricted * Insufficient fuel in tank
Engine does not give full power	Sticking valve(s) Worn piston rings and bores Incorrect valve clearance Sticking piston rings Injection timing incorrect * Engine overheating	Air in system * Faulty lift pump Fuel filter restricted * Faulty injector(s) Insufficient fuel in tank Dirty air cleaner * In-line pump control rod sticking Stop control pulled out slightly *
Engine idles imperfectly	Governor idling setting incorrect Injection timing incorrect Air leak in governor system Sticking valve(s) Broken valve spring(s)	Air in system * Fuel filter restricted * Faulty injector(s) Faulty lift pump Faulty pump

* Checks and jobs the amateur mechanic should be able to do.

THE PETROL ENGINE

Inboard petrol engines, and a growing number of outboards, are of the kind with a four-stroke cycle: induction, compression, power, and exhaust. They are divided into two types, having overhead valves which are (1) push-rod operated and (2) overhead-camshaft operated, as shown here.

Familiarize yourself with all parts noted on the two drawings, and you will see that many parts are common to both. The repair of the internal parts is not the province of everybody, but where there is a star against one of the reference letters, any yachtsman should be able to cope with that item's repair, service, and winterization.

The parts of the petrol engine

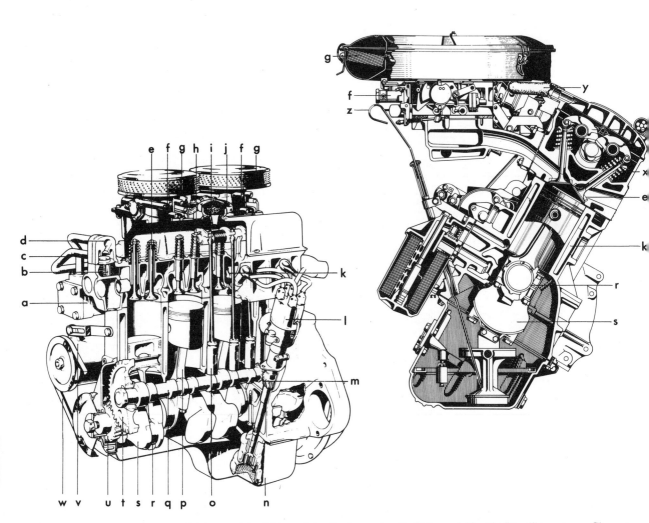

*(a)** Water-cooled exhaust manifold.

(b) Thermostat.

(c) Raw water to injection bend and exhaust pipe.

(d) Water-distribution housing. When the thermostat is closed on a cold engine, some water is distributed to the exhaust pipe to cool it.

(e) Valves: inlet for incoming fuel/air mixture and outlet (exhaust) for burnt gases.

(f) Carburettors. The push-rod engine has twin carburettors— see the engine manual for basic work that is possible. The overhead-camshaft engine has a sealed carburettor to keep the amateur out.

*(g)** Air filter/flame trap. Clean or replace filter as for diesel engine. Don't run the engine without it.

*(h)** Rocker arm that actuates the valves. Adjust clearance as for diesel rockers. Note first if this should be done on hot or cold engine (check manual).

(i) Push rod.

(j) Oil filler-cap on rocker cover. Check gasket on cover for leaks.

(k)* Water passageways in engine block.

(l) Distributor.

(m) Worm gear driving distributor shaft from camshaft.

(n)* Oil sump. Keep topped up to between the dipstick marks.

(o) Tappets or cam followers.

(p) Connecting rod.

(q) Camshaft. As well as operating the valves, it is sometimes used to drive the cooling-water pump.

(r) Big-end bearing.

(s) Crankshaft.

(t) Camshaft gear.

(u) Crankshaft gear.

(v) Alternator (generator).

(w)* Pulley belt driving generator and, on indirect-cooled engines, a fresh-water pump.

(x) Valve spring.

(y)* Oil breather pipe to exhaust oil fumes from the rocker box to the air intake in the air filter. Clean out once a year.

(z)* Dip stick. Keep oil between the marks.

Fuel pumps for both petrol and diesel engines

The mechanical, or cam-operated, pump used on most inboard engines is known as a diaphragm pump. A diaphragm is operated by a rocker arm driven from the engine camshaft. The diaphragm varies the volume of the chamber above it, creating suction on the downward stroke to suck fuel into the chamber through an inlet valve and ejecting the fuel through the outlet valve and into the carburettor. Although small outboard engines may be fed by gravity from a fuel tank above the engine, most engines (inboard and outboard) need a fuel-lift pump to pump the fuel from a lower, remote tank to the engine's fuel system.

Outboard two-stroke engines sometimes have their diaphragm pumps actuated by the pressure pulses created in the crankcase. Obviously, there must be no leaks in the pulse-line connection or in the diaphragm.

Parts of the pump that might require attention

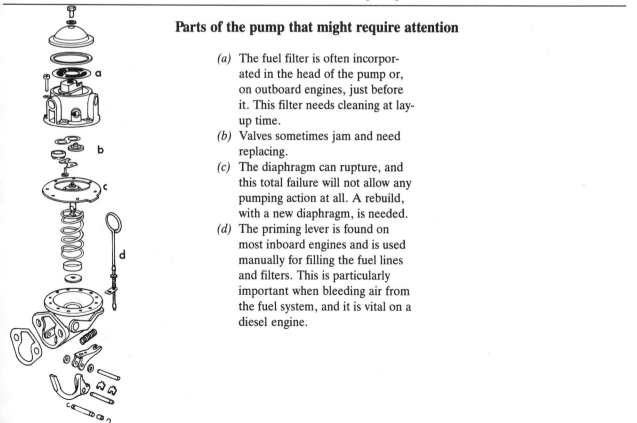

(a) The fuel filter is often incorporated in the head of the pump or, on outboard engines, just before it. This filter needs cleaning at lay-up time.

(b) Valves sometimes jam and need replacing.

(c) The diaphragm can rupture, and this total failure will not allow any pumping action at all. A rebuild, with a new diaphragm, is needed.

(d) The priming lever is found on most inboard engines and is used manually for filling the fuel lines and filters. This is particularly important when bleeding air from the fuel system, and it is vital on a diesel engine.

The carburettor

The carburettor is the heart of a petrol engine; so unless you are a carburettor heart surgeon, leave it alone. Carburettors vary in complexity. The sophisticated Solex 4A1 employed on some BMW outdrives has factory-sealed jets, but you can still check the pipes and the electric terminals. On simple carburettors it is possible to adjust the low- and high-speed needle jets and clean the float-bowl chamber.

Where the trouble occurs

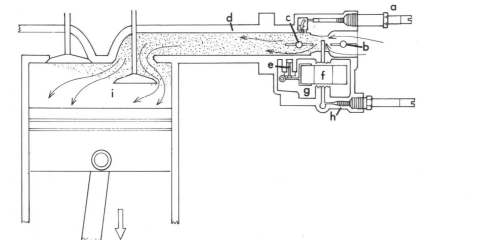

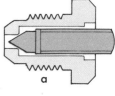

The working principle for a simple carburettor is shown here.

(a) Needle jets damaged by over-tightening will ruin the needle and the seating. The engine will not tune easily and running will be erratic. Jets in good condition generally need to be opened 1½ to 1¾ turns from a gently closed position, when you are tuning the engine.

 The high-speed jet is best adjusted when the engine is under load. Fine tuning for speed and fuel economy is best left to the service depot, as manufacturers often specify the use of special methods involving instruments the amateur is unlikely to possess.

(b) The choke is used to get a richer fuel/air mixture when starting the engine. It can be either hand- or electric-operated. Over-use causes flooding of the cylinder with fuel and wets the plug or plugs.

(c) The throttle adjusts the speed of the engine. Sloppy linkages do not allow smooth opening and closing. Keep the pivot points lubricated and the control cables in good condition.

(d) The inlet manifold needs proper gasketing, so that it is airtight. Air leaks will prevent or induce poor starting and erratic running.

(e) The float valve allows fuel to enter the float chamber—yet another orifice that can get blocked with dirt in the fuel, although many carburettors incorporate a small fuel filter (not shown) in the body to prevent this. Find out if your carburettor has one and clean it at the end of each season.

(f) The float moves up in the chamber as the fuel level rises and then it actuates the float valve to stabilize the fuel level. The float can be punctured by careless handling or it can stick on dirt, causing the carburettor and engine to flood. This is the reason for the carburettor drip tray, which prevents petrol and petrol vapour getting into the boat and causing an explosion.

(g) The float chamber tends to accumulate dirt at the bottom. Clean it out at lay-up time.

(h) Orifices in the carburettor casting must never be poked out with wire or other tools which will ruin them. Use a jet of air when cleaning.

(i) Suction, as the piston in a four-stroke engine travels down the cylinder and in a two-stroke travels up, needs to be good, so that it induces the maximum depression across the carburettor venturi. Badly worn and leaking pistons and rings, poor valve seatings, and broken two-stroke inlet valves (reed- or petal-type) in the crankcase will make starting difficult, if not impossible.

Safety with petrol

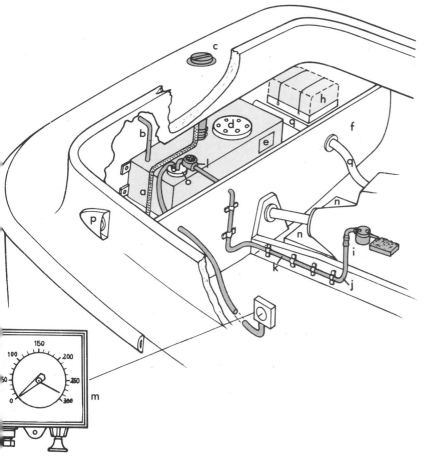

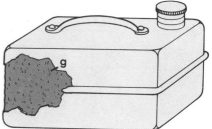

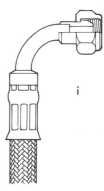

(a) All metal parts and the fuel filler should be bonded to the earth. The tank must be well secured.

(b) Vent pipe, with a minimum of 12 mm (1/2″) inner dimension, is positioned above the fuel-filler inlet level and covered with flame-arrester gauze. It must be clear of hatches and sources of heat.

(c) The fuel filler should be outside the coaming and marked with the word "petrol".

(d) Large cleaner plate for cleaning access, when Explosafe (see under g) is not used.

(e) Plate to show that the tank has been pressure-tested to a minimum of 0.25 kg per sq cm (3.5 lb per sq in).

(f) Fuel- and air-tight fire bulkhead to separate tank from engine space.

(g) "Explosafe" aluminium foil to fill both outboard and inboard tanks to prevent explosion.

(h) Loose tanks are never filled aboard, and when aboard they must be fully secured in a tray with straps across them.

(i) Use a solid swept bend in fuel lines. If you have a flexible metal hose, there is a danger that distortion may occur.

(j) Keep metal flexible hoses well clear of moving parts and free from chafe. Make sure that any bends have the correct radius—see the manufacturer's advice.

(k) Softened copper or stainless-steel fuel pipes, well clipped to minimize vibration and strain.

(l) Fuel shut-off valve. Electric solenoid type which is good for remote-control operation in case of fire.

(m) Fuel gauge calibrated by the tank manufacturer.

(n) Drip trays for the engine oil and carburettor. The latter tray should be protected with Explosafe or metal gauze.

(o) Outlet for fuel pipe and fuel-gauge pipe, well constructed.

(p) Full natural ventilation should be provided for the tank compartment.

(q) Water-cooled exhaust pipe passing through the tank space, well lagged.

Ignition

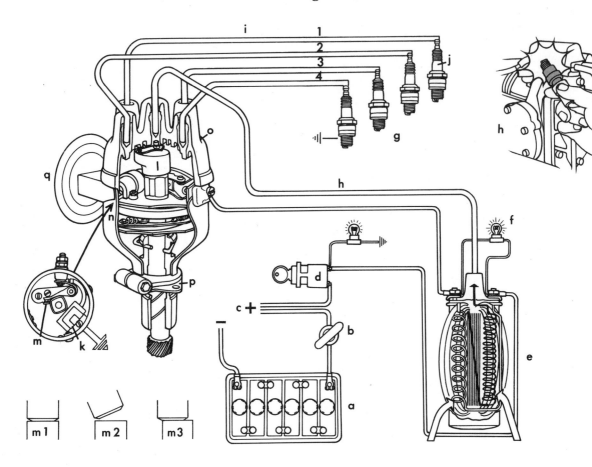

(a) Starter battery. This has to provide high amperage for a short time.

(b) Battery master switch. Use this as a safety precaution when the boat is left and when working on the engine.

(c) Fused control box.

(d) Ignition switch. Test this by connecting the side terminal on the switch to a tiny bulb and earthing the other lead from the bulb. The bulb should light when the key is turned on. In an emergency, the ignition can be shorted across the terminals to complete the circuit and start the engine. Do not oil, as the contacts can stick.

(e) The ignition coil, whose two circuits produce the spark at the plug.

(f) Light-bulb test for low-tension circuit in the coil.

1. Wire up a bulb which has the same voltage as that used in the system.

2. Remove plugs (so that the engine is turned over easily) and the distributor top.

3. Connect the bulb as shown to contacts on either side of the coil.

4. As the engine is turned over, the bulb lights when the contact points are closed, going out when they are open.

(g) The firing order is given in the engine manual. When removing high-tension leads from plugs, use masking tape to number them, if you are not sure where they go back.

(h) High-tension lead from coil and distributor. Test by removing the end from the centre of the distributor cap, holding it about 6–7 mm (1/4″) from the engine

block, and turning the engine. WARNING: High tension! Take care to hold the insulated part of the wire!

(i) High-tension plug leads (1, 2, 3 and 4). These age, harden and crack. The slightest crack will allow them to short to earth, giving misfiring or no firing at all in the engine, but a real fire or explosion if they ignite petrol fumes.

(j) Spark plug.

(k) Condenser. To test, undo the end of the condenser that is fastened to the distributor, leaving the wire to the points intact. Connect a test bulb between that end of the condenser and the earth. When power is on, the condenser is faulty if the lamp lights. Replace it.

(l) Rotor, which distributes high-tension current to each plug in the turn of the firing order. This can crack, make poor contact, or become pitted. Remove the rotor when you want to immobilize the engine to prevent theft.

m) Contact-points gap. The distance between the points is given in the manual. You measure the gap with a feeler gauge. To adjust, do the following:

Turn the battery off at the master switch, take off the distributor cap, turn the engine over until you see the cam opening the points to their maximum. Loosen the fixed point, insert the feeler gauge between it and the moving point, and when a sliding fit is achieved, re-lock the fixed point. Turn the engine over and check with the feeler gauge that the gap is correct. See that the alignment of the face of the points is correct.

m 1. Correct lateral alignment.
m 2. Lateral misalignment.
m 3. Misalignment of centres.
(n) Lower body. This contains the mechanism for automatic advance of timing—not the province of the amateur.
(o) Distributor cap. This needs keeping clean and regular inspection for hair-line cracks that allow the high-tension current to jump to earth. Keep the inside dry and look especially there for cracks (arcing can sometimes take place out of sight).
(p) Clamp ring. When this is undone, it allows the whole body of the distributor to rotate to alter the timing. Again, this is not the province of the amateur, especially as damage can be done to the engine if it is mis-timed. Without proper testing gear and tools, it is bad practice to tamper

with such things, especially on highly sophisticated modern engines.
(q) Vacuum diaphragm. This produces movement to automatically advance timing in the distributor, as the engine speeds up, or retard it as it slows down. The depression at the carburettor produces the atmospheric change which by means of a connecting tube is fed to the diaphragm. Simply see to it that the tube is intact, and not leaking.

Spark plugs

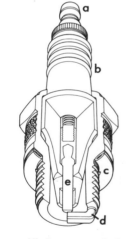

Electrode gaps

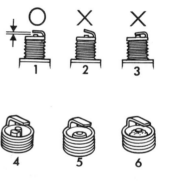

Each petrol engine uses a specific heat grade type of plug which will be given in the manual. Do not use any other type (although each plug manufacturer offers an equivalent from his own range).

Check that you have the proper connection between the terminal screw *(a)* and the high-tension lead.

The ceramic insulator *(b)* must not be cracked or damp. A cracked ceramic insulator is often the result of an ill-fitting plug spanner being used.

The gasket *(c)* provides a vital seal for the cylinder head and for the heat

path that transfers heat from the plug to the cylinder head. Do not over-tighten, as this will crush it needlessly. Use a torque wrench set to the manufacturer's recommendations.

To adjust the gap between the electrodes, you can bend the side electrode *(d)*. Never bend the central electrode *(e)*, as this will crack the ceramic insulator. If the edges of the tips of the electrodes are rounded (burnt off), replace the plug. Always carry a spare set, correctly gapped and ready for use.

1. Check that the gap is correct with the correct feeler gauge.

2. Gap too large. Adjust by bending the side electrode down.

3. Gap too small. Adjust by prising the side electrode up.

4. Central electrode torn. Replace the plug.

5. Central electrode excessively worn. Replace the plug.

6. Central electrode melted. Replace the plug.

PETROL-ENGINE FAULT FINDING

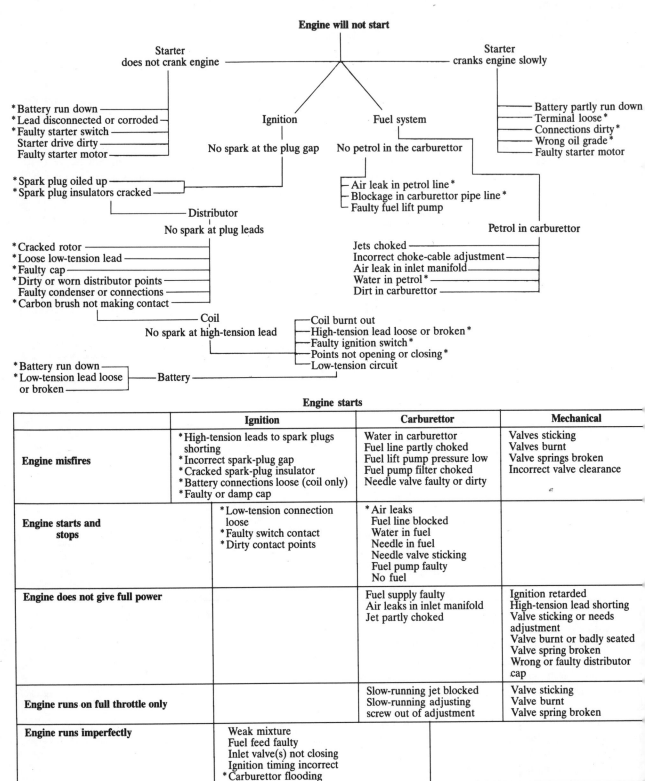

Engine will not start

Starter does not crank engine — Starter cranks engine slowly

*Battery run down
*Lead disconnected or corroded
*Faulty starter switch
Starter drive dirty
Faulty starter motor

Ignition — Fuel system

Battery partly run down
Terminal loose*
Connections dirty*
Wrong oil grade*
Faulty starter motor

No spark at the plug gap — No petrol in the carburettor

*Spark plug oiled up
*Spark plug insulators cracked

Air leak in petrol line*
Blockage in carburettor pipe line*
Faulty fuel lift pump

Distributor
No spark at plug leads

Petrol in carburettor

*Cracked rotor
*Loose low-tension lead
*Faulty cap
*Dirty or worn distributor points
Faulty condenser or connections
*Carbon brush not making contact

Jets choked
Incorrect choke-cable adjustment
Air leak in inlet manifold
Water in petrol*
Dirt in carburettor

Coil
No spark at high-tension lead

Coil burnt out
High-tension lead loose or broken*
Faulty ignition switch*
Points not opening or closing*
Low-tension circuit

*Battery run down
*Low-tension lead loose or broken — Battery

Engine starts

	Ignition	Carburettor	Mechanical
Engine misfires	*High-tension leads to spark plugs shorting *Incorrect spark-plug gap *Cracked spark-plug insulator *Battery connections loose (coil only) *Faulty or damp cap	Water in carburettor Fuel line partly choked Fuel lift pump pressure low Fuel pump filter choked Needle valve faulty or dirty	Valves sticking Valves burnt Valve springs broken Incorrect valve clearance
Engine starts and stops	*Low-tension connection loose *Faulty switch contact *Dirty contact points	*Air leaks Fuel line blocked Water in fuel Needle in fuel Needle valve sticking Fuel pump faulty No fuel	
Engine does not give full power		Fuel supply faulty Air leaks in inlet manifold Jet partly choked	Ignition retarded High-tension lead shorting Valve sticking or needs adjustment Valve burnt or badly seated Valve spring broken Wrong or faulty distributor cap
Engine runs on full throttle only		Slow-running jet blocked Slow-running adjusting screw out of adjustment	Valve sticking Valve burnt Valve spring broken
Engine runs imperfectly	Weak mixture Fuel feed faulty Inlet valve(s) not closing Ignition timing incorrect *Carburettor flooding		
Engine knocks			Timing too far advanced Excessive carbon deposit Loose bearing or pistons *Plug leads crossed

*Items you can check and remedy yourself.

COOLING SYSTEMS

Direct, or raw-water, cooling

This is the simplest water-cooling system, but it produces a less even temperature control and a higher rate of corrosion than does the indirect cooling system. However, provided that the engine manufacturer has put plenty of metal into the engine (which will result in a long working life) and provided that such an engine, if used in salt water, is flushed out with fresh water at lay-up time, this simple system is still excellent.

Parts of the direct-cooling system

a) Raw-water inlet valve.

b) Raw-water filter. Some manufacturers provide a separate unit, while others rely on a filter at the inlet valve.

c) Raw-water impeller-type pump.

d) Some engines may have a second circulation pump which is belt-driven. Drive belts break and wear, and so need seasonal attention, but the pump itself is a job for the professional.

e) Thermostat to control the cooling-water's temperature.

f) Distribution housing, to ensure that the exhaust manifold and exhaust pipe get cooling water, even when the thermostat closes due to the engine being cold.

g) Heat exchanger for oil cooling.

This is not found on all direct systems—see "Indirect Cooling" (next page). Cold water circulates over tubes containing hot engine oil, thus reducing the temperature of the oil. The same principle is used to cool warm air on some turbocharged engines and to cool oil in gearboxes. Tube stacks need to be kept clean, but a simple flush-through with fresh water at lay-up time is usually all that is needed.

(h) Exhaust water-injection bend. Some raw water is diverted to cool the exhaust gases as they emerge from the manifold. This also helps to silence the exhaust. The material in this bend is often subject to severe corrosion.

The thermostat

Found in both direct and indirect water-cooled engines and on some outboards, the thermostat controls the flow of water, so that the engine warms up quickly and maintains correct working temperature. Cooling water *(a)* flows from the engine past a bellows-type thermostat *(b)* which operates a valve *(c)* to regulate the flow of the water to the heat exchanger *(d)*.

Usually, thermostat failure results in the valve staying open, so that the engine does not warm up properly but runs cold. Replace the thermostat if this occurs. If overheating occurs, the reason might be a sluggish valve, due to debris in the cooling system. Flush the system out with fresh water.

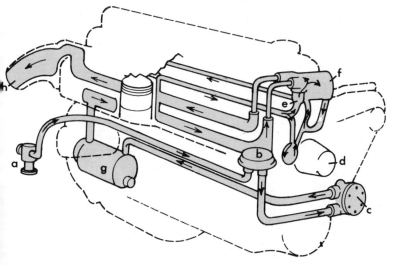

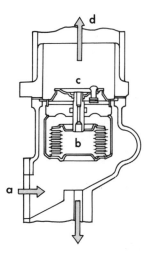

Indirect cooling

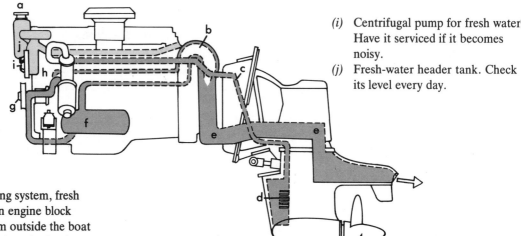

In the indirect-cooling system, fresh water cools the main engine block while raw water from outside the boat exchanges heat with it and other items (for instance the gearbox, oil coolers, and air coolers) through a heat exchanger before it finally cools the exhaust and is ejected overboard with it.

(a) The pressure cap on the header tank (filled with fresh water). Check that it is properly seated and that the spring inside is providing a proper seal. Failure leads to boiling and loss of coolant.

(b) Raw-water injection bend, where water mixes with exhaust gases. A corrosion point.

(c) Flexible water hose. This needs proper clipping to prevent leaks.

(d) Although an outdrive system is shown, the raw-water inlet could just as well be at a skin-fitting

inlet valve on a normal engine driving through a propeller shaft. This is where clean raw-water can be introduced at lay-up time to clean out the raw water.

(e) Exhaust bellows on the outdrive only. See the section on outdrives.

(f) Heat exchanger. Overheating may arise if the raw-water tube stack becomes clogged. Clean tubes with the recommended agent and rinse thoroughly in fresh water, or push in a thin rod in the opposite direction to the water flow.

(g) Raw-water impeller pump.

(h) Oil cooler (on some engines). Another type of heat exchanger. It needs the same care as (f) above.

(i) Centrifugal pump for fresh water. Have it serviced if it becomes noisy.

(j) Fresh-water header tank. Check its level every day.

NOT SHOWN, BUT IMPORTANT: Many small rubber hoses, held in place by stainless-steel hose-clips, join various parts of the fresh-water and raw-water systems. They harden with age, and then crack and leak. Replace them at the first signs of fatigue, before they let you down in some potentially dangerous situation. Check the clips regularly for tightness and see that they are at right angles to the axis of the pipeline.

Learn how to bleed air from the fresh-water side of the system—overheating is often caused when a system is not bled after refilling.

Heat exchanger in header tank

The drawing on the right shows how heat exchange takes place in the header tank.

(a) Header tank.
(b) Pressure/filler cap.
(c) Gasket.
(d) End cap.
(e) End-cap gasket.
(f) Rubber hoses.
(g) Stainless-steel hose clip.
(h) Engine-block gasket.
(i) Tube stack for raw-water flow.

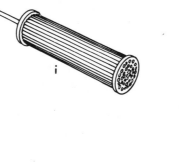

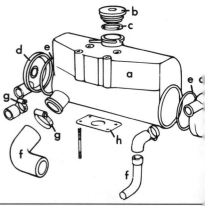

Impeller pump

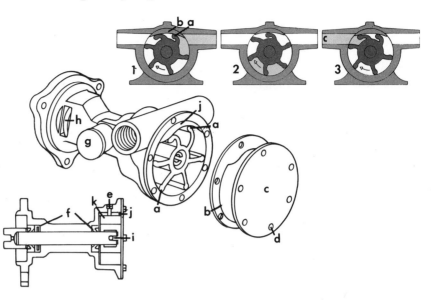

This type of pump circulates raw water in direct and indirect water-cooling systems. It is driven by a belt from the front engine pulley, or direct from the camshaft as shown here. Water is **(1)** sucked in by the blade *(a)* at the cam plate *(b)*, then **(2)** rotated and **(3)** pushed out the port *(c)*.

Parts of the impeller pump

a) Rubber impeller. Always remove this for the duration of the winter lay-up. Otherwise, the blades that are bent against the cam can become permanently distorted. Inspect blades for cracks at their base, and for friction wear (especially in muddy water) at their tip. If you suspect any damage, replace the impeller. Always carry spares. This is the item that goes first when you forget to turn on the raw-water cooling valve (due to the heat that will result from friction).

b) End gasket, usually made of paper. Replace at every rebuild and when you replace the impeller after the winter lay-up. Otherwise, you can make a temporary gasket of silicone rubber.

c) End plate. Inspect it for corrosion due to leakage.

d) End-plate screws. Check to see if vibration has loosened them.

(e) Cam-plate holding screw. Check for tightness; a loose cam can ruin the pump.

(f) Water seal. On shaft-driven pumps, water must not get past the water seals and into the engine. They are easily prised out for renewal.

(g) Greaser. Some pumps are fitted with a greaser to lubricate the shaft. Use it daily, if you have one.

(h) Water-slinger washer. Some pumps have this, to fling off any water that might get past the pump and the water seal. Keep the slot clean, so that water will not be trapped there.

(i) Impeller drive pin, in the centre of the impeller. Check that it is securely fixed and not worn. Some pumps have the impeller fitted on a splined shaft, which must be greased when the impeller is removed for the winter. Remove the grease when refitting, as it can damage the rubber in the impeller.

(j) Cam plate.

(k) Wear plate. Reverse this or replace it when the impeller has end play on its shaft.

Service the cooling-water filter regularly

a) Wing nuts provide quick access to allow you to clean the filter strainer. Ensure that they are tight.

b) Top plate. Keep its underside well greased for good bedding onto the gasket.

c) Gasket.

d) Filter-strainer basket for removing seaweed and small debris from incoming water. Clean it regularly.

e) Cooling-water inlet.

f) Filtered-water inlet.

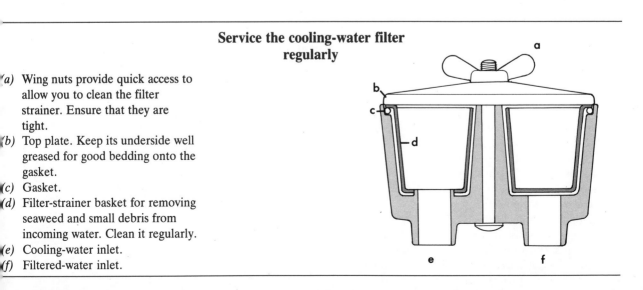

THE EXHAUST

Exhaust injection bend with engine on or below waterline

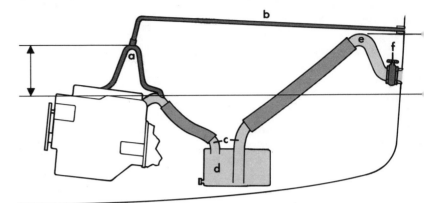

A water-lock system is shown here. Consult the engine manufacturer, as the design factors referred to are vital for safe operation. This system reduces noise from the exhaust. The rubber exhaust hose can be damaged by the heat if you forget to turn on the cooling-water seacock. Always use two stainless-steel hose clips on all jointed rubber sections.

(a) An inverted U-pipe leads to the exhaust. Its apex is a minimum of 25 cm (10″) above the waterline.
(b) A bleed pipe is connected to the apex of the U-pipe and has a constant fall of not less than 35.5 cm (14″) to the skin fitting.
(c) Exhaust pipe into and out of the water lock. The total volume of the shaded parts of the pipes must

be no more than the volume of the water lock.
(d) Water lock, which must be fitted with a drain plug at its base, so that it can be tapped at lay-up.
(e) Swan neck. Its height above the waterline must be sufficient to prevent waves getting back into the system and flooding first the

water lock and then the engine.
(f) Full-way valve at the skin fitting. This totally precludes the chance of waves getting into the system. It is a safety must on sailing boats, which have to heel in rough weather when the engine is not running. Never run the engine without opening the valve.

Exhaust system with engine above waterline

Corrosion is the big enemy of exhaust systems. The acids and gases active in the system work more corrosively when sea water washes over the the corroding surfaces.

A poorly designed exhaust system will allow too high a back pressure to be created, thus lowering the engine's efficiency. Vulnerable parts which you should keep an eye on are:

(a) The water-injection bend. Severe corrosion conditions arise where cooling water causes an impingement attack on the metal opposite the point of injection. Inspect the outside of the bend for fracture. Some castings are well designed and have annular injection into the gas stream. This cuts down the impingement attack.
(b) Support for the piping must be well placed, so that its weight is not taken solely on the engine manifold. If the exhaust pipe passes through bulkheads, it must

be protected from chafe and sealed in such a way that fire and fumes cannot pass into adjacent compartments.
(c) The best position for the silencer is at the engine manifold, but this is not possible on many designs. The alternative will be described below.
(d) The pipework in the exhaust system must have constant fall to the outlet, with no sags where water can collect.
(e) All too often, a full-way exhaust valve is not installed at delivery.

This is a must, as it prevents flooding from the skin fitting, should a leak develop. Even when the system is above the waterline, you should have a full-way exhaust valve or a hinged flap over the exhaust hole on the outside, because waves can cause water to slop up the pipe when they hit the transom. This has been known to cause sinking.

Positioning the silencer

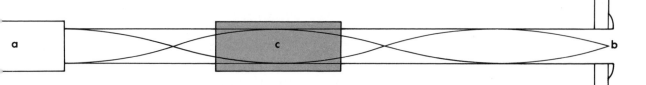

The silencer should be placed at an anti-node point of the exhaust sound. This is a point along the exhaust pipe where there is maximum change in the pressure wave between the manifold (a) and the outlet (b). One such point is at the manifold itself, but another can be found as follows:

. Measure the length of the exhaust pipe from manifold to outlet (say 4 metres).

2. Multiply this by 0.4 (4 × 0.4 = 1.6).

3. Measure the length of the silencer (say 0.8 m) and subtract half of it from the last figure (1.6 – 0.4 = 1.2).

4. This gives the distance from the manifold to the beginning of the silencer (c). In the present example, this will be 1.2 m, and as the silencer is 0.8 m long, the distance from the end of the silencer to the outlet fitting will thus be 2.0 m.

If it is not possible to place the exhaust at this point, due to the design of the boat, then the next best thing is to place the silencer at 4/5 the total of the system.

AIR CLEANER/FLAME TRAP

This has two important functions. The first is to clean the air as it enters the manifold on a diesel engine or the carburettor on a petrol engine. The second is to prevent a backfire setting fire to the boat or causing an explosion. Except when you are cleaning them, they must always be kept in place, to prevent accidents when you are tuning the engine. The two types of cleaner are illustrated.

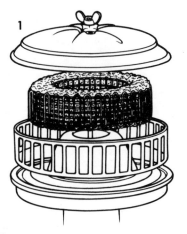

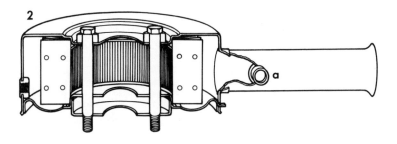

. The oil-wetted mesh type. To clean it, you must remove the mesh, wash it in paraffin or diesel fuel, drain it thoroughly, wet it with engine oil, drain again, and replace. This is done annually when winterizing.

2. The pleated-paper element type. This operates more quietly, trapping valve noise. You replace it with a new element. Under normal boating conditions, it should last three or four seasons before it needs replacing. Check it annually, as a clogged filter will reduce engine performance and cause high fuel consumption. A screw

or (as here) bolts in the top cover allow access to the element after unclipping the crankcase breather pipe (a).

When winterizing, seal the air cleaner with a plastic bag or cling film.

ENGINE VENTILATION

In many craft, especially sailing boats, the engine room is merely a crammed space just large enough to accommodate the engine and some ancillary equipment. Little or no proper ventilation is provided other than that which is ingested into the space by the engine itself from the accommodation spaces. Check your local legislation (e.g. U.S. Coast Guard Rules) to make sure that your boat meets the minimum requirements.

All yachts should have mechanical ventilation backed up by plenty of static ventilators that prevent the ingress of water, even in the worst conditions.

The effects of poor ventilation

1. The exhaust will be smoky and the engine will be unable to develop its full power.

2. The service life of the engine will be shortened if components are run at excessive temperatures.

3. Corrosion from condensation will be enhanced.

4. Elevated temperatures will shorten the life of the electrics, especially of the batteries.

5. Wooden parts of the boat will be subjected to moisture and eventually to rot.

6. Cabin linings, soft furnishings, and sails stored below will be subjected to mildew.

7. Crew inefficiency often results from the bad air down below—smells contribute to seasickness.

8. Flammable gases—butane, propane, petrol vapour—can gather and perhaps explode.

9. If gas heaters, cookers, etc are not properly serviced or ventilated, carbon-monoxide poisoning can kill the crew.

Ventilating water-cooled engines

Two things need to be considered, the combustion air and the cooling air.

1. Combustion air is the air that the engine consumes. For effective work, the engine requires a certain amount of combustion air. Multiplying the engine's brake horsepower (bhp) by 2.5 gives this amount in cubic feet per minute, and multiplying again by 0.0283 gives it in cubic metres per minute.

2. Cooling air is the air needed to maintain safe temperatures in the engine compartment. Its amount depends on the ambient temperature and climate. In a cold/temperate climate, the amount of cooling air in cubic feet per minute should be 5.5 times the bhp; in a warm/temperate or (sub-) tropical climate, the factor is 8.25 or 11 respectively. (Multiplying these by 0.0283 gives the amount in cubic metres per minute.)

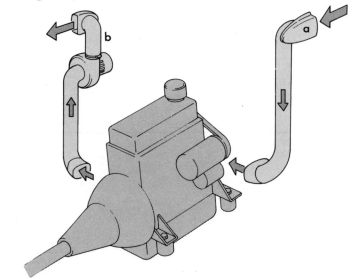

The total supply requirement (fan intake) for engine and engine compartment is the sum of 1 and 2 above. The exhaust requirement (fan extraction) is simply 2 above.
(*a*) Clamshell intake on cabin side.
(*b*) Exhaust fan and outlet.

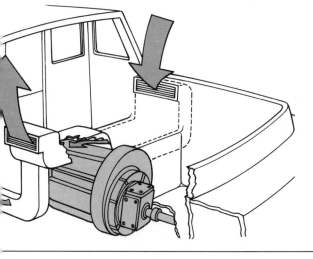

Air-cooled engines

These have to be installed with air supply and extraction according to the manufacturer's instructions to retain the validity of the warranty and to ensure a safe working life. Cleaning the ducting and fins in the cylinders is a must at the end of each season.

Battery ventilation

If there is a powerful battery, or more than one ordinary battery, then fan-assisted ventilation is vital. A spark-proof fan placed outside the battery compartment should blow air via a duct into the bottom of the battery compartment, and at least two vents should be installed at the top of the compartment to allow air and hydrogen to escape.

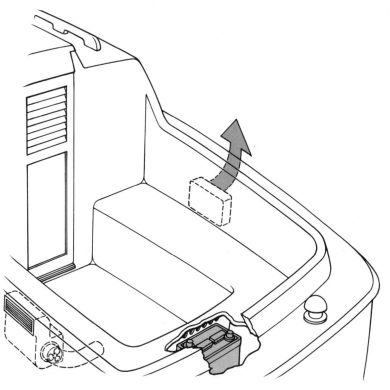

Battery compartments

A charging battery gives off hydrogen, which will explode if exposed to a flame or a spark. Natural ventilation by means of vents placed above the batteries is acceptable for small battery compartments, as hydrogen is lighter than air and will rise. Larger battery installations should have a centrifugal gas-extraction fan mounted outside the compartment, with switch controls also outside the compartment. The capacity of the fan is determined by an equation: $Q = 0.25 \times N \times I$ where Q is the air supply in cubic feet per minute, N is the number of cells in the battery, and I is the maximum charging current in amps.

Flammable gases

Petroleum vapour, butane, and propane are heavier than air, so the extraction point must be low down in the bilges. The fan can be of the centrifugal type, but with a sealed motor and impeller that would not spark should it come loose. The fan must discharge the extracted gas into the open air, away from possible ignition sources, such as cabin-heater flues.

Lubrication

A coarse filter (a) in the sump prevents large pieces of debris being drawn into the oil, or gear, pump (b), which generates pressure in the oil to feed it through the oil filter (c) which removes metal debris, varnishes, water, and acids from the oil before it is transported to the engine (d). The dip stick (e) determines safe oil levels in the engine, gear box, and outdrive legs.

Oil filters are of two types: (f) a renewable filter element which you put in a plastic bag for clean disposal, and (g) a canister that is twisted off to renew. A new canister is easier to fit if you smear some grease on the rubber gasket (h).

Oil filters are renewed as per the manufacturer's recommendations or at the end of each season. NEVER leave dirty oil in an engine during the winter.

The filter relief valve (i) allows lubrication to continue if, for reasons of neglect or failure, the filter becomes clogged. This prevents ruining the engine from lack of lubrication.

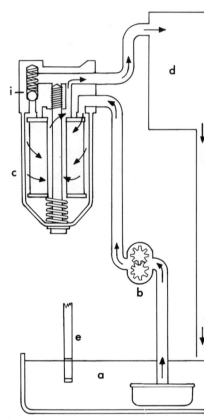

Lubrication hints

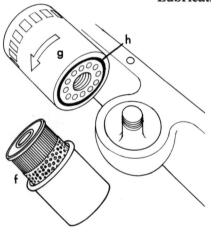

Never overfill with oil! Check daily—or whenever you start the engine, if not daily—that the oil is just up to the maximum marked line on the dipstick. An occasional check is not enough—an oil leak is no respecter of occasional checks!

When uncertain of how clean an engine's lubrication system is, use a proprietary flushing oil to clean it out. Follow the manufacturer's instructions exactly, as this is not a powerful lubricant. Flushing oil is not recommended for diesels.

ROCKER ADJUSTMENT

On four-stroke engines (both diesel and petrol), the valves which let air (on a diesel) or a fuel/air mixture (on a petrol engine) into the cylinder, and the valves which let the exhaust gases out, are operated by rockers driven by a camshaft or a pushrod. On some engines, these are self-adjusting, but the majority need occasional adjustment to check that the gap between them and the head of the valve stem is maintained to the manufacturer's specification.

Adjust the rockers only when the engine has been run up to working temperature. Any rocker must be fully off the cam or pushrod before you adjust it, so that it will be fully rocking. The following is a useful tip when you want to establish the order in which the rockers should be adjusted.

If you have a four-cylinder in-line engine with two valves per cylinder and the no. 1 cylinder is farthest from the gear box, then remember the number 9 in order to know which valve is fully rocking and therefore ready for adjustment.

With no. 1 valve fully depressed, you will find no. 8 valve rocking and ready for adjustment (1 + 8 = 9).

With no. 2 valve fully depressed, you will find no. 7 valve rocking and ready for adjustment (2 + 7 = 9), and so on.

Likewise, if you have a six-cylinder in-line engine with two valves per cylinder, the magic figure is 6 × 2 + 1 = 13. When valve no. 1 is fully depressed, adjust valve no. 12 (12 + 1 = 13), and so on.

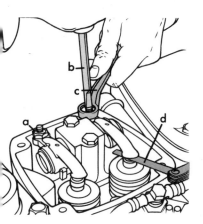

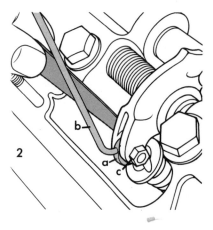

1. The thread-and-nut type of rocker *(a)* is adjusted with a screwdriver *(b)*, a ring spanner *(c)*, and a feeler gauge *(d)*.

2. The cam type of rocker *(a)* is adjusted by a lever *(b)* inserted into the cam. The nut *(c)* is tightened when the clearance is correct.

The clearance is an important part of the "tune" of an engine and should be adjusted as frequently as specified in the manual.

Other points to remember

Check the gasket on the cover of the rocker box. This is often made of cork, which compresses and hardens with age. Oil then leaks out onto the engine. Replace in good time, and seal the new one with gasket-jointing compound.

Remove the cover when laying-up the engine for the winter, and give the rockers and tappets a good dousing of clean, fresh oil to preserve them over the winter. Pouring oil through the normal filler hole in the box does not always do this.

ELECTRIC STARTERS

Both petrol and diesel inboard engines and many large outboards rely solely on electric starting. This means that, from the safety point of view, the proper care and servicing of the system, from battery to final gear starter wheel, is imperative. Starter failure in an emergency situation can be fatal.

Remember to make sure that all the controls are properly set BEFORE you use the starter.

Care of electric starters

The solenoid switches the light current from the starter button into high-amperage current to power the starter. Cleaning the cable contacts, tightening the terminals, and protection with petroleum jelly at the battery end make sure that the full electric power flows.

The heavy-duty cables to the starter must be of adequate cross-section to pass the current. See to it that they are not chafed and never run them through the bilges.

When the starter button is first pressed, the starter pinion slides forward to engage slowly with the gear ring of the flywheel. Any problems with engagement should be referred to the service agent as this is where damage usually occurs.

With age, both pinion and starter ring become rounded. This causes increasing backlash in the gears. The parts must be replaced, which is a job for the service centre.

An over-anxious finger on the starter button really damages the starter motor. If a start fails, always wait until the motor has come to a complete rest. Trying to engage the starter pinion before this happens will cause milling on the gear teeth. This results in a situation where the starter will not engage at all or will fail to disengage. Fortunately, most starter motors are protected against the latter by an overspeed cut-out, but be warned and be patient—or you will have a ruined starter. The golden rule is: If the engine fails to start, do not go on pressing the starter button, but ascertain the cause.

POWER TRANSMISSION

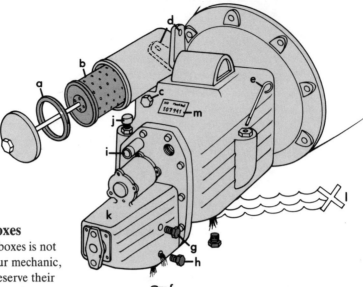

Marine gearboxes

The inside of marine gearboxes is not the province of the amateur mechanic, but you can do a lot to preserve their working life. One basic type, the mechanical gearbox, is simpler and less bulky than the other type which is shown here. This is the oil-operated gearbox, often called a hydraulic box. Oil in the box lubricates the gears, and shifts the clutch to provide forward and reverse gears. Points to consider for an oil-operated box:

(a) The filter's oil-sealing ring, usually square in section, must be replaced after renewing a filter, to avoid oil leaks.

(b) The filter element, if fitted, needs replacing as the manufacturer recommends. But replacement every couple of years at lay-up time is usually adequate, since engine hours are generally few.

(c) The oil-pressure relief valve, under the cover nut, may need adjustment when the gearbox is wearing, to maintain the recommended oil pressure. Otherwise, adjustment is best left to a mechanic with calibrated pressure-testing equipment.

(d) The gear-shift lever's travel movement must be as stated by the manufacturer to achieve full engagement of gears. When the gears do not engage properly, check the cable and mechanical linkages for backlash, before suspecting the gearbox.

(e) The main gearbox filler/dipstick needs checking only weekly. But look daily under the gearbox for oil leaks—sump plugs have been known to fall out!

At lay-up time, fill only to the lower mark; top up when launching the boat.

(f) Sump plugs are on the main gearbox and, in this drawing, on the reduction-gear box. Do not strip the threads by overtightening in fear of oil loss! Some main boxes have a lift pump for easier emptying, but the dirtiest oil on the bottom must come out at the sump plug.

(g) Among other plugs on the box may be one for draining the cooling water from the reduction housing. This is important to prevent frost from cracking the casing.

(h) The oil-level plug exists on some reduction boxes instead of a dipstick. It weeps oil when the level is correct. If you have poured in too much oil at (j), let it run out until the level is right.

(i) The cathodic protection/cooling-water hose connection exists on some boxes which handle high power and often need water-cooling or a heat-exchange type of oil cooler to control working temperatures.

Cathodic protection prevents electrolytic corrosion by the raw cooling water and mixed metals in the system of light-alloy gearbox and copper cooling pipes. In the example shown, the alloy stub connection into the gearbox, intended for a rubber hose connection, also acts as an anode. It is designed to wear away to a set limit, and then needs replacing. You should know these points on your engine and gearbox, and replace as necessary.

(j) The oil breather/reduction-box filler must be kept free of dirt, to equalize the air pressure inside and outside the box.

(k) The gearbox's reduction section, if fitted, is lubricated as outlined above. The seal at the output flange must not become gritty or be painted; just keep it wiped clean and look for oil leaks, which indicate the need to replace it.

(l) The gearbox underside will corrode seriously if it is immersed in salty bilge water. Otherwise, the casting is usually made of light alloy and will not corrode if kept clean and painted.

(m) The manufacturer's identification and number plate should be noted so that you can order spares easily.

Engine controls

Many boats use cable controls for the engine throttle and gear shift, and as a stop control on diesel engines. These should be maintained well to ensure safety. Inspect all terminals at both ends for wear or signs of fatigue. Points to check:

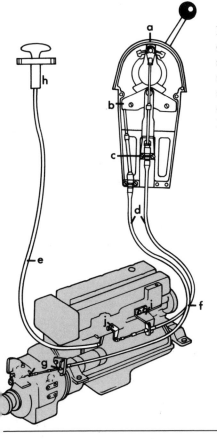

(a) Throttle terminal.

(b) Clutch terminal. Check that the fitting-plates are not getting too much backlash through wear.

(c) Cable clamps should be tight. Thread sealant will counteract vibration.

(d) Cables are lubricated for life, but corrode if water enters them. Check rubber seals on their ends, and spray metal parts with aerosol preservative—especially in exposed positions.

(e) Bends should have the minimum safe radius recommended by the cable maker, typically 200 mm (8″). A larger radius favours easy action and long life.

(f) Keep cables well clear of revolving machinery, and of hot exhaust pipes.

(g) The total movement of the gear-shift terminal must be matched to the gearbox-maker's specification, to produce full engagement ahead and astern.

(h) The diesel-engine stop control. Check that, when it is at rest, the stop arm on the injection pump is fully open.

(i) Cable clamps and support brackets. Check the screws on engine block and gearbox for tightness.

(j) The throttle cable must give total open-and-close movement to the throttle lever. Lubricate the pivot point at its terminal end.

The propeller shaft: solid gland to solid mounted engine

(a) Half-coupling key. Keep greased for future disassembly.

(b) Lock pin. A bad fit may allow this to be flung out. Secure it with liquid bush-retainer (from an automotive supplier).

(c) Half-coupling (other half is on the engine). Precise alignment of shafting and engine is necessary.

(d) Gland nuts and studs. Tightening these compresses the gland packing to keep water from entering the boat down the distance tube. Overtightening causes excess wear on the shaft and makes the bearing run hot.

(e) Gland and bearing. Bad engine alignment will cause excess wear on this and the shaft.

(f) Gland packing, which is compressed to provide the seal. Compress it only enough to exclude water.

(g) Lubricator tapping. Connect to a remote greaser, which can be

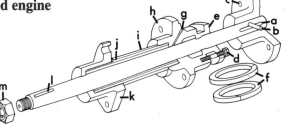

given a turn every day to grease the bearing. Water is sometimes bled from the engine for lubrication.

(h) Forward housing, fixed to boat hull. Check that fasteners are sound, especially if wooden reinforcing plates have been used.

(i) Distance tube.

(j) Aft bush. This keeps the shaft running sweetly in the distance tube and aft housing.

(k) Aft housing, fastened to the dead wood. Fasteners are subject to corrosion and should be checked along with *(h)*. Sometimes the housing with the bush is specially

water-lubricated by outrigger scoops. See that these are kept free of fouling, and clean out at the end of each season.

(l) Propeller key. Special underwater greases should be used on the key and tapered shaft where the propeller fits, so that the propeller is easy to remove.

(m) Castle nut, used to secure propeller. This must be secured with either Monel wire or a split pin (bronze for bronze shaft and fittings, stainless steel for stainless-steel shafts and fittings).

Shaft brakes for sailing boats

Engine gearbox makers state whether their gearboxes can "freewheel" during sailing when the engine is not driving them. The slipstream over the propeller causes this rotation. It does not harm some boxes, but others receive no lubrication and are seriously damaged by being trailed. Check your gearbox handbook!

To prevent rotation, a shaft brake is installed. Shown here is a hand-operated model. Remote electrical and hydraulic models also exist for easy operation from the cockpit. Maintenance is minimal, but necessary to avoid seizure and excessive wear on the shafting. Do not try to start the engine with the shaft brake on!

(*a*) Propeller shaft.
(*b*) Shaft-brake mounting.
(*c*) Brake-tightening screw.

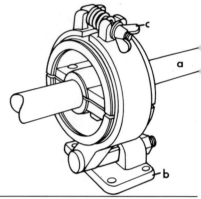

Flexible couplings

A single flexible coupling will isolate engine vibration and noise. It is not designed to accommodate misalignment, but will tolerate a very small amount. Flexible couplings isolate extremely well; they can be used on a flexibly mounted engine with solid inboard gland, if proper shaft alignment is made. Marine flexible couplings are designed to take both forward and reverse thrust.

(*a*) Propeller shaft.
(*b*) Half-coupling to engine.

Marine constant-velocity joint

The Svenska Aquadrive CVA drive can be installed to run at a down angle of 16 degrees. The engine can then be installed parallel to the waterline, saving height and allowing a lower wheelhouse or cockpit floor. It also takes the thrust from the propeller in the thrust bearing and relieves the gearbox.

(*a*) The thrust bearing, rubber-mounted, isolates inboard gland and shaft noise. Its support must be solidly built into the boat to take this strain.

(*b*) The shaft coupling clamps onto the propeller shaft, but can be supplied with flange coupling.

(*c*) The constant-velocity shaft is maintenance-free. Its two CV joints will each run through 8 degrees angle.

(*d*) Gearbox flange, to suit the engine.

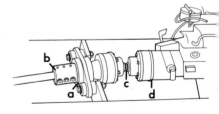

SAILDRIVE SERVICING

For servicing and winterization of the saildrive, follow the owner's manual as well as the preceding sections.

(*a*) The power head will be either petrol or diesel four-stroke, although British Seagull did make some small two-stroke units some years ago.

(*b*) Dipstick for drive leg. The leg has oil levels which should be maintained; for the correct filler hole and method of filling, see the engine manual. The oil should be drained out, through a plug on the bottom of the leg, after 100 hours of running and at the end of each season.

(*c*) The reduction gear and clutch, in the top of the leg, need no attention from the amateur except as noted above.

(*d*) Flexible mountings should be kept free of oil and fuel, which soften them if left for long. Many small units have three-point mounting as shown here.

(e) The rubber diaphragm is the vital part of a saildrive, being a thin layer between you and the water. See that all fouling is gently removed at the end of each season, and do not anti-foul! There are usually two separate cord plies for extra safety; one manufacturer has a facility for inserting a warning device if one ply is punctured. Renewal must be done as recommended by the maker, every 5 to 7 years. You should consider in advance how easily the drive can be lifted out for this job; some yachts have engines built in with no thought of later maintenance.

(f) The drive leg, on most units, is made of light alloy (aluminium). Never use a copper anti-fouling on the leg or boat! This would set up electrolytic corrosion that eats away the drive leg. Legs are well-painted when produced, but you must keep small scratches overpainted to prevent pitting corrosion, and use a recommended type of anti-fouling.

(g) The engine base is glassed onto the hull. Check that the joint is well done by the builder, with no fatigue cracks.

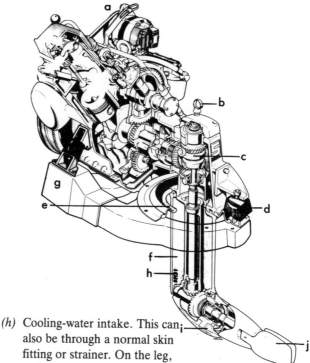

(h) Cooling-water intake. This can also be through a normal skin fitting or strainer. On the leg, make sure any fouling is gently cleaned out.

(i) Cathodic protection. Zinc anodes must be replaced when 50% is eaten away, and they must never be overpainted or anti-fouled, which would prevent them from working.

(j) The folding propeller needs service at the end of each season. Saildrives are also supplied with conventional propellers.

Servicing the saildrive propeller

Proceed in the following order:
(a) Undo and remove the locking screws.
(b) Gently knock out the pivot dowels so that the blades can be removed.
(c) Remove the split pin and *(d)* nut from the propeller shaft.

(e) Slide the spacer sleeve off the shaft.
(f) Remove the zinc anode only if renewal is needed: undo screw *(g)*.
(h) When replacing the anode, clean the surfaces so that good contact is made.

(i) Grease the splined propeller shaft for the winter, and cover with a plastic bag. Take the propeller home for winter. Reassemble in the reverse order, using underwater grease for dowels, spline, and propeller-blade bearing.

PROPELLERS

Propellers usually have important data—diametre and pitch—stamped on or near the hub. Note these dimensions in your boat's log, for easy reference when you need to buy a replacement. No matter what design it has, a propeller must be completely cleaned and serviced at the end of each season.

A propeller that is in reasonable condition will sound like a bell when each blade is struck. A dull sound usually indicates severe trouble—either cracks or corrosion.

Slight surface imperfections cause a loss of efficiency. Small surface repairs can be carried out on bronze propellers using special bronze epoxy putty.

Removing a propeller

A propeller on a splined shaft should slide off fairly easily, if an underwater grease was used when it was put on. If this is difficult, use a puller which you borrow from a tool-hire company or a garage. This is a specialized, expensive tool. A two-armed model is used for a two-bladed propeller, while a three-armed one is needed for a three-bladed propeller.

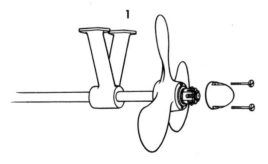

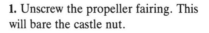

1. Unscrew the propeller fairing. This will bare the castle nut.

2. Remove the split pin on the castle nut on the propeller shaft.

3. Undo the castle nut three or four turns, but leave it in place to protect the starter thread on the shaft.

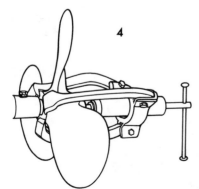

4. Slack off the puller arms and place the ends behind the propeller boss.

Slowly tighten the centre of the puller to take up the slack.

Put full pressure on the outside end of the shaft at the castle nut with the sliding "T" bar.

Propeller care

Opinions differ as to the use of antifouling systems on propellers. My advice is not to use antifouling. Changing the relative areas of different metals underwater—stainless-steel shafts, bronze stern gear, and maybe aluminium bronzes and unknown stainless steels used for fastenings on rudders—can cause an unholy mix. If the metals on these underwater units have been stable when exposed, then let them alone.

Remove the propeller when you lay up the boat for the winter; otherwise thieves will do it for you. If you want to run the engine ashore, whether it be inboard, outboard, or saildrive, it is always best to remove the propeller, to avoid accidents. In many countries, it is unlawful to have a propeller exposed while the boat is being transported on a road trailer. Padded covering is required.

Bronze propellers should be cleaned off immediately a boat is taken from the water. Scotch-brite pads are ideal cleaners. When the propeller is dry, grease it to protect it from corrosion during the lay-up. Shafting should always be greased and protected when it is exposed.

On boats where "A" or "P" brackets are used on the outboard end of the propeller shaft, a visual check should be kept on the brackets and on the hull to see that no fatigue cracking is developing, especially if the boat has been run hard aground or has hit an obstruction at speed.

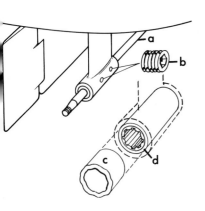

1. Any movement of the propeller shaft (*a*) when moved from side to side could indicate that the rubber or polyurethane water-lubricated bearing is worn and needs replacing.

2. Clean off the anti-fouling to locate any grub screws (*b*) that hold the bearing in place.

3. Find a short length of steel tube (*c*) the same diametre or fractionally less than the diametre of the bearing. When the propeller and shaft have been removed, use the tube with a puller to push out the bearing (*d*).

4. A silicone grease which does not affect the rubber or plastic in the bearing can be used to help ease the new bearing back into the bracket where it is re-secured with the grub screws.

Propeller-corrosion repairs

It is often possible to have corrosion damage professionally repaired, if the metal is not too far gone. Additional metal is then welded onto the surface and then ground down to conform to the original contours.

Corrosion comes mainly from two sources, electrolytic corrosion and cavitation. Boats are usually provided with cathodic protection against electrolytic corrosion, that is, they are provided with protective anodes that will wear away before the part they are protecting will be attacked by the corrosion. The anodes are made of zinc for use in salt water, and of magnesium alloy for use in fresh water.

You can also find zinc anodes in some engine-cooling systems, protecting the mixture of metals found there, and even on outdrive legs. If your boat is not equipped with cathodic protection and you notice that this kind of problem is starting, check that you have not got an electrical short that is causing the propeller to earth. See pages 181–182.

Cavitation is a complex phenomenon that causes local high shock on areas of the blade, resulting in pitting and erosion.

The basis of good engine beds

(a) In modern glassfibre construction, large free panel areas act as sounding boards. Reducing their area, by reinforcing top-hat sections and intercostal beams, will reduce noise and spread the engine load.

(b) Top-hat section near the waterline, a safety feature, also reduces panel areas.

(c) Stress load at the end of intercostals is spread by a large area of glass-reinforcing mat.

(d) Intercostals should be provided under the engine across keel spaces.

(e) Limber holes should be sealed against water ingress, so that all parts drain.

(f) Engine beds should not terminate sharply but spread their load well aft and forward of the main engine load. Some sailing yachts have beds of very inadequate length.

(g) Engine drip tray rests in the keel intercostals.

(h) Glassfibre lamination must always be held in compression. The main reinforcement is hardwood, shown here with a steel strip—preferably stainless—running along its top. This is tapped to take bolts to hold flexible engine mountings.

(i) Solid hardwood bearers need a plate, strip, or angle for reinforcement on top, to take engine mounts. A gallery cut in the engine bed takes a nut for the securing bolt above.

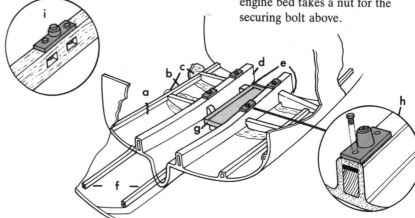

Improving engine access

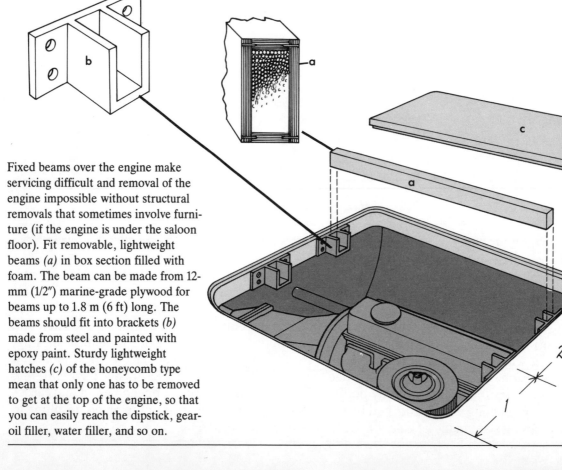

Fixed beams over the engine make servicing difficult and removal of the engine impossible without structural removals that sometimes involve furniture (if the engine is under the saloon floor). Fit removable, lightweight beams (a) in box section filled with foam. The beam can be made from 12-mm (1/2″) marine-grade plywood for beams up to 1.8 m (6 ft) long. The beams should fit into brackets (b) made from steel and painted with epoxy paint. Sturdy lightweight hatches (c) of the honeycomb type mean that only one has to be removed to get at the top of the engine, so that you can easily reach the dipstick, gear-oil filler, water filler, and so on.

Reducing noise from the engine

When engine spaces are enclosed to reduce the emission of noise, full compensation must be made to provide forced air ventilation. Each of the steps below will contribute to noise abatement, but it is the sum of all the steps that will really reduce airborne noise from your engine. Remember to use only fire-retarding foam products for insulation.

1. The engine area should, as far as possible, be encased by bulkheads that are free from bolted-on equipment, which would mean that the areas underneath have had to be left without sound insulation. Insulation material should be fitted over the total surface of the engine-room bulkheads, not merely in conveniently clear areas.

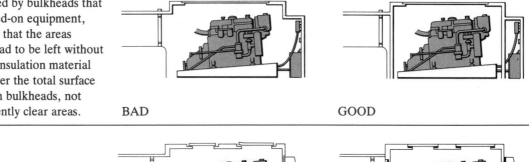

BAD   GOOD

2. Hatches and companionways must fit neatly, with noise-tight cushioning (marked in heavy black) on the lands.

BAD   GOOD

3. If you have an engine box, remember that the noise will flow under the general deck area. Bulkheads should continue right down to the hull, and, if necessary, there should be limber holes at the bottom of the bulkheads for bilge water. Insulate down to, but not into, the bilge water.

BAD   GOOD

4. Fuel and water tanks collect and amplify noise, so insulate between them and the engine. Also, avoid "caverns" on either side of the engine. Drop a removable, insulated bulkhead beside the engine.

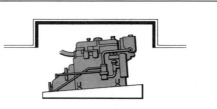
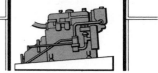
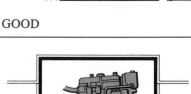

BAD   GOOD

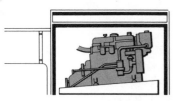
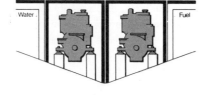
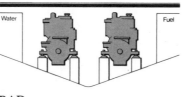
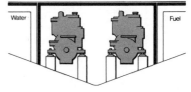
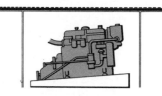

5. Power craft, especially with twin engines, will benefit enormously from a double layer of insulation, the upper layer being attached to a false deck or hatch, with a good 150 mm (6″) in between the layers.

6. If you have twin engines, try to keep them in separate, insulated compartments, with removable bulkheads in between.

7. Having insulated the engine room in as many of the above ways as possible on board your boat, further sound insulation can be achieved by fitting special insulation matting between cabin carpeting and the actual deck.

Engines

THE OUTBOARD ENGINE

Choose an outboard with a drive leg long enough to suit your boat. When the boat is travelling at speed, the anti-cavitation plate should be about 50–75 mm (2–3″) below the surface. If it is too deep, the propeller will find it heavy going and will not reach the right speed. If too shallow, the engine will start to vibrate and race, thus leading to over-heating, and the propeller will easily begin to cavitate.

Trimming

The angle at which the propeller works in relation to the waterline may have to be adjusted to produce the best results. Change this angle by swinging the drive leg towards or away from the transom. Larger engines have hydraulic-powered trimming such as Powertrim, but smaller engines must be trimmed manually, by moving a cross-bolt.

The propeller produces a sideways as well as a forward thrust, making the boat turn slowly in the direction of the thrust. You may counteract this by placing the outboard a little off-centre, to the side in which the boat is turning.

Basic jobs for any type of outboard

Always read the owner's manual. If anything goes wrong, consult it as a first resort, not as a last.

If the engine is not running well or does not start at all, you have problems either with spark plugs, fuel supply, or cooling-water supply.

1. Remember that the tank's air-inlet screw must be open when the engine is running.

2. Condensation forms easily, and water and sediment gather at the bottom, under the fuel, and can be sucked up with the fuel. On a two-stroke, oil mixed with the petrol provides the lubrication. If the fuel is allowed to stand for too long, the oil will form a gummy deposit. So keep the tank clean, emptying it regularly, and rinsing with petrol.

3. Check that the fuel line is not clogged. If it is, take off the pipe and blow through. Open and clean the fuel filter. Can fuel flow freely to the fuel pump?

4. Engines with the fuel tank on top do not have fuel pumps, otherwise the pump and filter are often part of the same unit. Dismantle it and check that the pump is not clogged and that the membrane is unbroken.

5. Disconnect the fuel pipe from the carburettor. Press the starter switch or pull the starter rope a few times and see if fuel is reaching the carburettor.

6. Inspect the spark plugs. If they are wet with fuel, the carburettor is flooded. Turn off the fuel tap, screw in the slow-running jet needle (read about this in the manual *before* you do anything!), and turn the engine over with the starter switch or the rope, to dry the spark plugs. Open the slow-running jet 1½ turns, open the fuel tap, and start the engine.

7. If the air-fuel mixture is wrong, the engine will be hard to start. Dismantle the carburettor and blow through all holes, preferably with compressed air. If necessary, clean the jets with a suitable solvent. Replace and check that the needles are properly seated. Check also that the float can rise and fall freely in the chamber and that the needle actually closes when the float rises.

When you have reassembled the carburettor, tighten the slow-running jet gently, then open it 1½ turns.

8. Test spark plug(s). First remove a plug, replace the rubber cap containing the high-tension lead, and hold the plug against bare metal on the engine case while you turn the engine over with the starter switch or the rope starter. *Hold the plug by the rubber, otherwise you'll get a shock.* A sharp, blue spark should come from the plug. If no spark is generated, check the points.

Clean the points with a fine file or abrasive paper. Change them, if necessary. Consult your manual for the correct gap and, using a feeler gauge, set the points to this gap (usually about 0.40 mm or 0.015″).

Inspect the spark plugs (see page 127). If necessary, adjust the electrode gap, using a feeler gauge. Consult the manual for the correct gap (usually around 0.6 mm/0.022″).

1. Gear-shift lever. Needs lubrication. Check that the linkages are intact and have minimum of backlash.
2. Cooling-water inlet. Keep clean.
3. Bevel-gear and clutchhouse lubrication oil plug.
4. Lubrication-oil level plug.
5. Cooling-water pump. Check the impeller blades at the end of each season.
6. Mounting brackets. Check for cracks and lubricate the screws. Consult the manual to see if the propeller has the correct immersion.
7. Choke control.
8. Low speed adjustment control.
9. Recoil start. (Many engines, especially the larger ones, now have electric starters).

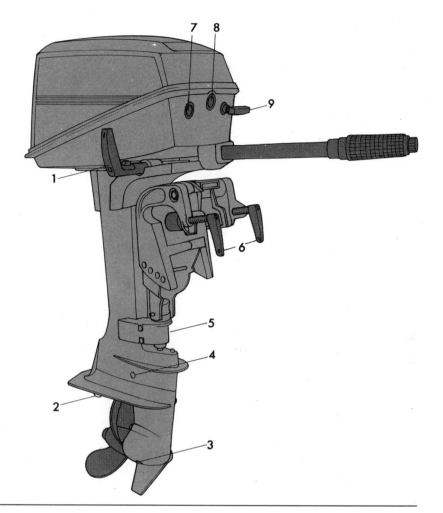

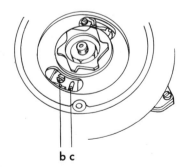

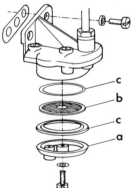

Servicing the ignition

Inspect the points. On small outboards, they are usually under the flywheel, which has an inspection hole through which you can examine them. Bigger multi-cylinder engines have distributors, just like a car engine.

Clean them, or replace them, if necessary. Check the gap (*a*), and adjust it by opening the locking screw (*b*) and adjusting the eccentric positioning screw (*c*).

Fuel pump with filter

Small engines operate on gravity feed, larger usually use a diaphragm pump.
(*a*) Cover.
(*b*) Filter.
(*c*) Gasket.

The basic instruments shown here are those we consider essential for the safety of your engine and for your own peace of mind. Some manufacturers give you less—you can always add what you need. Some give you a lot more—take notice of them all.

1. Engine oil-pressure gauge and gear-box oil-pressure gauge. As you start the engine, the needle should quickly climb to the engine's normal reading. Similarly, an oil-operated gear box with a meter should show a reading as its pump idles with the engine. If there is no reading, stop the engine immediately. The reason may be simple, such as a lead dropping off the sender on the engine or the instrument head. On the other hand, you might have lost all the oil from the engine or forgotten to fill it up after the winter lay-up.

2. Temperature gauge. This indicates what is happening to the coolants and is sometimes used for oil-temperature readings. From start-up, it should climb steadily to normal working temperature, at which stage you will be ready to move off your mooring or dock. In an indirectly cooled engine, the gauge will be on the freshwater side and tell you if the thermostat is behaving. Persistent low readings can indicate that the thermostat has failed in the open position. A climbing reading that is becoming dangerously high tells you to stop as soon as you can in a safe place for investigation. The following possibilities then arise:

(a) A rubber hose has perished and the coolant has been lost. Always carry spares! Replace.

(b) The pressure cap has not been fully secured on the header tank. Secure it properly.

(c) The water-inlet valve or inlet on the outdrive leg is blocked with a plastic bag or similar debris. This is when it is handy to have a scuba-diving crew member.

(d) The engine's centrifugal pump is not circulating water on the in-direct cooling systems or the impeller pump has packed up on a raw-watercooled system. You have either a broken drive or a broken impeller. Again, you should have spares on board. Replace.

(e) The thermostat has failed to open fully. There is probably corrosion on the stem. Replace the thermostat.

(f) You have not bled all the air from the indirect system when you refilled it.

(g) The oil level is too low.

(h) Blocked or partially blocked heat exchanger/oil cooler. Clean.

(i) If it is a petrol engine, it could be seriously out of tune. The valve/ ignition timing is wrong. You may be using the wrong grade of fuel for ignition setting. If you have a diesel engine, the injection timing might be wrong.

(j) You may have a carelessly secured clip on the water hose, which allows air to be drawn into the cooling system.

3. Tachometer. This is much more than just a rev counter. Properly calibrated, it can give useful information about speed over water and the best rpm for economic operation. If it fails, check the sender and the wiring.

4. Engine-hours meter. This gives you some indication of the wear that has taken place on a well-used engine so that service periods can be noted. With so few hours run by most boating people, major services are more likely to take place when corrosion is being attended to rather than because the engine has been run for a certain number of hours. However, it is interesting for an owner to know how many hours his engine runs each season. If anything goes wrong with this meter, it will probably be a complete failure that demands replacement. Enter the total number of hours run on your log at the time of replacement.

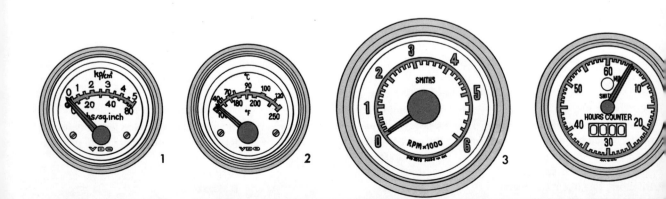

CHAPTER 9

Electrics

Most boats delivered today have insufficient electrical capacity to meet the demands of modern boat owners, who want to be able to use more and more electrical equipment. Sooner or later, the addition of just one more appliance will prove too much, and the system will not be able to provide enough power. Furthermore, the inevitable workings of the damp and salty environment will cause a certain amount of power to be lost, so that not all of the electricity produced will reach its point of use.

The heart of the electrical system is the battery, which has to function under very difficult working conditions, which reduce its ability to charge and distribute power by about 50 per cent within a couple of years.

Salt water and electricity simply don't get on, and the water always wins in the end. However, you can keep problems at bay if you see to it that your electrical system is so dimensioned that it can produce, store, and distribute the current that you require.

All too often, the generator (dynamo) supplied with a new boat is too small and/or wrongly installed, so that it cannot produce sufficient current. Otherwise, the most common problems in an electrical system are faulty battery installation, incompatible types of battery, and cables of insufficient cross-section.

Despite all this, it *is* possible to have a properly functioning electrical system on your boat, and this chapter will show you how. We shall go step-by-step through all the problems that normally occur, and examine what can be done to avoid them and to provide the boat with a proper power installation. Finally, we shall look at what is necessary to maintain everything in proper working order.

Electrical circuits on a yacht

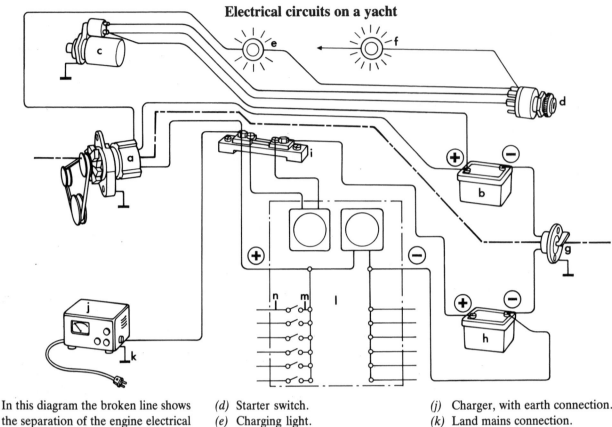

In this diagram the broken line shows the separation of the engine electrical system (above the dashed line) from the on-board mains system (below).

(a) Generator, with earth connection.
(b) Starter battery.
(c) Starter, with earth connection.
(d) Starter switch.
(e) Charging light.
(f) Oil pressure light.
(g) Main switch, with earth connection.
(h) On-board service battery.
(i) Shunt, with ammeter (A).
(j) Charger, with earth connection.
(k) Land mains connection.
(l) Mains distribution, with voltmeter (V).
(m) Fuses.
(n) Switches.

Some electrotechnical terms

The following pages are going to contain a number of electrotechnical terms, such as:

Electricity is a form of energy. Energy is effect × time = work.

Current flow is measured in amperes, usually shortened to amps or, in writing, the letter A.

Potential, or *voltage*, is measured in volts (V).

Effect is the product of potential and current flow (volts × amps) and is given in watts (W). **Capacity** is the product of current flow and time. When discussing batteries, we talk of capacity in amp-hours (Ah). A battery with 60 amp-hours capacity can in theory deliver 60 amps in 1 hour or 1 amp for 60 hours. In practice, capacity is worked out by the so-called C 20 test, which measures how much current is delivered during a 20-hour period before the potential drops to 10.5 volts.

If this is a 12-volt battery, we can, in theory, expect to receive 720 watt-hours (Wh). That means, for instance, that your battery should be able to power a 10-watt stern light for 72 hours. In practice, it is often less.

Save electricity!

Even if your on-board electrical system produces enough power for your present needs, you should know how much power each appliance uses. Then, you can reduce your boat's electrical consumption by quite simple means. First, look at the total power load.

In Table 1, we show the total power load for a medium-sized boat without refrigerator or heating. If the battery on board can produce 100 amp-hours, then running all the electrical equipment for 4 hours will drain the battery so much that it is in danger of being ruined. Make a table like this for your boat and work out your total power load.

Table 1: Total power load on a 10-meters sailboat	
2 side navigation lights of 18 watts	36 watts
1 stern light	18 watts
1 masthead light	18 watts
1 anchor light	10 watts
1 deck light	20 watts
2 below-deck lights of 20 watts	40 watts
6 below-deck lights of 10 watts	60 watts
1 compass light	2 watts
1 ventilation fan	24 watts
1 radio receiver	6 watts
1 VHF communications radio	26 watts
1 log	0.5 watts
1 echosounder	1.5 watts
1 autopilot	18 watts
Total load	**280 watts**

Obviously, you don't use all the equipment at the same time. In Table 2, we show how much power this particular boat consumes during a typical twenty-four-hour period. Total consumption is 600.5 watt-hours, which means that a 12-volt battery will produce

$$\frac{600.5 \text{ watt-hours}}{12 \text{ volts}} = 50.04 \text{ amp-hours}$$

that is, your battery's capacity is 50.04 amp-hours. At the end of those twenty-four hours, the battery will be pretty flat.

Table 2: Total consumption during 24-hour period			
Side lights	36 W × 4 hours	=	144 Wh
Stern light	18 W × 4 hours	=	72 Wh
Masthead light	18 W × 0.5 hour	=	9 Wh
Anchor light	10 W ×·7 hours	=	70 Wh
Deck light	20 W × 0.25 hour	=	5 Wh
Below-deck lights	40 W × 0.5 hour	=	20 Wh
Below-deck lights	60 W × 3 hours	=	180 Wh
Compass light	2 W × 4 hours	=	8 Wh
Ventilation fan	24 W × 0.5 hour	=	12 Wh
Radio receiver etc.	7 W × 3 hours	=	21 Wh
VHF, sending	26 W × 0.5 hours	=	13 Wh
VHF, stand by	0.5 W × 14 hours	=	7 Wh
Log	0.5 W × 4 hours	=	2 Wh
Echo-sounder	1.5 W × 1 hour	=	1.5 Wh
Autopilot	18 W × 2 hours	=	36 Wh
Total consumption			**600.5 watt-hours**

So how can you reduce your total power load? A systematic inspection of your electrical installations will indicate where you can make savings. See how much you can reduce the wattage on each appliance. For instance, if you have a sailboat, you must have two side lanterns and one stern lantern for night sailing. If you install a tricolor mast-top lantern for use instead, you will save two bulbs at 18 watts per bulb, in other words, 36 watts. On a motorboat, you could install a combined red/green lantern, thus saving one 18-watt bulb.

The anchor light can be replaced by a paraffin lantern, saving a further 10 watts. Alternatively, you can fit your electric anchor light with a photo-cell or timer so that it is lit only when it is dark.

Belowdecks, great savings can be made. Many lamps contain two 10-watt bulbs. Take out one; there will still be enough light. Other lamps can be fitted with 5-watt bulbs. Your eyes will easily adapt to working in weaker light. Alternatively, you can install fluorescent lighting instead of ordinary bulbs, but that light is often too harsh. A better alternative is to install halogen lamps, which will soon be available on the market. Halogen lighting offers superior light yield to that received from ordinary bulbs.

Table 3: Total consumption after energy-saving steps			
Tricolor light	18 W × 3.5 hours	= 63	Wh
Stern light	18 W × 0.5 hours	= 9	Wh
Masthead light	18 W × 0.5 hour	= 9	Wh
Deck light	20 W × 0.25 hour	= 5	Wh
Below-deck lights	20 W × 0.5 hour	= 10	Wh
Below-deck lights	30 W × 1 hour	= 30	Wh
Radio receiver etc.	4 W × 3 hours	= 12	Wh
VHF, sending	26 W × 0.5 hours	= 13	Wh
VHF, stand by	0.5 W × 14 hours	= 7	Wh
Log	0.5 W × 4 hours	= 2	Wh
Echosounder	1.5 W × 1 hour	= 1.5	Wh
Autopilot	18 W × 2 hours	= 36	Wh
Total consumption			**197.5 watt-hours**

Table 3 shows the results of these savings. The total power load has been reduced by almost two thirds, and the battery does not have to produce more than about 17 amp-hours per twenty-four hours, which means that you can spend a weekend sailing without having to recharge.

THE TWIN-CIRCUIT SYSTEM

Most boats use a twin-circuit electrical system: one to provide current to start the engine and one to power all the other electric appliances. In principle, the starter battery should always be fully charged, and you ensure this by preventing it from being discharged together with the general-services battery. The simplest way to do this is to fit a blocking diode in each circuit (Illustration 1), so that current can only flow in one direction. This is not a good solution, because it causes a drop in voltage, thus reducing the effect. A better solution is to disconnect the diode on the general-services circuit and connect it in parallel to the diode on the charging (starter) circuit (Illustration 2). This reduces voltage drop and improves the balance between power requirement and ability to accept charge.

The best solution, however, is to replace the diodes with breakers, as shown in Illustration 3.

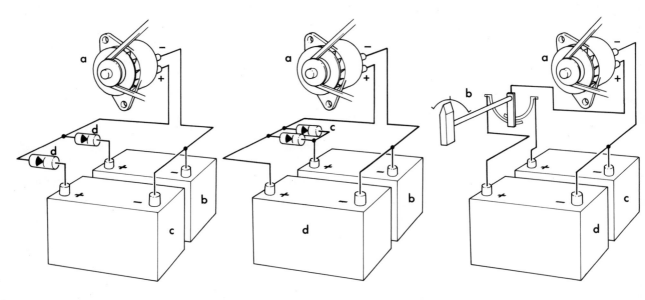

1. Typical two-battery charging circuit

Two batteries can be charged by the same generator *(a)*, and the method shown here gives priority to the starter battery *(b)*, ensuring that it is fully charged before the general-services battery *(c)* receives any charge.

Diodes *(d)* separate the two batteries, so that one cannot "steal" current from the other.

2. Improved two-battery charging circuit

This method is an improvement on that shown on the left, using exactly the same components. Current flows from the generator *(a)* to the starter battery *(b)* via the two diodes *(c)*, which are connected in parallel. This reduces the voltage drop that always occurs when current passes through diodes. The general-services battery *(d)* will now receive about 0.3 volts higher charge than the starter battery, which gives a better balance between the two batteries.

3. The best two-battery charging circuit

The best method is via a four-way switch, which permits the current to flow directly from the generator *(a)* to the relevant battery. The switch *(b)* has one position, usually marked "All", which enables the generator to have contact with a receiver all the time. (Because if you break contact between the one battery and the generator in order to switch over to the other battery, the diodes in the generator will blow.)

Never use the "All" position during charging. This is a frequent reason why batteries are ruined. If you connect two batteries with such different characteristics as the starter battery and the general-services battery, they will very quickly be ruined. *(c)* Starter battery. *(d)* General-services battery.

MORE BATTERIES

Nowadays, boating people expect more and more comfort on board, and most want to have a refrigerator, a heater, water pumps, and even TV. A refrigerator requires about 100 watts to function properly, a heater perhaps half that when it is connected to a thermostat. (The heating coil requires 100 watts or more every time it starts.)

On most boats, the starter battery usually has too much capacity, while the general-services battery does not produce enough power for the various appliances. The starter uses only about 1 amp-hour at each start, and you can, therefore, use the engine for weeks without having to recharge the starter battery. However, every time you install a new appliance that is a heavy consumer of electricity, you should install another battery on the general-services circuit. For instance, if you install a refrigerator and an electric heater, the battery requirement is at least 200 amp-hours and you should, in fact, allow for about 300 amp-hours.

The only practical way to achieve this capacity is to install several parallel-connected auxiliary batteries. There are special batteries available that are suitable for tractionary use, so-called tubular-plate or monobloc batteries, but these are heavy and expensive. Use ordinary starter batteries instead, installing them as auxiliaries on the general-services circuit. These batteries are smaller, lighter, and cheaper, and they should last for about five years under proper working conditions. The best thing about them is that they are much easier to charge, and take less time to be charged than do the heavier batteries.

Installing auxiliary batteries

As just mentioned, auxiliary batteries to provide more on-board electricity are installed on the general-services circuit and should be connected in parallel. By connecting batteries in parallel (plus to plus and minus to minus), you keep the potential the same and increase the capacity. (Connecting in series—plus to minus—does the opposite: increase the potential and retain the capacity.)

If you further increase the number of electrical appliances on board and you need even more batteries, never add them on to the existing bank of batteries. Parallel-connected batteries tend to "fight" among themselves, if they are not completely similar. You must therefore exchange *all* the batteries in the battery bank, when you require more electrical capacity.

When you buy batteries that are to be parallel-connected, be sure that they have been manufactured in the same batch. (The production number is stamped on each battery.)

Battery types

The normal battery found on the market is gradually being replaced by the so-called maintenance-free battery, which differs insofar as it usually has calcium-reinforced grids, and therefore can take a higher voltage before gassing. Maintenance-free batteries don't "use" as much electrolyte as do ordinary batteries. They also have more electrolyte, and usually do not have screw tops for refilling with distilled water. They are not, however, hermetically sealed. The level of electrolyte should be checked once a year and topped up, if necessary.

Batteries with calcium-reinforced grids have a more stable potential and are easier to recharge. This makes them well suited for marine use. However, they cost more than ordinary batteries. The major disadvantage is that they must not be allowed to become totally flat. If that happens, they will be ruined. The potential should never be allowed to fall below 10.5 volts.

In recent years, re-combination batteries have come on the market. These are hermetically sealed, the battery gas being constantly converted to water inside the battery. This type of battery is ideally suited for use on board boats but is considerably more expensive. It, too, has calcium-reinforced grids and therefore must not be allowed to be heavily discharged.

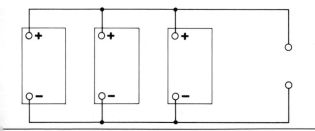

If you parallel-connect three 12-volt batteries with 100 amp-hours capacity each, you will have 300 amp-hours capacity.

Batteries should be placed in sturdy boxes that are well clamped down. On fast motorboats and ocean-going sailboats, the batteries themselves should be firmly clamped inside the box, which is in its turn held by independent clamps.

On ocean-going sailboats, batteries should be mounted so that their cells are pointing in the same direction as the keel, that is to say that the batteries are placed athwartships. The reason is that these boats can often be heeled on the same tack for days, with the risk that one tip of the cells could project above the level of the electrolyte and dry out, thus causing loss of capacity.

Installing a battery

Batteries should be placed as close to the engine as possible, but preferably not in the engine room, where the heat and vibrations can damage them. Some countries *forbid* you to have your battery in the engine room, if the engine runs on petrol.

Most batteries emit gas — a mixture of oxygen and hydrogen — which is highly explosive. Ventilation is, therefore, important. You may keep your batteries in the engine room if you have a diesel. Then, as long as the engine is running and the battery charging, the engine's combustion will cause enough ventilation.

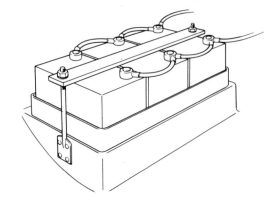

Batteries must be securely fitted in sturdy trays or boxes. In fast motor-boats and ocean-going yachts, they should be screw-clamped in position, as shown.

Batteries on boats with petrol engines must have a fan-assisted ventilation system and be placed in a tightly sealed compartment (see page 135). Never place batteries under a bench or in a cabin.

CHARGING YOUR BATTERIES

Most boat batteries are seldom charged to more than 70 per cent capacity, and you should never drain your battery so that it has less than 20 per cent of its capacity left. So a battery of, say, nominal 100 amp-hours capacity is charged to only 70 amp-hours, and you should not use more than a further 50 amp-hours without recharging. Which means that you have only a safe 50 per cent from your 100 amp-hours battery.

This is due to the charging potential. Most boat engines are fitted with a generator or dynamo of the kind used on car engines. In a car, the battery is installed near the warmth of the engine and the wires between the generator and the battery are short. Furthermore, the engine, and therefore the generator, runs very often and for long periods, more or less constantly recharging the battery.

The regulator protects the battery from excessively high charge rates. While the battery is charging, a counter voltage is built up in the battery.

When it reaches 14.4 volts in a 12-volt battery, the battery is fully charged. If you continue charging, water in the electrolyte will evaporate, and the battery will be ruined. You will then have gone above the so-called gassing voltage. This is prevented by the regulator, which automatically cuts off the charging process.

Many generators have built-in regulators which take their current from the D+ terminal on the generator's tridiodes. In a car, the charging process is cut off when the battery reaches 13.7 to 14.0 volts, which leaves quite a safety margin. This is too low to charge the battery fully. With a charging current of 13.8 volts, you need to charge for 5 hours to get the battery up to 70 per cent capacity. To charge fully, you must approach the gassing voltage, 14.4 volts. We are talking here of raising the voltage by only some tenths of a volt to achieve full charge, but since most boats have several metres of wiring between the generator and the

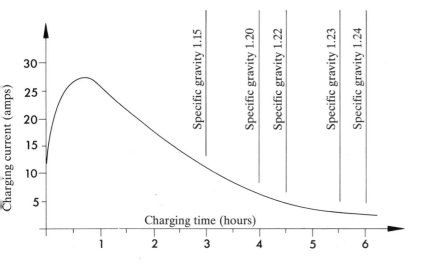

From the curve, it can be seen that even with a strong charging current, the specific gravity of the electrolyte does not reach 1.24 until after six hours' constant charging. At this stage, the charging curve is more or less straight, and the battery's capacity is still on 70 per cent, that is, 38.5 amp-hours. The lesson to be learnt from this is that the charging current must be increased. The reason that this is not possible is that most marine-charging equipment comes from the car industry, which has different requirements. If we are to approach the gassing voltage of 14.4 volts, the charging regulator must be able to withstand a stronger load and to be sufficiently adaptable to the charging current.

Graph showing how a battery is easier to charge the greater the charging current. The battery's capacity is 55 amp-hours and the charging potential is 14 volts. The dynamo is 55 amps.

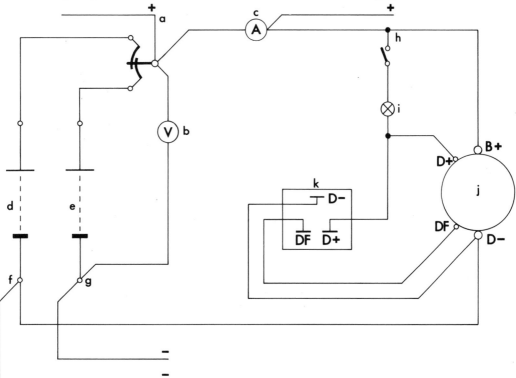

This is the kind of charging regulation that you find on most boats. The regulator receives and stores voltage from the D+ and the D− terminals on the generator. Under load, the voltage between B+ and B− on the generator will drop. A further voltage drop occurs between the battery and the generator. The "appetite" for current will fall as the charging voltage drops, and the time needed for charging will be longer. A regulator connected in this way will simply not be able to service the batteries properly. To do this, it must be made to deliver a higher voltage, so that the charging voltage at the battery is high enough.

(a) Starter +.
(b) Voltmeter.
(c) Ammeter and general-services +.
(d) Starter battery.
(e) General-services battery.
(f) Starter −.
(g) General-services −.
(h) Ignition switch.
(i) Charging light.
(j) Generator.
(k) Regulator.

battery, a drop in voltage of a half a volt easily occurs. If there is a blocking diode in between, then another half a volt is lost. If the current that leaves the generator's terminals is 14 volts, it will have sunk to 13 volts by the time it reaches the battery. You can charge for days at this level and only manage to recharge the battery to 50 per cent.

The regulator

The best solution is to install a new charging regulator, especially trimmed to get the battery completely recharged. It should be adjustable, and because a battery's ability to accept a charging current decreases with falling temperature, the charging regulator should be able to compensate for temperature loss. A regulator that pulse charges is the most effective and makes a high charging current possible without risk of ruining the battery.

The wiring system

Due to the resistance that every wire has, every cable through which a current is passed causes a loss of effect in the form of voltage drop. The finer the cable (i.e., the smaller its cross-section), the greater the resistance and the drop in voltage. A 4 per cent drop in voltage is the maximum you should accept on board your boat. This means that if your boat runs on a 12-volt system, the maximum voltage drop acceptable is half a volt, and if you are to keep it at that level, you must use wiring that is thick enough, i.e., has a sufficient cross-section. The nomogram on this page will enable you to find the correct cross-section at given effect and length of cable in a 12-volt system. (In a 24-volt system, you can double the effect from the relevant cross-section.)

Remember that you must double the length when calculating the distance the wiring covers, because on board a boat you have positive and negative wires. If the length covered by the cable is 5 metres, then you must reckon on 10 metres, and so on, because the current has to get from the battery to the appliance and back again, a "return trip".

Reduction of the cable's cross-section is one of the most usual causes of voltage drop. This occurs most often where one or more wires in the cable have broken, perhaps because of being constantly bent to and fro by the movement of the boat, or because of working loose at a terminal connection.

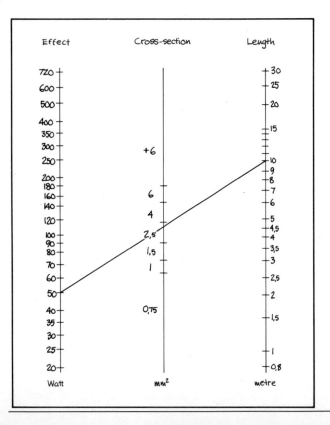

This nomogram shows the relationship between cable length, cable cross-section, and the effect required.

If you draw a line between values on the two outer scales, the required cable cross-section will be crossed on the middle scale. The example shows that a cable cross-section of 2.5 sq mm is necessary to lead 50 watts a distance of 10 metres. Remember that the currect must go in both directions, therefore the actual cable length must be doubled on the nomogram.

1 sq mm = 0.00155 sq inch

1 m = 3.28 ft

EXPANDING THE ELECTRICAL SYSTEM

Do you need a new generator?

Most boats are delivered from the factory with a generator of about 50 amps. This is sufficient as long as you don't use too much current, but when you install a refrigerator, electric heaters, a television, and even an electric anchor windlass, the generator will soon be under-dimensioned. In principle, the generator can be as big as you want; the batteries regulate how much current they want to receive, but a 20–30 amp charging current per 100 amp-hours battery capacity is optimal for a 12-volt system.

Make sure that the generator works at a high enough rpm. It works best around 8,000 rpm and at that rate receives the most efficient cooling, too. Such high revs are rare on the slower diesel engines that are often found on sailboats. If the engine's running speed produces only 2,000 rpm, the V-belt's pulley on the flywheel should have four times the diameter of the pulley on the generator.

The V-belt must be correctly tensioned. You should only be able to depress it about 1 cm (1/2"). Always have a reserve belt on board. On most small boats, the V-belt usually powers the water pump at the same time as it drives the generator, so if you drive without a belt, the engine will be ruined.

Engine wiring

The cables that are delivered with the engine are usually properly dimensioned. However, check your start cable. If it has too small a cross-section, exchange it for one of suitable dimension. Say the starter motor has a half horsepower, which equals 370 watts. In the nomogram, you can see that a 6 sq mm cross-section cable is not sufficient for such a motor after 1.75 metres of cable (i.e., 3.5 metres on the nomogram). To be on the safe side, you should take 1.5 metres as the maximum length.

Check all terminal connections. Salt and corrosion cause a highly resistant coating that should be scraped or sanded clean, both on the cable terminal connector and on the appliance's terminals. Fit them together again and spray with thin Tectyl.

Charging circuitry

Again, this is usually comes with the engine. Check that it is in good condition by measuring the current at the battery poles when the engine has been running for a long time and the battery therefore should be fully charged. If the current is lower than 14.2 volts, you should rebuild your entire charging system, as described earlier.

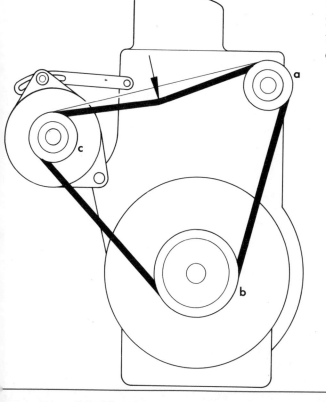

If you press the V-belt on the generator, it should not give by more than 10 mm (1/2").
(*a*) Water pump.
(*b*) Flywheel.
(*c*) Generator.

General-services circuitry

The circuit that distributes current to all the appliances on board except the starter is the biggest current thief of all, because it has so many branches and points of distribution where voltage drop may occur. Check that your cables are of the right dimensions and inspect all terminals. If you see a corroded terminal or one with a coating, take apart, scrape or sand clean, put together, and spray with anti-corrosion oil. Check especially the connection between the cable and the terminal connector. If you suspect that there is poor contact between them, clip the connector off with a pliers and replace it. A crimping pliers with an assortment of crimp connectors costs very little but is invaluable.

Never solder a terminal connector or a cable end that has been stripped of its plastic covering, if they are to be fitted into screw or crimp connections. The junction between the solder and the wire is a notorious weak spot, where breakage easily occurs. Furthermore, solder paste contains fluxing agent, which is acid and becomes extra active in a marine environment.

Remove all fuses. Clean the fuse connections as well as the fuses' ends. Change them if necessary. Then put in the fuses and spray with anti-corrosion spray.

Battery terminals

The terminals on the battery are often corroded. The hard, greyish coating has a very high resistance. You can buy a special cutter that fits on a power drill to clean up the lead on the battery terminals, but you can also scrape the coating off with a knife. Work down to clean metal. An alternative is to use emery paper. Carefully scrape inside the battery wire's terminal connector, or use a round file to do it. Terminal and terminal connector must be covered in anti-corrosive grease before being fitted together again.

External wiring

External cables should be curved downwards before entering navigation lights from underneath, so that water cannot run along the cable

---

Connecting terminals

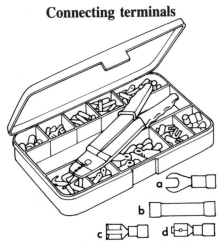

A crimping pliers and a set of cable joints are a must if your connections are to be well made and safe. Usually, you can buy a complete crimping box, as shown. The pliers will cut wire, strip it of its plastic insulation, and crimp connecting joints of various cross-sections.
(a) Fork-type terminal connector.
(b) Sleeve for covering joins.
(c) Female flat joint.
(d) Male flat joint.

Crimp-connecting cables

(a) The cable is stripped, exposing about 7 mm (¼″) of the lead.
(b) The joint is slid over the wire, crimped where it covers the lead (see black arrow), and then crimped where it covers the wider insulation of the wire (see open arrow).
(c) Shown without its insulating cover, the crimp connection secures the lead at one point and the wire insulation at the other point.

Battery terminals

Positive and negative terminals of storage batteries are usually marked, but they can also be identified by their different sizes, as shown here. The positive terminal always has the greatest diametre.

Keeping water out of electrical fittings

a) This navigation light has its cable routed through an entry at the bottom to stop water from running along the cable into the gland.

b) A waterproof connecting plug, and a socket with a waterproof cap, are specially designed to keep the water out of external fittings, such as the leads to navigation lights. They are normally required when a mast is stepped on deck, so that the leads can be quickly uncoupled.

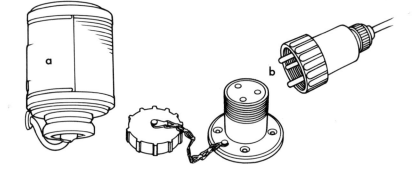

into the light. Even then, you can't be certain that the light will remain watertight, so open it and dry it out carefully before cleaning the cable connector and the bulb holder. Cover the wire connections with Tectyl and spray the bulb-holder with an anti-corrosion spray.

The water that gathers inside a navigation or deck light is usually condensation. If the light is positioned where sea spray won't be hitting it from underneath, it is worthwhile drilling a couple of tiny holes (2 mm) in the bottom of the light, so that condensation can run off.

Electric deck-plug connections are designed to be watertight, but don't count on them always being that. Take them apart and dry and clean them. Spray with anti-corrosion spray and spread watertight grease on all gaskets before putting them together again.

FAULT FINDING

When some electrical appliance malfunctions, approach the problem systematically and logically. If a light is not working, the simplest explanation is that the bulb has gone. If not, use a test lamp to check if there is current between the terminals in the bulb holder. If not, check if the fuse has blown. If not, the problem must be in the switch or somewhere along the cable.

If a fuse blows every time you switch the current on, you have a short-circuit somewhere in the system. Turn each switch on, one after the other, until you locate the section where the problem is. The breakdown has occurred either in the cable or in the appliance to which it is carrying the current.

Check the first possibility by disconnecting the appliance and connecting up another appliance, such as a test lamp. If it lights, the cable is in order and the problem is in the appliance. If the fuse blows again, then the cable is defect.

Connect the two ends of the cable to a multimeter in ohm-position. If the cable is OK then the multi-meter's reading will fall towards zero. If the cable is broken, the reading will be infinite resistance. If the cable is partly severed, a high resistance is indicated on the multi-meter, and that resistance can be high enough to blow the fuse, without having caused a short-circuit.

Whatever the reason for the problem in the

Testing with a multi-meter

This instrument can be used for bulbs and fuses as well as circuits and other items. Its probes are pressed to the terminals of, for example, the fuse as shown here. For measuring resistance, the instrument contains a battery, which should be replaced at regular intervals.

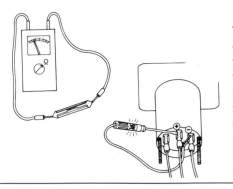

Using a test lamp

The wiring to electrical and electronic devices can often be checked simply with this aid. When the probe and the wire of the test lamp are connected to the terminals on the device, the lamp will light if there is a normal voltage difference at the terminals. However, a fault inside the device itself can only be detected by other test equipment such as a multi-meter.

cable, it will have to be replaced. Don't compensate for this kind of problem by installing a stronger fuse than is suitable for the circuit. Another thing to remember is that the fuse can blow if all the appliances on the circuit are working at the same time. (This happens when you have connected more appliances to the circuit than it can take.) In that case, you must expand the fuse-box's capacity by installing more fuses—not stronger ones.

If the starter refuses to turn the engine over, despite the fact that the battery is fully charged, the simple explanation may be that the battery terminals are corroded. If this is the case, a clicking start relay will confirm. Of course, the self-starter can have seized, but this is not usual, unless you have been mistreating it. (Never keep the starter running for more than 15 seconds. Then let it cool for 30 seconds, before trying again.)

Cable cross-section in sq mm (fixed)	Maximum fuse size	Cable cross-section in sq mm (movable)
0.75	6	—
1.5	10	0.75
2.5	16	1.5
4.0	20	2.5
6.0	26	—

Maximum fuse sizes in relation to fixed and movable electric cables.

MAINTENANCE AND CARE

The battery

For years, the hydrometer was the instrument used for determining the state of the charge in a storage battery, but it is actually useless if you want to check the condition of the battery. The hydrometer only tells you how much charge you have in the battery in relation to the battery's present condition. Besides, on modern maintenance-free batteries which are sealed, it is not easy to use a hydrometer.

The voltmeter is the only instrument that will do the job properly. Don't use the battery at all for a couple of hours and then measure the voltage. If it shows 12.7 volts, then your battery is fully charged. If the reading moves down towards 12 volts, the battery is flat.

Check the capacity of the battery in the following way. Start with the fully charged battery that you have just measured at 12.7 volts after a couple of hours' rest. You don't want the engine to actually start, so on a diesel engine you press in the stop button or pull out the stopper control and run the starter motor for 10 seconds. On a petrol engine you disconnect the cable between the coil and the distributor, and turn on the starter for 10 seconds. If the voltmeter reads 12.7 volts within a couple of minutes, then your battery is in good condition.

Charging the battery

A good electric system should be fitted with both voltmeter and ammeter. One often sees the ammeter connected in series to the main current cable, but this is wrong. One should never draw such a heavy current long distances from its source, and, besides, there is risk of fire if you draw it to a little instrument under the dashboard or control panel. The correct way to connect the ammeter is to use a block shunt, as shown in the diagram.

The ammeter tells you how much current is

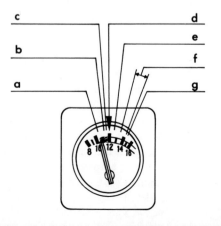

Reading a voltmeter

(a) Completely discharged at 10.5 volts (battery damage).

(b) Charge at 11.4 volts! Do not discharge below this level.

(c) At-rest voltage, 11.6 volts (battery empty).

(d) The onboard nominal voltage, 12 volts.

(e) At-rest voltage, 12.7 volts (battery full).

(f) Charging voltage, 13.8 to 14.1 volts.

(g) Gassing voltage, 14.4 volts.

The shunt-connected ammeter

With zero as its central reading, the on-board ammeter measures the current taken from the battery (readings to the left) or the charging current (readings to the right). The shunt is simply a resistance inserted into the measuring point. Two standard-sized leads join it to the ammeter. Note that the leads supplied with the ammeter should not be shortened, as this would change the readings.

(a) Ammeter (front).
(b) Ammeter (back).
(c) Shunt.
(d) Line to on-board mains battery.
(e) Line to charger.
(f) Line to generator.

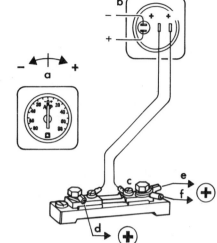

flowing into or out of the battery, indicating the balance between charge and discharge. Use it together with the voltmeter, which tells you the state and charging of the battery, when you want to know what is happening in the electrical system. When using electricity, never allow the voltage to drop below 10.5 volts before you recharge.

When the engine is running and the ammeter swings over to the plus side, it is showing the charging current, i.e., how much current is flowing into the batteries at any time. If the batteries are low,

the current (amps) is high and the potential (volts) is low. You can now see if the generator is producing as much current as it should. As the batteries become more charged, the voltage increases and the current decreases. When the voltage tops 14 volts, the current is low, and it takes quite a long time for the battery to be charged with the final ampere-hours. In the end, the voltage approaches 14.4 volts, but it should not go above that limit. At this stage, the current is almost nil.

Ampere-hour counter

This is a recently introduced device that functions in the same way as the fuel gauge on a car. A little computer works out how much current the battery is charging or discharging.

The ampere-hour counter is also fitted with a block shunt and measures both current and voltage. It can be set at zero, and indicates then the ampere-hours: they decrease as the batteries are discharged and increase as they are charged. It can also show voltage and current strength at any time. Every boat with an electrical system that is a cut above the rudimentary should have one.

The ampere-hour counter is connected to the circuit as shown in the diagram. The shunt comes with the instrument and is connected between the negative pole on the battery and the engine block. If you have a twin-circuit system, connect it to the general-services circuit. This means that you won't have a constant check on the state of the starter battery, but this is of less interest, as you don't use this so much as you use the batteries on the general-services circuit.

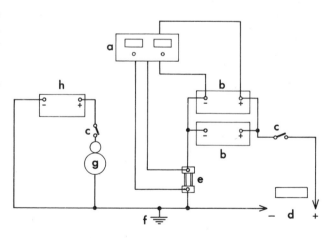

When you connect the shunt between the minus on the battery and the engine block, the instrument indicates how much current is flowing into and out of the battery.

(a) Ampere-hour counter.
(b) General-circuits battery.
(c) Switch.
(d) Electrical appliance.
(e) Shunt.
(f) Engine block.
(g) Starter.
(h) Starter battery.

Alternative charging methods

Don't count on solar cells solving all your electrical requirements. They produce far too little electricity in relation to the amounts you need on board your boat. However, solar panels are excellent for charging the last few ampere-hours when the boat is not in use, and they maintain the batteries in a high state of charge, when the boat is left unattended.

A wind charger, which consists of a wind turbine linked directly to an alternator, can produce a higher current. The alternator connects to the battery through a standard charging circuit. It can provide a useful power supply in harbour—as long as your reason for being there is not lack of wind. The chief problem is that the exposed vanes must be mounted clear of human contact. If left working at sea, the vanes can foul the ropes.

Water-powered alternators also provide power when under way on a sailboat, or even when moored in a tideway. There are two types. One has an impeller which is towed astern, like the traditional log, with the alternator connected directly to a linking line between the impeller and the yacht. The other is a generator driven from the free-wheeling propeller shaft. This is usually belt driven, and of course also provides power when the engine is in use.

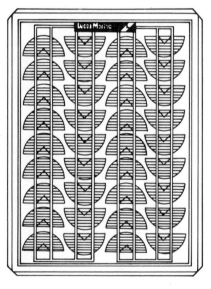

Solar panels for use on boats
Lucas Marine solar modules are specially designed for marine use to keep the batteries in a high state of charge when the craft is left unattended.

Wind-driven generators
Ideal for charging 12-volt batteries on boats are the L.V.M. Aero-Gen 25 and Aero-Gen 50. They have a corrosion-proof construction with cast-aluminium body and glassfibre fan-blades.

Water-powered alternators
A towed water turbine requires little installation except for waterproof wiring connections.

INSTALLING ELECTRONIC EQUIPMENT

The more electronic equipment a boat owner buys, the greater the necessity of correct installation. Find out if the appliance is waterproof, splashproof, or neither. If neither, then it must be installed in a protected place. Only hermetically sealed instruments that are filled with an inert gas, like nitrogen, can be installed in an unprotected place, such as the cockpit.

Antennae and their cables must be fitted where they will not cause interference. A VHF antenna induces a powerful magnetic field when being operated, and that can affect the function of other electronic equipment nearby.

Install the compass so that no deviation is caused by magnetic or iron objects in the vicinity. If it is impossible to avoid this, then the compass must be corrected and a deviation table worked out.

Simple electronic equipment often has its fuse inside the instrument, and it is sometimes difficult to get at it with dismantling the whole thing. It is worth your while to discard this fuse and to fit a fast fuse of the same capacity as the original on the cable that runs into the appliance.

All electronic equipment must be earthed properly. It is not enough to earth it to the engine block or some other part of the engine. The best earth is provided by fitting a special earth plate on the outside of the underwater hull, so far down that it is always underwater. If you don't want to do this, then you can connect the earth to the through-hull fittings, but you must keep a close eye on them, so that they are not eaten up by galvanic corrosion.

Electrical interference

There are many possible sources of electrical interference on board a boat, the most important being the generator, the starter motor, and the propeller shaft, but bunches of live electric cables can also cause interference. It is fairly easy to isolate the major causes on your boat, but much more difficult to cure the problem.

The two major ways of curing interference are screening and filtering. Screening consists of building the source of interference into a metal case or of earthing the chassis to those instruments that you want to protect.

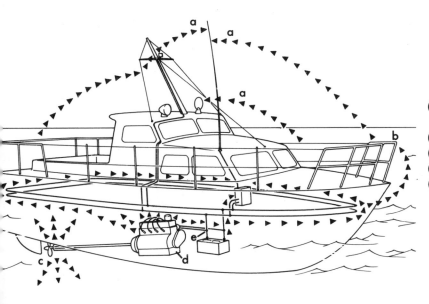

Interference sources on a yacht
- (a) Re-radiation to antenna and d/f loop.
- (b) Radiation to ship rail, or lifelines.
- (c) Radiation from propeller shaft.
- (d) Generation by engine ignition.
- (e) Conduction to receiver.

Filtering means fitting condensors to the offending equipment.

You can do all this yourself, but serious cases of interference should be referred to an expert.

Decca, Navtex och other long-wave signals are particularly sensitive to interference and, here, the position of the antenna is vital. It should be as far away as possible from any transmitting antennae, such as VHF.

Protection

Sensitive electronics are especially prone to tension peaks, or transients, in the system, especially when the current comes from an outboard engine where the flywheel continues to rotate after the ignition is switched off. Starter motors on the bigger diesel engines can also cause this problem.

Tension peaks are often the cause of "inexplicable" electronic breakdown, so it is important to protect your equipment. Do this inexpensively by connecting an 18-volt epoxy transorber in parallel on the current-supply cable to each appliance, i.e. between positive and negative. It should be fitted so near the apparatus as possible, preferably where the cable connector is attached to it, to avoid induction in the cable.

CHAPTER 10

Safety and Maintenance

A well-maintained boat is a safe boat, so the section on safety is followed by a section on annual maintenance. Regular inspection of the hull, standing and running rigging, and the engine are an important safety measure during the sailing season, and if you find some problems that can wait until you take the boat out of the water, these should be noted on your repair list for fixing during the winter.

If you live in a warm climate, you do not need to take the boat out of the water for the duration of the winter, but every boat should be taken out of the water annually to check the underwater fittings. Besides, it is much easier to carry out maintenance work in a yard ashore.

Remember that when a boat is taken out of the water, it is out of its natural element and needs handling with much greater care. In the water, the boat is supported evenly over the whole hull, but on land the support has to be concentrated in localized areas which must be chosen carefully. Even the lifting operation and, later, the launching operation should be carefully planned to avoid trouble.

It is surprising how little safety equipment may be fitted to new yachts. A new owner is expected to deal with this himself. Fire extinguishers are usually standard, but liferafts, lifejackets, and flares have to be purchased separately and installed on board. Even with fire extinguishers, it is a good idea to check their location and number. Safety is primarily the concern of the owner, and cannot be left to the boatyard.

FIREFIGHTING

Fire extinguishers should be light enough to use with one hand, because you may need the other hand to hold on with. The gas and powder types are best for boat use, although the powder type can compact with the constant movement of the boat. One should be placed in the galley area, where the risk of fire is greatest, and the others near the companionway or wheelhouse door. They are handy in this position when you escape from the fire and turn round to tackle it. The galley extinguisher can be supplemented by a glassfibre fire blanket, to cope with small fires on the stove.

Apart from the galley, the engine compartment is the main source of fire. Here the fire may not be detected until it has a good hold. You can fit automatic extinguishers which are turned on by heat sensors built into them. More sophisticated systems incorporate an alarm, allowing either manual or automatic operation of the extinguisher from outside the compartment. These extinguishers should be mounted above the engine and have enough capacity to completely flood the compartment with the inert gas.

The engine should be stopped before operating the extinguisher, if the fire has not already stopped it. Otherwise it sucks more air into the compartment, feeding the fire and diluting the gas. For the same reason, you should look at the air inlets of the engine compartment, and prepare a method of sealing these off—but do not do this while the engine is running. It is not always easy to seal off the compartment completely, but consider the possibilities. Finally, any wiring used for a fire-alarm system must be fireproof.

Firefighting equipment
                                               Keep fire extinguishers handy

(a) Hand-held BCF extinguisher.
(b) Automatic BCF unit. This should be installed with the diffuser facing downwards.

(c) Fire blanket for use in fighting galley fires.

Apart from the galley, these should be stowed just inside the companionway.

LIFERAFTS

The liferaft is one of your most important pieces of emergency equipment. The plastic-casing type offers better protection for the raft inside, but it can be difficult to find space for. The flexible packs must be stowed in a locker—but make sure that the liferaft is easily accessible, and that the package is well-protected from chafe.

Generally, the rigid packs can be stowed on the coachroof or transom of a sailing yacht, or on the wheelhouse top or cockpit of a motor cruiser. Once you have identified a suitable location, make up wooden chocks to support the liferaft pack, to keep it clear of the deck. These chocks should be firmly bolted down, as you do not want to lose the raft in a heavy sea. The webbing securing-straps should be good and strong, fitted with a means of tightening them securely to prevent motion. At the same time, it should be possible to release the straps quickly and easily in an emergency. At least two independent straps should be used so that, if one comes adrift, the other will keep the raft secure.

This may seem troublesome, but the stowage can be swept by solid seas, and your life may depend on it holding. Do not forget to make the liferaft painter line secure, which also requires a good connection. Finally, liferafts can be attractive to thieves in harbour, so a locking bar over the casing may be wise—but take the lock off at sea!

Chocks for a liferaft

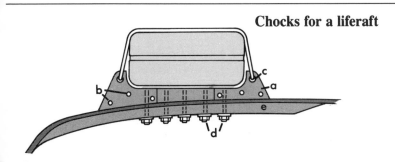

Your liferaft can be swept overboard in severe conditions, and it is not enough to have a lifeline with two—or even four—small eyebolts. Even eyeplates can be inadequate if they are too small, or are held by undersized bolts through a flimsy deck. A good arrangement is to use chocks as shown here. They may be made of hardwood, with short grain where the end lips curve up to prevent the liferaft from sliding off, and these ends should be reinforced. Remember that the lashings must have a quick means of release. For safety, there should be two means, such as a heavy-duty snap shackle and a rope lashing which can be cut.

(a) Wide chocks to spread the load; a pair forms a strong cradle and should have thin metal plates on one or both sides for reinforcement.
(b) Through bolts to hold the plates.
(c) Countersunk holes in the ends for the liferaft lashings.
(d) Five or more countersunk bolts.
(e) Under-deck stiffener, tapered at each end.

A lifejacket with part inflation, part inherent buoyancy, is a good compromise of safety with convenience.

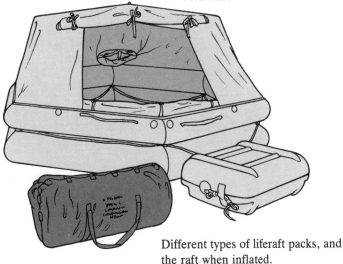

Different types of liferaft packs, and the raft when inflated.

LIFEJACKETS

Lifejackets are a further line of defence in the battle for survival, and should receive proper care and attention. A special stowage should be allocated to the lifejackets, somewhere near the cabin or wheelhouse exit, free of rubbing and chafing. The choice of lifejacket types is between full inherent buoyancy, partial inherent buoyancy combined with partial inflation, and full inflation. The latter are the most convenient as regards stowability and wearability in bad conditions, but will not work if the air chamber gets punctured. The combined type is a good compromise.

Distress flares are another item which should be stowed just inside the door for ready access. The parachute type is best, because it is much more visible both day and night. Since you may need one in a hurry, at least one or two should be in a clip stowage ready for instant use. Smoke flares for daylight use should be similarly located.

Flares stowed in clips

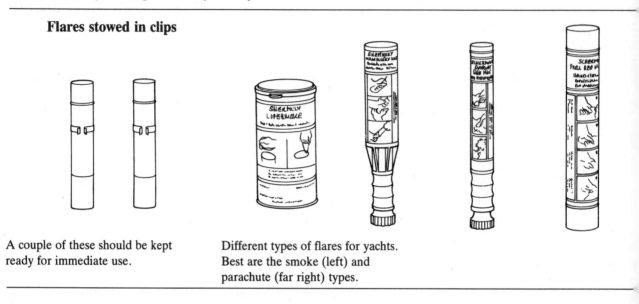

A couple of these should be kept ready for immediate use.

Different types of flares for yachts. Best are the smoke (left) and parachute (far right) types.

Emergency equipment does not last forever: it needs periodic servicing or replacement. Liferafts should be serviced annually, and this must be done at a service station. You may be able to inflate the raft and see what is inside the pack before sending it back. But check with the service station first, because there will probably be an extra charge for servicing an inflated liferaft.

You can check a liferaft yourself by looking carefully for wear or deterioration. Check all stitching. Inflate the buoyancy chamber and hold it under water, watching for bubbles that indicate leaks. If an air bottle is used for inflation, this should be replaced annually. Flares have a two-year life, after which they need replacing. Most flare suppliers offer a disposal service for old flares. Do not fire these off, as you might alert the emergency services unnecessarily.

You hope you will never need it, but when you do, you want it very badly. Emergency equipment is not something to take for granted. A little care and attention will serve you well in times of difficulty.

Servicing a winch
Lightly oil and grease all working parts monthly during the season. If you sail often, you should strip, clean, and re-lubricate two or three times during the season. At lay-up time, examine all the parts for damage, clean thoroughly, and re-lubricate.

(a) Circlip.
(b) Top cap.
(c) Pawl.
(d) Pawl spring.
(e) Spindle.
(f) Drum washer.
(g) Roller bearing.
(h) Drum.
(i) Key.
(j) Centre stem.

MAINTAINING AND REPAIRING DECK EQUIPMENT

All yachts have equipment and machinery on deck, where exposure to wind and water can cause rapid corrosion. Adequate maintenance is therefore a prime necessity, although it has been greatly reduced by modern materials such as stainless steel and plastics.

On a modern windlass, for instance, all of the moving parts are enclosed in a sealed oil bath, which keeps out water and grit. The only maintenance required is to check the oil level and change the oil according to the instructions of the manufacturer. When you do this, check the shaft bearings for any signs of an oil leak, which would probably mean that you must change the oil seals. This is a job you can do yourself, if you have a suitable instruction book. It is best done by removing the windlass from the boat and taking it to a warm workshop.

With an electric windlass, the connecting terminals should also be checked. These carry a high electrical load, and should be kept clean and free from corrosion. A smear with Vaseline will help to keep corrosion at bay.

Little maintenance is needed on anchors and chains, except to check that all shackles are correctly housed or otherwise locked. At the annual refit, it is wise to check that the inboard end of the chain is still firmly secured to the boat. If the anchor or chain is going rusty, as is almost inevitable with time, the only long-term solution is to have it regalvanised. A temporary expedient is painting with silver paint, after careful surface preparation. When checking the anchor and chain, make sure that the bow roller and any other fittings move freely and easily—but do not lubricate them with oil or grease, which would be washed everywhere by sea water.

Winches, in order to run smoothly, should be stripped occasionally and greased. Modern types are made almost entirely of corrosion-free materials. But on older boats, the bearings may need renewing if sea water has found its way into the mechanism. For both stripping and greasing, the handbook should be followed closely.

Most winches are dismantled by removing a circlip around the handle socket, after which the drum can be lifted off. Take care that the springs and pawls do not fly out and get lost. All of these small items need careful cleaning in paraffin (kerosene) or a degreaser, and then reassembling with fresh lubricant.

During the annual lay-up, the mooring lines should be checked for wear, and either shortened to remove the bad parts or else replaced. Fenders also need checking, because ropes get cut or damaged and, sometimes, the fender itself gets punctured. Most modern fenders have a screw air inlet so that they can be deflated. At the same time, check the sealing strips on hatches and windows. Any damaged or worn portions eventually leak—if they do not already—and replacement usually means digging out the old seal before inserting a new one (see page 75). These seals can normally be obtained made-to-measure from the manufacturer of the hatch, but are sometimes sold in strips.

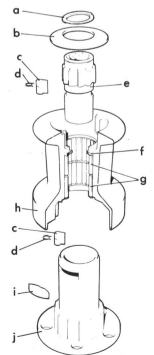

DINGHIES

The dinghy is probably one of the most neglected items on the boat, and tends to be repaired only after it has let you down. Regular maintenance can save heavy repair bills, and the work is not difficult. For glassfibre dinghies, this is largely a matter of grinding out any chips in the gel coat and filling with new gel coat (see page 54).

At the same time, check for any cracks in the gel-

Maintenance on a glassfibre tender is similar to that on a yacht hull, but the places where it rubs against the davits should be checked particularly for wear.

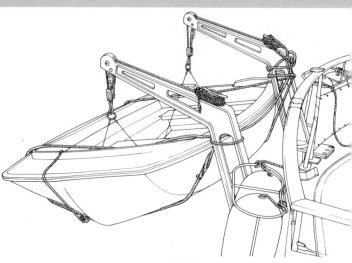

coat surface, and treat these in much the same way. Any major damage is treated in the same manner as damage to the yacht hull (see page 41).

With wooden dinghies, the work largely involves painting and varnishing the hull after carefully cleaning and rubbing down the surface. On the rigid type of folding dinghy, the areas to check are the joints where the fabric hinges allow folding. Any cracking or wear in the fabric must be fixed immediately, and probably by returning the boat to its manufacturer.

With inflatable dinghies, even major repairs are within the capabilities of the average owner. Maintenance consists of generally cleaning the boat thoroughly with water and detergent, then checking it for leaks. You can do this by simply inflating the boat and seeing if it retains its pressure over a period of time. A quicker way is to "paint" the boat with a half-half mixture of water and liquid detergent. Any leaks will be revealed quickly by a stream of bubbles. While doing this, check for any chafe in the fabric, particularly where the floor boards rub. These areas can be identified by white fabric showing through the rubber. But no action is required if the chafe is on a doubling strip, unless it is very bad.

Small leaks or chafe are repaired with a simple outside patch. Clean the area around the leak by rubbing down with sandpaper, then clean with a solvent such as Toluene. Give the same treatment to the patch, and apply the adhesive to both surfaces. Allow to dry, then apply a second coat. When this is tacky dry, apply the patch, and roll or hammer it to remove any air bubbles. Excess adhesive can be removed with the Toluene. Most manufacturers supply a suitable adhesive, but the two-component glues are best. If possible, carry out such repair work in a warm dry place.

Repairing an inflatable

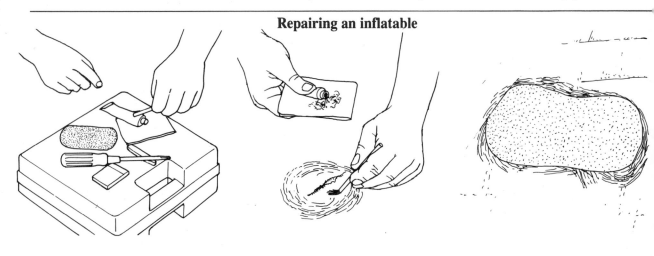

1. First mix the adhesive.

2. Apply two coats of adhesive to both the patch and the tube.

3. Then apply the patch to the tube, rolling or hammering to remove air.

Winter lay-up

You have a number of choices when laying-up the boat for the winter. The main choice is between leaving the boat in the water and taking it out. This decision will be influenced first and foremost by the climate of the area in which you live and then by the available facilities. If you have to pay for your marine berth by the year, keeping the boat there all year round may be attractive. And if the boat stays in the water, you need not close it down completely; you may be able to use it on the fine days which occur in winter, particularly if you have a heater on board.

Another important factor will be your insurance company. Insurance companies prefer a boat to be out of the water for the winter, and will then generally offer reduced premiums. There is always a greater risk of a boat being damaged in wintertime when afloat, due to storms and freezing conditions. You are also likely to sleep better at night if you know that the boat is safe ashore.

If you do decide to keep the boat in the water, several precautions must be taken. You can tie up the boat securely, with adequate fendering against storms, but protection against ice is much more difficult. Fresh water will freeze, and sea water may do so. A boat in frozen water can be distorted by the ice, if it gets thick, but further danger arises when the ice breaks up and rubs against the hull. Bubbling systems can prevent ice from forming except in severe conditions, yet installing and operating them involves additional expense.

Equally, if the boat is kept on shore, there are added costs such as cradles or supports, covers, and renting the required space. Whichever lay-up procedure is chosen, you will have a fair amount of work to do before leaving the boat for the winter.

This work is apart from the annual inspection and maintenance. In most cases, it should be done before the boat is laid up, to avoid deterioration during the winter months. You may be tempted to leave this work until the spring refit, but the damage may be done by then. (See page 174.)

When a sailboat is laid up for the winter, its mast and rigging are normally removed. One very practical reason is that the boat can be covered much more easily with its protective awning when the mast and rigging are not in place. Another reason is that the mast and all fittings can then be thoroughly checked before the next season.

The mast will normally be removed by the yard crane. But with the modern method of putting the mast step on deck rather than on the keel, you can lower the mast by yourself, only if the mast step is suitably designed to allow the mast to hinge. Check this out carefully before starting, either with the builder of the boat or mast, or by exact measurement. You do not want to get the mast halfway down only to find that the hinge will not allow further movement (see over).

First remove all the connections to the mast, such as the boom and electrical cables, so that the mast will be free once the rigging is let go. At this stage the forestay can be released, and a tackle rigged between the end of the forestay and the deck, with a line long enough to lower the mast to the horizontal. The remainder of the rigging can now be disconnected and the mast lowered, using the tackle to control the descent and a person on each shroud to steady the mast.

Lowering in this way is fine until the mast is nearly down, when the forestay is almost parallel to the mast and has little effect. With a light mast, it

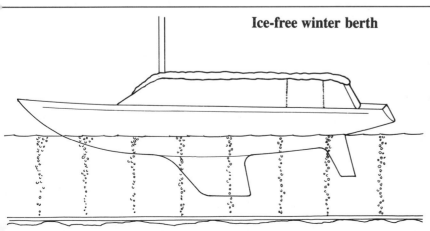

Ice-free winter berth

Maintain water circulation around the boat. This helps to keep ice at bay if the boat is left afloat during the winter.
You can either pump air through a coil of holed tubing (as shown) from a land-based pump, or you can keep the water moving by a special propeller (again powered from land) that is lowered into the water.

Lowering your mast

Lowering a mast with a tackle on the forestay is fine until the mast is nearly horizontal, when it becomes ineffective (dotted lines). A frame *(a)* fitted to the bottom of the mast gives the tackle a much better lead even when the mast is horizontal, and this type should be used for larger masts.

Mast steps

(Right) The type of mast step shown at the top will not allow the mast to be lowered on the hinge pin *(a)*, but the type shown at bottom will.

is simple for the mast to be lowered the last bit by hand; but with a heavier mast, it could be lowered into a crutch high enough to catch the mast before the forestay becomes ineffective. An alternative is to take the lowering tackle to a high point ashore, to give a more effective angle—but the boat should first be tied up very securely. In any event, lowering the mast in this manner should be carried out only in very calm conditions.

Once down, the mast should be laid on trestles in a horizontal position. It must be absolutely straight on the trestles; otherwise it will acquire a slight bend. Do not place the mast alongside the boat, where it might make a convenient stepping-place up into the boat. Masts are designed to take a very heavy downward thrust from the sails and rigging, but are not particularly strong or rigid in other directions, so treat your mast with care.

Even on a powerboat, it is a good idea to remove the mast for the winter lay-up. This makes it easier to fit the cover, and allows the fittings on the mast to be checked. Removal may not be easy when antennae are fitted to the mast, and the problems of mast removal should be taken into account when installing electronics.

The boat ashore

Laying up ashore starts with getting the boat out of the water. There are three main methods: lifting by crane or Travel Hoist, hauling ashore on a slipway, and taking the boat out on its own trailer. The choice will probably be dictated by the yard doing the work, but with the first two methods you need to know what the underwater areas of the boat look like.

Slings must be positioned carefully to avoid damage. There is usually no problem with the forward sling, because the hull is normally straightforward in this area on both sailboats and powerboats. At the aft end, you have to contend with propellers and shafts, rudders, log impellers, and keels or skegs, so the placing of the sling can be critical. When you have the boat lifted for the first

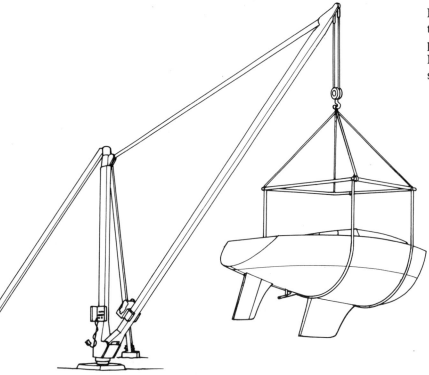

Lifting-slings must be placed where they will not put any loading on the propeller, rudder, or other fittings. Note the use of spreaders on the slings.

time, hopefully from land to water so that you can see what is happening, mark the correct place for the slings so that you will know in the future. Whilst you may be able to thread a sling between a propeller shaft and the hull on dry land, you will not be able to do this afloat, so look for an alternative position.

Putting a boat on a slipway cradle is usually no problem with a sailboat, because the weight can rest on the keel and the boat is steadied by the uprights. A bilge keeler might be a bit more difficult, and much will depend on the type of slipway cradle. A powerboat may have its propellers and rudders extending below the bottom of the boat, and the yard will want to know this before hauling out.

Once ashore, the boat must be supported properly. Glassfibre hulls are much less critical to distortion when on dry land than on wooden boats, but they are out of their element, and careful support will reduce any chance of damage or distortion. Since the supports are resting on the ground, this ground must be hard—otherwise the supports will gradually sink in, giving uneven support with the possibility of damage. When arranging the supporting of the boat, remember that you may need additional ground clearance if the rudder is to be removed. This usually drops down for removal, and it may be possible to get the required clearance by digging a pit.

Laying up a boat on its own trailer is only applicable to smaller craft. But it has the advantage

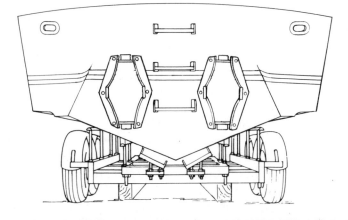

For smaller boats, a road trailer can make a good winter berth, but remember to place some sturdy blocks of wood under the axles, to spare the springs and the tyres.

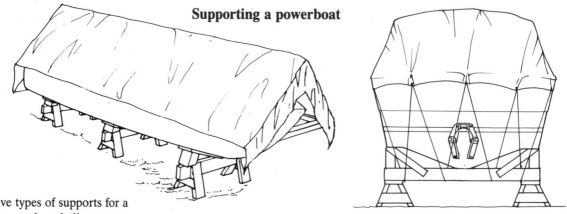

Supporting a powerboat

Alternative types of supports for a deep-vee powerboat hull.

that the supports are tailor-made for the boat, and you are able to move the boat around as required.

A sailboat will sit comfortably with the main weight taken on the keel. The bottom of the keel has a small area, so the weight is concentrated and needs to be spread out by placing strong timbers under the keel. The aim is to spread the load as wide as possible to reduce the ground loading.

The keel of a sailboat connects with the hull over a comparatively small area, leaving the rest of the hull unsupported. Extra support is thus necessary at the bow and stern, and along the bilges at each side. Timber is the traditional supporting material, in the form of round or square baulks. These are positioned under the hull in the required places, and the weight taken by each support is adjusted by hammering in wedges. The position where the support meets the hull should ideally be in the region of a strong point in the hull—perhaps at a bulkhead, frame, or stringer—to help spread the load in the hull and reduce the chance of local distortion. The bottom ends of the supports should have plates in order to spread the load over the ground.

The alternative to these individual supports is to have a special cradle. This can be of timber or steel, and allows the boat to be mainly supported on its keel, with side-support from shaped sections running along the hull under the turn of the bilge. Bilge keels require little or no support, and perform much the same function as the cradle.

For a motorboat, the normal long straight keel makes an ideal support for the hull. It may be necessary to place blocks of wood under the keel in order to raise the hull, both to give clearance to the propellers and rudders, and to allow work to be done on the hull. In addition to the keel support, you need only support and steady the hull under the turn of the bilge or the chine. Take particular care to provide adequate support under the engines of a twin-engine installation, where there is a local concentration of weight.

THE SUPPORT CRADLE

So you have decided to take your boat out of the water for the winter and to lay it up ashore. If you have a nice hard concrete area to stand the boat on, you can rely on simple props to support the boat adequately, confident that the supports will not sink into the ground during the winter. However, the chances are that the boat will be stored on soft or uneven ground, and here the use of a cradle is the best solution.

A cradle is a self-contained support, rigid enough to span any unevenness in the ground and able to provide support on soft ground. It holds the whole weight of the boat and can do so not only for winter storage, but also to transport the boat on a truck. Constructing such a cradle is not difficult. The first step is to obtain plans of the boat showing the locations of the main bulkheads and stringers, and the centre of gravity of the boat.

Starting first with a sailboat, you can assume that the centre of gravity is roughly at the keel. The weight of the keel must be spread over a wide area, and this is best done with sturdy blocks of wood, such as old railway sleepers.

The bilge supports are best cut from timber, which is easiest to shape to the correct contours of the hull. Alternatively a steel tube could be shaped to fit, if you have tube-bending facilities. A metal rod or light plywood can be used to make a pattern for the hull shape. When cutting the wood or bending the tube, remember to leave room for padding to be inserted between the frame and the hull.

Thus you have the basis of the cradle, with the keel and bilge supports. The latter should extend just beyond a bulkhead, if possible. Now these units must be linked together into a rigid structure, with transverse bracing at the bow and stern, and side-bracing on each bilge support. If the boat has long overhangs, you may need to incorporate bow and stern supports; but most modern glassfibre hulls are rigid enough, unless there are local concentrations of weight in these areas.

For a powerboat, the main support must be under the engines. Transverse supports, triangular in shape, are normally used for a deep vee hull, with cut-outs for the spray rails. Alternatively, longitudinal supports can be used, fitting under the chine or the outer spray rail. For other types of hull shape, a cradle similar to a sailboat cradle can be used, or strongly built transverse chocks can be made.

A boat cradle may be constructed in wood or steel or a combination of these. Welded steel, using channels and tubing, will make a good strong cradle which will last for years. Wood may be less durable, and should generally be used in combination with steel to provide high local strength when needed.

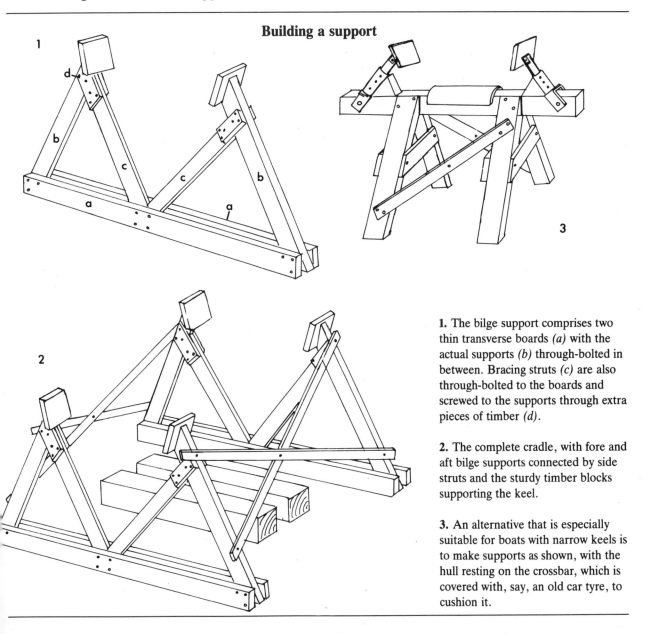

Building a support

1. The bilge support comprises two thin transverse boards *(a)* with the actual supports *(b)* through-bolted in between. Bracing struts *(c)* are also through-bolted to the boards and screwed to the supports through extra pieces of timber *(d)*.

2. The complete cradle, with fore and aft bilge supports connected by side struts and the sturdy timber blocks supporting the keel.

3. An alternative that is especially suitable for boats with narrow keels is to make supports as shown, with the hull resting on the crossbar, which is covered with, say, an old car tyre, to cushion it.

Once supported, the boat also needs a cover. Wood is the obvious material for building a frame which will support the cover and keep it clear of the hull and superstructure. However, tubular steel is better and will last a lifetime. Covering fabric that is left rubbing against the hull all winter can cause nasty marks on the gel coat.

Simple triangular supports, notched onto the toerail, will be adequate for a sailboat, but the wheelhouse on a powerboat may require more complex framing. Longitudinal battens will lock the whole thing together. The support should extend over the side of the boat so that the cover does not rub on the hull. The cover should be lashed down very tightly to secure it against winter gales. If possible, it should be a one-piece cover to reduce the chance of damage. Leave the ends open to let air circulate, as the cover is intended to keep the boat fresh and dry while protecting it from rain, snow, and dead leaves.

Wooden support frame

First of all, remove the lifeline and stanchions from the boat. Then put the support frame together, fitting its notches over the toerail and bolting it together at the apex. Fit longitudinal battens (a) at the apex and outside the toerail, to hold the cover away from the gel coat. Now fit on the cover and lash it to the cradle and to ground pegs, or, as in the illustration, hang large paint or oil cans, filled with water, from the cover.

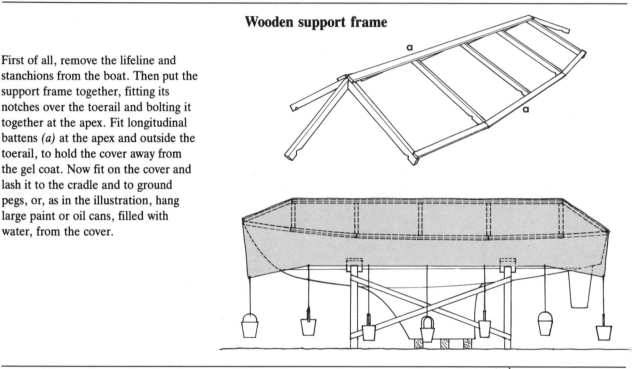

Tubular-steel support frame

Another way of supporting the cover is to have a large tubular A-frame (a) at the stem and stern and shorter A-frames (b) which attach to the longitudinal apex support-tube via special end fittings (c). The length of the shorter A-frames can be adjusted (d) to stand securely on the deck. They are fitted with rubber protection caps so that the deck is not damaged. A neat way to keep the cover away from the hull side is to insert special fittings (e) into the stanchion holders, and to screw a longitudinal plank (f) to the fittings.

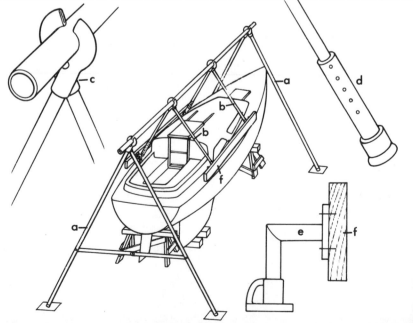

Winterizing the boat

Preparing your yacht for winter lay-up is vital if the yacht is not going to deteriorate during the long winter months. It is no good just taking the boat out of the water and thinking you can leave everything until the spring. If you do, you could find yourself facing some hefty repair bills.

The first thing to do when the boat comes out of the water is to clean off all the dirt and marine growth. A high-pressure water jet is best for this, perhaps accompanied by careful use of a scraper. When removing the marine growth, pay special attention to the stern gear, particularly the small water inlets which allow water to flow through the propeller-shaft bearing, if this is the water-lubricated type. Clean the echo-sounder transducer and the log impeller very carefully, and do not use metal scrapers on these items.

Once clean, the outside of the hull should be examined carefully for chips and scratches in the gel coat. Shallow ones can be left until spring, but any which expose the laminate underneath must be treated *before* lay-up. If water enters the laminate and then freezes, it will start a process of delamination, which could cause serious trouble if left unchecked. The treatment is to grind or sand out the affected area, and then apply gel coat to seal the wound (see page 54).

Water, when it freezes, is one of the greatest enemies of glassfibre boats. The water expands and can open up small cracks, which then allow in more water. Apart from the hull surface, check around the deck and superstructure, to make sure that there are no areas where water can lie and cause trouble.

Water in the engine-cooling system must be drained off (see page 185). This applies to both the freshwater and the salt-water systems. The former can be left in if there is anti-freeze in the system, but check its strength. The water tank and domestic plumbing system must also be drained, and here you must pay special attention to the calorifier, if fitted, where the water on both sides must be drained. The toilet should also be drained.

It makes sense to remove the battery, so that it can be put on charge occasionally to keep it in sound condition. Moreover, the battery can freeze up if left on board at sufficiently low temperatures, particularly when in a discharged state. The remainder of the electrical system does not require much attention. A spray with a silicone-grease aerosol around exposed terminals and junction boxes will help to keep corrosion at bay. The same spray can usefully be used on engines to prevent corrosion. Electronic equipment is best removed from the boat, to protect it from both damp and thieves. The same applies to external fittings such as navigation lights, but antennae of different types can be safely left in position.

Preventing theft from a boat laid up for the winter can pose a dilemma, because you should leave the boat with fresh air moving through it, while also making it secure against intruders. You may be able to introduce fresh air through cockpit lockers left open, but the air should circulate right through the boat, so you need an exit as well as an entry for air, and the solution will vary from boat to boat. Removing all the loose equipment from the boat is a chore, but at least this leaves you free from worry.

Check through every locker and clean it out. Do the same with the bilges, to ensure that no nasty smells mature during the winter. Once you have cleaned out the inside of the boat, leave all the lockers and hatches open, allowing air to circulate. Much wood is used in the construction of glassfibre boats, and this can rot even if the laminate itself can survive damp conditions.

Make sure that all seacocks are left open to prevent water collecting, and check that the cockpit drains work.

Work all the seacocks a number of times to prevent them jamming. Ideally, you should treat varnish and paintwork at the winter lay-up, to prevent further deterioration; but this work is normally left until the spring.

Finally, when you are done with the inside, wash down the outside of the superstructure and hull, and wax it as though you were going to give it a good polish. However, save the polishing for the spring, and leave the wax in place as further protection during the winter.

It requires discipline to carry out all this work on the boat at the lay-up. But you will be very thankful that you did so when the spring comes around. Your task of refitting will be greatly simplified. Also, while you are laying up the boat and can plan future work, it is a good idea to make a list of what must be done in the spring.

Winter checklist

– Have you got all the tools you will need for cleaning, electrical repairs and so on?

– Are the hull shores or cradle secure, with the hull weight distributed evenly? If the yacht is afloat, are the mooring warps sound?

– Is the cover free from chafe, and are the eyelets firmly in place?

– Are all the limber holes free? (If water tends to collect at a low point on a teak deck, where it could cause rot, this can be prevented by a piece of towelling lead through a scupper, allowing surplus water to "wick" over the side.

– Are the floorboards, berth boards etc. lifted up to allow air circulation?

– Are the lockers emptied and open for ventilation?

– Are any objects left on wooden or laminate surfaces where they could cause discoloration?

– Is the compass stored at home, or safely away from metal objects?

– Is the fire extinguisher on board and in working condition?

– Is the gas bottle stored away from the boat? If it is aboard, are all of the connections sound?

– Have you taken the flares ashore? (In the wrong hands they could be dangerous.)

– Are all the cable clips of marine quality, and uncorroded?

– Will the sacrificial anode last through your lay-up period?

– Have you removed the battery, or else ensured that it is kept on charge—perhaps by a wind generator—with the terminals clean and protected by Vaseline?

– If the engine is diesel, are the tanks full to prevent condensation? (If the engine is petrol, do not leave fuel in the tanks.)

– Is there anti-freeze in the cooling system? Is it the correct type of anti-freeze for your engine?

– Have you taken the sails ashore? If not, take them off now for inspection, cleaning and storage.

– If the mast is standing, are halyards rove? If so, remove them and reeve a messenger in their place.

– Is the standing rigging dressed?

– Is the yacht secure in your absence? (Remember that thieves and vandals can do more harm than the worst winter.)

– Is the boat insured for the winter? Have you complied with all the rules of the insurance company?

Winterizing petrol and diesel engines

While the boat is in the water

1. Run the engine until it reaches working temperature, preferably off mooring, so that the gearbox oil also circulates. Return to dockside.

2. If the engine is secondhand and its interior cleanliness is unknown, drain the engine oil and fill the engine with flushing oil to the lower dipstick level. Run the engine at a light load for the recommended time. This done, continue as you would if you were familiar with the engine and knew how clean it was.

3. Empty the engine of all its oils: engine-sump, gear-box, and reduction-gear. Outdrive legs must be emptied ashore.

4. Renew the engine-oil filter, the fuel filters, and any gearbox filter. Fill the engine with oil to the lower dipstick level. Also fill any reduction gear with normal-grade oil recommended by the manufacturer; or else, if the engine is to be laid up for longer than six months, fill it to the lower dipstick

level with preservative oil, which must be pumped out and replaced with normal-grade oil when the engine is put into commission.

5. Connect the raw-water side of the cooling system to a freshwater hose (from a dockside tap, a large oil drum, or the boat's own freshwater supply).

6. Run the engine, still connected to the freshwater supply, to circulate all the new oils.

7. Some manufacturers recommend that, while running the engine (especially on a raw-water cooling system), you add an emulsifying oil (Esso Cutwell or Shell Donax) to the water in a proportion of 1:5 to give the system better corrosion protection. Another tip is to connect a small reservoir of diesel-injection preservative oil before the primary filter, to protect the pump and injectors from corrosion.

8. All raw-water engine-cooling systems MUST be left dry. The exception is the indirect system, which may be left wet, if an antifreeze is added, or dry.

Stop the engine, spraying preservative into the air intake or carburettor as it comes to a halt. Protect the generator and other electrics with cling film.

Close off the raw-water cooling supply and open the cooling drain-cock on the engine block. There may be raw-water drains on the gear box, too. Use them, as all raw water must be removed to avoid frost damage.

On an indirect cooling system, the freshwater side is left either wet or dry. Before the last run (point 6 above), if leaving the system wet, drain down the freshwater and fill the system with the correct antifreeze/freshwater solution (see manufacturer's instructions). This gives frost protection for two whole years, but the specific gravity of the solution must be tested each season to ensure that dilution has not caused a dangerous lowering of the necessary protection level. Check that the raw-water side of the system is drained and dry.

With the boat on land

9. Coat the engine with aerosol spray.

10. Clean or renew the air-cleaner filter element, then reseal the electrics and air intakes.

11. Winterize the impeller pump (see page 131).

12. If possible, disconnect the exhaust hose from the manifold and seal the end after spraying into it with preservative oil. Otherwise, condensation and damp air will attack the valves and the cylinder.

13. Winterize the gear box (see page 138).

14. Dry out the bilges to keep the atmosphere dry around the engine.

15. Cover the engine with waterproof canvas to keep off dust. Do not use plastic, which keeps damp air and condensation beneath it.

16. Open the seacock to give some ventilation to the bilge area. Do this only if the boat is ashore!

17. Diesel fuel tanks are best kept free of condensation if they are filled to the top for the winter. Petrol tanks, on the other hand, should be emptied completely, for safety.

18. Use a heavy grease to seal the threads on the fuel-filler caps. A weighted inverted plastic carton can further help to keep water out.

19. Seal off the fuel-tank breathers.

20. Protect the engine-room air intakes from drifting rain and snow.

21. Winterize and protect the electrics of a petrol engine. See below.

22. Note all spare parts that you will need for the following season and order them now, before the rush for the new season starts.

Engine cleaning

1. Seal off the electrics and orifices with clean rags and a waterproof plastic bag, as illustrated.

2. Use a proprietary engine cleaner and water to degrease and clean the engine.

3. Remove small parts so that they can easily be cleaned and painted in the workshop.

4. Use a wire brush on an electric drill to remove loose paint and corrosion.

5. Very small ferrous parts can be boiled in a solution of water and soda. This removes the paint.

6. Arrest and prevent further corrosion by treating light alloys with etching primer and by treating ferrous metal with one of the proprietary products containing phosphoric or tannic acid.

7. Use a heat-resistant primer/paint system. Best of all is if you can obtain the same paints as those used by the engine manufacturer.

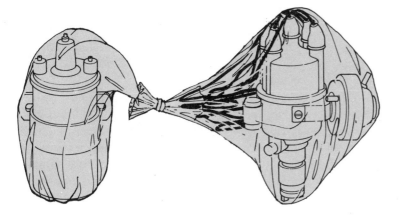

SPRING OVERHAUL

The first days of spring give you the urge to get your boat back into the water. Off come the covers, and you are faced with the seemingly monumental task of restoring the boat to its seaworthy condition. This can be a daunting prospect but, if the boat was laid up with due forethought, the work will not take long. Mark up and store covers, cradle sections, etc., so that you can easily identify them when the autumn comes.

You should already have a list of the work and repairs to be done. If not, the time to make one is now. Divide the tasks into those which can be done inside and those requiring fine weather. Many of them will be simple checkouts, but these will give you peace of mind in the sailing months.

Outside, go over the hull surface carefully, marking any small defects or scratches. Treat them by grinding out if necessary and filling them. Polishing the topside will improve the appearance and remove the winter grime. Anti-fouling should be applied on the underwater surfaces.

Checking the stern gear is vital, as this is the last time you will see it during the season. Check the propeller carefully for cracks or damage; make sure that the nut is tight and the locking pin is secure. Inspect the shaft bearings for wear and, if they are water-lubricated, see that the water passages are clear. The rudder bearings should also be checked for wear; if there is even slight play, have them renewed or adjusted. Otherwise they will only get worse, and the same applies to the rest of the steering system.

Sacrificial anodes should be replaced if they are more than half-worn. If a stern drive is fitted, check the anodes on the underwater unit. Also on stern drives, check the rubber sealing-gasket for wear or damage. All seacocks should be worked and lubricated; while doing this, check the hoses connected to them, and their securing clips. Make sure that the log and echo-sounder fittings are clean and bright.

On deck, the guard rails and stanchions should be checked for security, particularly where the wires pass through the stanchions. All the electrical fittings on deck should be secure against leakage, and the seals on the water and fuel filters should be inspected. This is a good time to look at the anchor and cable, with special reference to the securing of the inboard end. Freshen up the depth marks on the cable. Finally, carry out a hose check on the windows and hatches, to make sure there are no leaks.

The routine for checking the engine will be in the handbook, but a careful visual check of all the hoses and pipework will provide reassurance. In particular, the exhaust system should be inspected for leaks or deterioration. Have a look at the engine mounts to make sure that there is no sign of movement if they are solid mounts, or that there is no wear and tear in flexible mounts.

The electrical system is often a neglected area. All the wiring and fittings should be checked for corrosion or wear. In particular, look at the wiring where it passes through a bulkhead or wherever it might chafe. On electrical fittings, look for the telltale green signs of corrosion; if you find them, renew or clean the fitting, but more importantly you should seek the cause. Maintenance is unlikely to be needed by the electronics, but this should be checked in the handbooks.

Safety equipment is vital and requires a thorough check. Look at the renewal date on flares, and have the liferaft serviced if this has not already been done. Fire extinguishers should be weighed to make sure that they still hold their charge. The contents of the first-aid box may need replenishing. See that the bilge pump and gas detector work. This is a good time to brush the gas-pipe joints with soapy water and ensure that there are no leaks.

Hydraulics are now found on both powerboats and sailboats. These should be checked for leaks, and the system topped up and bled if necessary. The navigation lights should be in working order. Give particular care to the masthead light, which may not be readily accessible once the mast is in place.

Lastly, when all the checking and repairs are done, the boat can be cleaned and painted to make it look smart. After the boat has been relaunched, a few things remain to be done. With a rigidly mounted engine, the propeller-shaft alignment should be checked, and this must be done with the boat afloat. All the water hoses connected to the seacocks should be checked for leakage. Before you go off to sea, do have your compass adjusted to bring the corrections up to date.

THE WOODWORK

Whilst glassfibre laminate is largely maintenance-free and needs only a good polish to keep it "as new", the monotony of the cold laminate is often relieved by wood which does require careful maintenance. Bright woodwork can highlight a yacht, whereas dull woodwork gives an air of neglect.

It is the exterior woodwork which suffers, and there are various methods of treatment. Much will depend on the type of wood, but teak is the only wood which can be left bare and still retain an attractive finish. Main methods are to use oil or to apply the traditional varnish finish.

Teak is widely employed as a material for deck covering. The traditional teak-laid deck is still in use, with its pleasing pattern of planking as a beautiful contrast to the starkness of the glassfibre laminate. Left bare, teak will tend to become grey with time and lose its warm look, but the attractive colour can be retained by simply scrubbing the deck regularly. If the surface becomes dull even after scrubbing, then light sanding will restore the colour, but this should be done sparingly. Because of the wear and tear it takes, the toerail is often left bare, but a more attractive method is to attach a bare teak strip above a varnished lower section.

Oil stains on wood are unsightly and difficult to remove, since the oil will soak right into the grain. A light solvent such as carbon tetrachloride or tolurene can help to remove the oil, followed by treatment with a mild bleach. Use bleach cautiously as it can leave the wood looking patchy.

There are several proprietary products on the market for treating wooden decks, and they are generally good. Leaving wood bare is practical only if the wood is genuine teak. On other woods, the surface colouring can deteriorate quickly, and regular oiling is an alternative. Use one of the special oils for this purpose. Regular oiling is important—otherwise the surface may deterioriate to the point where laborious sanding down is necessary.

Varnish work requires even more careful preparation and maintenance, one of the reasons why this is a less popular finish today. In general, it is best to limit varnish work to vertical surfaces, as varnish on horizontal surfaces will deteriorate very rapidly and require constant maintenance.

Gold and silver cove lines are used on hull topsides to give a traditional appearance and to relieve the starkness of plain laminate. These colours are normally applied as an adhesive tape, replacing the laborious and skilled process of applying gold and silver leaf. If you decide to replace the lines, then carefully remove the existing tape, thoroughly clean the surface with a solvent, and apply the new tape, unrolling a little at a time. It must be positioned carefully, because you do not get a second chance. For patterned areas, the tape or sheet must be cut to size before application. After application, rub it down into position very carefully, so as to remove air bubbles and to seal the edges.

LEAKS

Leaks should not occur on a well-built yacht, but they do arise from time to time. You should never ignore the evidence of a leak. It will certainly not go away, and it could indicate that something serious is going wrong. It may require detective work to locate the source, but you ignore it at your peril.

One of the major difficulties with any leak is locating its real source. On a modern yacht which has linings throughout the sides and under the deck, a leak starting in one place may show up some distance away—or if the leak is running into the bilges, its first sign is a steady rise of water in the bilge.

Finding and curing leaks can be a tedious process. In trying to trace leaks, remember that they cannot occur through the moulding except after damage, so look at the joints. The obvious places are the join between the hull and deck mouldings, around windows and hatches, around bolts where fixtures have been made, and from pipe fittings which are open to sea water.

Looking first at leaks through the deck or the deck joint, you will see the point at which the water is showing on the inside, and you know that water cannot flow uphill. Generally, leaks run from either a forward or an aft area towards the lowest amidships point, although the forward-to-aft direction is generally most common. In a sailboat, you should ask: does the leak occur only when the boat is heeled to one side? This may indicate that water is entering when the lee deck is underwater. Does the leak occur only when it is raining? This is the sort of detective work you must go through.

One way to trace a leak is simply to remove the lining inside the cabin. But this can be difficult to remove and even harder to replace. An alternative is to look for possible sources of the leak on deck, and then apply coloured water to each point in turn. You can do this by building a miniature dam around the fitting with putty, and filling it with water. Allow some time for the water to percolate through at each point before moving on to the next point. Eventually you will strike lucky, and the coloured water will show through. From then on, it is just a matter of repairing the leak.

Once you have identified where a leak is coming from, the cure may be comparatively simple. A temporary cure is easy to devise with the modern sealing materials available. Clean and dry the affected area thoroughly, and apply the sealant to close the gap. You can then lie peacefully in your bunk without water dripping on you.

The problem with any such temporary solution is that you may find the leak recurring during the next season. A sealant cannot be forced right into the gap, nor can the space be cleaned out completely. The sea has a nasty habit of discovering any weaknesses, and you might as well resign yourself to doing a proper job in the first place.

If the leak is around a fitting attached to the deck or superstructure, the only real solution is to remove the fitting and bed it down in fresh sealant. With many modern boats, the fitting is not always easily accessible inside the boat—but the effort is worthwhile. Otherwise you are likely to have con-

Checking for leaks

Build a putty dam around a fitting and fill it with coloured water, which will show on the inside if this fitting is causing the leak.

tinual trouble, and the water seeping through may start to attack the exposed laminate.

Most fittings are secured with bolts. When applying new sealant, be sure to apply it also around the bolt holes and under the heads of the bolts. With stanchions or window frames, sealant is often spread only under the flange, leaving water free to find a way down under the bolt heads. Stanchions suffer from this problem when they are subject to strain and movement.

If a leak is found between the hull and deck mouldings, this requires special treatment. You cannot open up the joint and reseal it, but the next best thing is to remove the fender strip which covers the gap, lightly grind out the affected area, and then apply an epoxy sealer to the cleaned surfaces. As an added precaution, the fender strip can be bedded down in sealant when it is replaced.

CORROSION

Although glassfibre is not a material which suffers from corrosion, metal fittings are still essential on a boat, and these can indeed be subject to corrosion. Sea water is an extremely corrosive liquid, and salt spray can attack most metals. The presence of oxygen is also needed for corrosion to form, and the generally damp atmosphere on a boat can be a breeding ground for corrosion.

Two main types of corrosion occur on boats. In common corrosion, salt water reacts with a metal. The most usual form of this is rust, found on iron or steel. In electrolytic corrosion, a battery-like reaction occurs between metal parts of the boat, with the sea water serving as an electrolytic conductor.

The best way to prevent common corrosion is to use metals which are not attacked by sea water. Stainless steel is among the best materials in this respect. As it also has strength properties greater than ordinary steel, it is widely used for yacht fittings. Bronze and other copper alloys are reasonably corrosion-free, although a film of surface corrosion builds up which forms a barrier to further corrosion. This means that the metal does not retain a clean, shiny appearance like stainless steel, and the use of bronze for yachts is diminishing.

Boat builders have learned the hard way about corrosion, and external fittings are now almost universally made of stainless steel. Special aluminium alloys are used for some items such as cleats and fairleads, where stainless steel would be too expensive. However, corrosion problems can result unless compatible metals are used for the fastenings of these items.

The real problems with corrosion tend to occur inside the boat, where standards may be lowered. Cheap fittings may be used, a typical instance being the clips used to secure flexible piping. Plated steel clips look bright and shiny when new, but sea water can soon initiate corrosion—and a failure of such a clip could let water in, and possibly allow the boat to sink.

Finding this type of corrosion is generally a simple matter of checking through all the fittings at the annual inspection. Any discoloration is a sign that all is not well, and the remedy is simple: replace the fastening or fitting with one made of stainless steel.

Electrolytic corrosion is more difficult to identify and cure than common surface corrosion. First, it is caused by combining two metals with different electrical "potentials". These are listed generally here for various metals. Any metals used underwater should be as close together in this table as possible. For example, copper and aluminium have wide differences, but stainless steel and bronze are close together.

This kind of corrosion occurs when electrical current flows from one metal to the other through sea water. But current takes the easiest path, so if you link all the metal components on the hull with a sizeable earth bonding strip, current will prefer this path and the corrosion will be reduced.

Of course, on glassfibre boats only the fittings are made of metal, such as the propeller and skin fittings. However, if the boat lies alongside a steel pontoon, this can cause problems. The solution is to provide a metal surface on the hull of the boat which will act as a focus for the electrolytic corro-

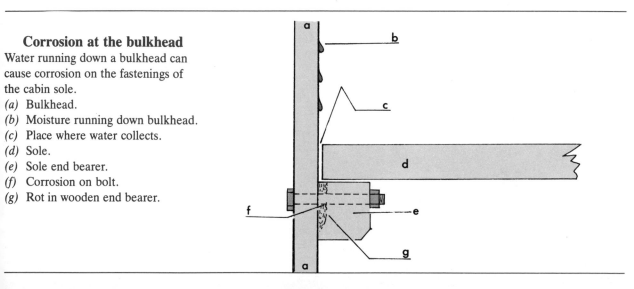

Corrosion at the bulkhead
Water running down a bulkhead can cause corrosion on the fastenings of the cabin sole.
(a) Bulkhead.
(b) Moisture running down bulkhead.
(c) Place where water collects.
(d) Sole.
(e) Sole end bearer.
(f) Corrosion on bolt.
(g) Rot in wooden end bearer.

sion. Zinc anodes are generally fitted on a steel rudder blade and on the hull near the propeller. These anodes take the brunt of the electrolytic corrosion, leaving the important boat fittings intact.

The anodes should be linked into the electrical bonding circuit along with the other skin fittings. Part of the annual check should be to ensure that these connections are in good order and electrically sound. The anodes will be steadily eroded, showing that they are doing their job, and will need replacing at regular intervals. If they are bolted through the hull, make sure that you effect a good seal when the securing bolts are hardened up.

Currents flowing between the metal hull fittings will cause electrolytic corrosion, and can be greatly amplified if there is any leakage from the electrical system in the boat. This could result in major corrosion. By always switching off the battery at the master switch when leaving the boat, you will reduce the chance of such leakage, and also the chance of a flat battery. High-voltage mains systems could be even more damaging if any leakage occurs, and it is not a good idea to leave these supplies connected when the boat is not in use.

Matching your metals

	Metal	Electrical potential	Metal	Electrical potential
Metals that are closest together in this table will cause least electrolytic corrosion when combined.	Magnesium	− 1.60	Yellow brass	− 0.26
	Magnesium alloy	− 1.60	Admiralty brass	− 0.26
	Zinc	− 1.10	Aluminium bronze	− 0.26
	Galvanised iron	− 1.05	Red brass	− 0.26
	Cadmium	− 0.80	Copper	− 0.25
	Aluminium	− 0.75	Monel metal	− 0.20
	Mild steel	− 0.70	Stainless steel (passive)	− 0.20
	Cast iron	− 0.70	Silicon bronze	− 0.18
	Lead	− 0.55	Nickel (passive)	− 0.15
	Tin	− 0.45	Silver	0
	Manganese bronze	− 0.27	Gold	+ 0.15

Installing anodes

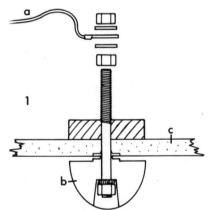

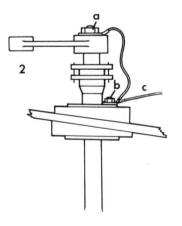

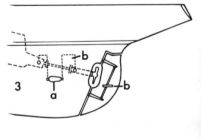

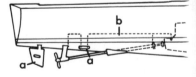

1. Through-hull mounting.
(a) Wire connection to the boat's electrical bonding circuit.
(b) Sacrificial anode. This must not be painted. It is best to bolt or screw the anode in place, so that it can be more easily dismounted when it needs to be replaced.
(c) Hull.

2. A flexible earth link between the rudder stock (a) and its housing (b) and then to the bonding circuit (c).

3. The bonding system on a sailboat and on a powerboat.
(a) Sacrificial anodes.
(b) The electrical bonding circuit.

DRASTIC ENGINEERING

Servicing and replacing parts becomes difficult when corrosion or incompetence has stripped or damaged engineering threads. Nuts, bolts, and threads sometimes need drastic remedies before they can be replaced, even if the correct-size spanners are used and screwdrivers have the correctly shaped heads for the screws.

Avoid having to use the drastic remedies below by careful treatment of the threaded components.

Restoring corroded or damaged threads
Heli-Coil screw thread inserts are used by

manufacturers of quality outboard, inboard, and outdrive units, in which stainless-steel fasteners have to be inserted into light alloy components. Screw threads into bare alloy castings are, at best, weak, and therefore the insert can strengthen and spread the load into sound material better than if you simply re-tap the hole to a larger bolt size.

Bronze plugs are sometimes used as sump plugs in gearboxes and other sump-drain points. Over-enthusiasm with a spanner will soon strip the threads. They can be restored by inserting Heli-Coil screw-thread inserts as shown.

1. Drill a hole, using a standard drill of the same diametre as the bolt.

2. Tap the hole with the appropriate size Heli-Coil tap.

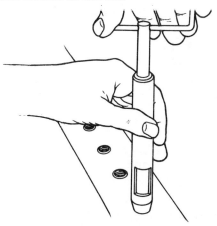

3. Wind in the insert with the aid of the inserting tool that you buy with the inserts. The end of the last coil should be 1/4 to 1/2 a pitch below the surface.

Removing badly corroded or stuck nuts

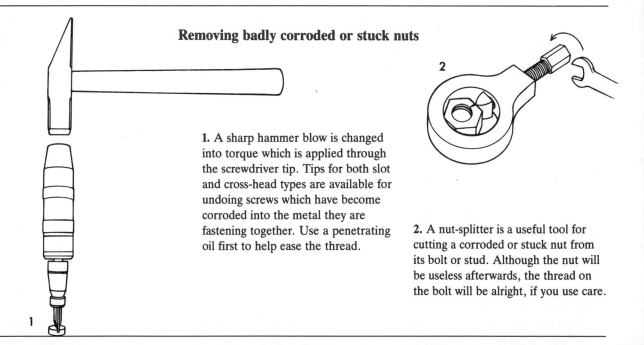

1. A sharp hammer blow is changed into torque which is applied through the screwdriver tip. Tips for both slot and cross-head types are available for undoing screws which have become corroded into the metal they are fastening together. Use a penetrating oil first to help ease the thread.

2. A nut-splitter is a useful tool for cutting a corroded or stuck nut from its bolt or stud. Although the nut will be useless afterwards, the thread on the bolt will be alright, if you use care.

EMERGENCY REPAIRS AT SEA

Hull damage

Probably the worst emergency you can have at sea is a leak below the water-line. When water is pouring into the hull and the bilge pumps cannot cope, the situation is urgent and helps to concentrate your mind. Quick action is needed to stop, or at least reduce, the flow of water, to give you time to devise something more permanent which can hold up until you reach harbour.

Hull damage that might cause a leak can come from several sources. Impact with floating debris is one of the most likely, and could produce a gaping hole in the bow. Moreover, damage to the rudder or the propeller shaft and its bracket could displace hull fixtures and let water into the hull. This may be a result of grounding, which on a sailboat can loosen the keel fastenings and might let in water. Probably the only other such problem is the failure of a skin fitting or its associated pipework, but this is among the commonest causes of yachts sinking when they are unattended.

One advantage of glassfibre laminate is that, when it receives an impact, the damage tends to be confined to the immediate area of impact. Even with a very heavy impact, much of the laminate may bend inward but will not break off. You may then be able to force these pieces back into the hole to reduce the leak. But a large hole calls for fast action. Grab anything available to force into the hole and stop the flow of water. Pillows or lifejackets are fine.

An inflatable lifejacket might be inflated in the hole to make an effective seal, although the sharp edges of the hole could puncture the air chamber—and remember, you may soon need the lifejacket! Further, in your haste to try and stem the initial flood, try not to do anything which might compromise the longer-term repairs necessary to get you home.

Probably the best way to stop any flow is to tackle it from the outside. Canvas tied around the hull can provide an effective seal, if you can stretch it tightly and securely. Modern canvas covers tend not to have lacing eyes, and it may be difficult to secure rope lashings to the canvas. Nor will the slippery surface of a glassfibre hull give the canvas any grip.

The alternative is to work from the inside. Make a pad from canvas or bedding, or any other handy material, and jam it into the hole, securing it by a plywood sheet held down with wooden props. You can obtain umbrella-shaped repair patches, which are put through the hole in closed form and then opened on the outside. This is an effective solution, and such items should always be on hand.

Smaller holes in the hull create less panic, and they can be fixed by some of the above methods. A useful repair item to have on board is a tapered wooden plug, perhaps 65 mm (2½″) in diameter at the large end, tapering to 10 mm (⅜″). Even in an irregular hole, such a plug can be an effective seal when hammered home. The plug and hole will tend to adopt the same shape if the plug is made of soft wood.

This type of plug is useful for many purposes. It has the right shape to make a temporary seal if you have trouble with a skin fitting. It can be used similarly if the rudder and stock are lost, leaving the rudder gland open to the sea. Indeed, such a plug can close any round, or nearly round, opening in an emergency.

If leaks occur through loose securing bolts for the keel or on the propeller brackets, you must try to secure the loose item as well as stemming the leak. This may be possible by hardening down the nuts, if enough thread is left and the bolts do not turn at the same time. Before hardening down a nut, ease it off and wrap some string around the bolt under the washer. This will help to make an effective seal.

In any situation where water is coming into the boat, the bilge pumps are vital. Keep the electric pumps switched on. If a crew member can be spared to work the hand pump, keep him at it. At all costs, try to prevent the water from reaching the battery, because you may need this to power the radio for a distress call. When you have time, check the bilges for any debris which might choke the bilge pump.

If you have a big influx of water, inflating the rubber tender might help to keep the boat afloat. The liferaft could be used for this purpose, but it is best kept ready for abandoning ship if the situation becomes desperate.

Superstructure damage

Heavy seas have been known to smash ventilators on deck, allowing water to get below. Rags can be

Fixing a hole from the inside

An umbrella-shaped sealing device has a canvas body that is held by wooden or metal arms which can be opened outward. After positioning, the in-board end is lashed tight to a strong point.

A plywood patch can be held in place by timbers wedged under the deck or another part of the boat structure. A seal can be made from a foam-rubber pillow or a mattress.

Water pouring through a broken window can be stopped if you have prepared for it. Keep a suitably sized piece of plywood (a), pre-drilled to take wing nuts and bolts (b), that can be tightened up against the window frame by a couple of pre-drilled battens (c).

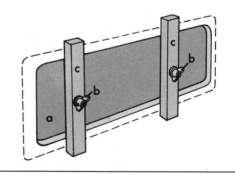

Working from the outside

A piece of canvas could be lashed in place to fix a hole from the outside. You will probably have to add extra sealing on the inside. The difficulty is to get the canvas in place, especially in heavy weather. You need a crewman on each side to "float" the canvas under the prow. A scuba-diving crew member is a big help in a situation like this.

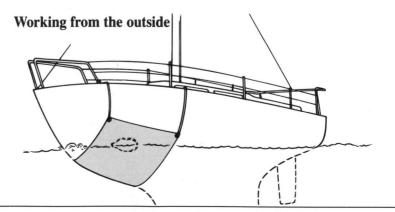

jammed in the hole as a temporary solution. A stronger substitute is a metal or wooden plate with a hole drilled in the centre. Tie a line through the hole and secure it tightly in the cabin. You could put something under the plate to improve the seal, but you can probably put up with dripping as long as water is not pouring through.

A similar solution can be used if a window is smashed in by the sea. If it is a side window or a porthole in the hull, you may need something strong which cannot be displaced by the waves. Use two pieces of plywood, one inside and one outside, with two or more long bolts to lock them together. For this type of repair, it is useful to have a selection of bolts and pieces of plywood available on board.

Damage to the steering

Whilst damage to the hull may be the most serious problem you have to face, a yacht is a complex vehicle and can require many other kinds of emergency repairs. Anything is possible, from the mast coming down to the loss of steering. A long step towards solving the problem when it arises can be taken by thinking it through beforehand, in relation to the particular features of your boat.

Damage to the rudder can happen at any time. If the rudder falls off, temporary steering must be rigged. Much harder to cope with is a rudder jammed in the hard-over position. There are several methods of emergency steering. The simplest is for a twin-engined boat: you run one engine at half speed and adjust the speed of the other engine to give steering control.

On a sailboat, some steering can be obtained from the sails by balancing the foresail against the main. But something more positive is needed to get you into harbour. Lashing a piece of wood onto the spinnaker or main boom can provide a "steering oar" which is pivoted on the stern to provide steering at slow speeds.

A traditional method of emergency steering is to tow a form of drogue astern on a bridle. By pulling on one leg or other of the bridle, you can steer the boat. A drogue is probably the only way to cope with a rudder jammed hard over. By adjusting its pulling position along the side of the boat, you should be able to balance out the steering effect of the rudder. A drogue can be made up from canvas or a strong bucket.

A problem in any other part of the steering system may be solved by rigging an emergency tiller. The rudder stock should have a square at the top, and in an emergency you could fit a large spanner over the square. If the boat is steered by a tiller anyway, you should consider what you have available to replace the tiller if it breaks.

A powerboat could have problems with one of the large wheelhouse windows breaking. Again, plywood is best for covering the hole if possible. But you could lash a piece of canvas over the area on the outside to stop most of the water.

A broken mast

Losing part or all of the mast on a sailboat can be a major emergency. You must get rid of the broken-off section as quickly as possible, before it does further damage. Either cut it adrift, or bring it safely on deck. Powerful wire-cutters are essential to cut away the rigging, and these should be in your emergency tool-kit.

If you have fuel and a working engine, this is the obvious means of reaching harbour. However, you may have to devise a jury rig. How to do this depends on what is available. Masts rarely break off at the base, so you can use the remains of the mast to support a sail. First, make sure it has adequate support. If necessary, rig some additional shrouds and a forestay. Tackles are good for this purpose, as you can set them up tight to prevent movement.

The spinnaker pole or the boom can be lashed to the remains of the mast, to make it higher. But rig a block and halyard before you raise it. With any jury rig, you cannot make good progress to windward, but you will be able to proceed.

In any emergency situation, you will have to sail gently after making a temporary repair. If the hull is damaged, try to keep the repair on the high side if the boat is listing. On the other hand, you may feel that the repair is less strained if kept on the lee side, away from wave impact. Slow speed will reduce the strain, and you should look for the nearest shelter rather than trying to continue your passage.

Methods of rigging emergency steering

1. An extra tiller, holed to suit the top of the rudder stock, should always be carried.

2. In an emergency, a pick-handle, length of timber, or spinnaker pole can be lashed to the rudder stock as a jury tiller.

3. If you have no jury tiller, this system can work.
(a) A self-grip wrench is fastened to the rudder fixture.
(b) A suitable rope is fastened to the wrench handle and goes via blocks to winches on either side, which provide the necessary power.

Raising a jury mast

Emergency steering with a drogue

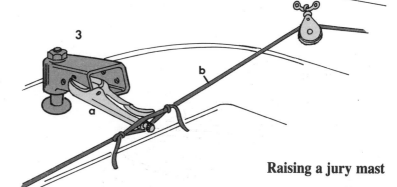

The drogue is attached to the boat by a bridle. Steering is effected by pulling on one bridle line or the other. When held to one side, the drogue can counter the steering effect of a rudder jammed hard over.

A spinnaker pole can be used to make an emergency mast as shown here.
(a) Forestay.
(b) Shrouds.
(c) Wedges inserted to tighten lashings.
(d) Backstay.

Gaskets and leaks

If you do not have spare gaskets from the manufacturers for engines, pumps, and ancillary equipment, emergency repairs can be carried out with modern sealants. A wide range of thread sealants and gasketing compounds is available from the automotive trade.

1. Paper gaskets can often be cut by tapping a piece of thick paper over the casting it is to seal with a ball-pein hammer gently. Cut out the paper gasket with a sharp knife. Rub grease into the paper.

2. Paper gaskets can often be replaced by high-temperature silicone rubber simply by squeezing this onto the gasket area. Do not use for cylinder-head joints.

3. The epoxide-resin family are excellent for emergency repairs to leaks in tanks, pipework, and engine parts that are not under severe stress. Some even set under water or on contaminated surfaces. Always have a kit of this with you. Check the manufacturer's recommendations and follow them, especially any safety instructions.
  (a) Tank with leaking join, which can be temporarily repaired with epoxide resin.
  (b) Mix the resin and hardener as per the manufacturer's instructions.

A

abrasive paper 19 34-35
acrylic glass 29
Airex 14
aluminium, fastening
    fittings to 97–98
ammeter 161
ampere-hour counter 161
anchor
    box (bulkhead for) 18
    security 32
anchor-chain roller 27
anode (sacrificial) 28 31 184
antifouling 45 48–50
    how to apply 49 50
aramid fibre 18 19

B

balsa 14 15
battery 135 149–161
berth 18
    crossover 84
bilge 57
    pump 89
blistering 28 29 30 51–52
boat survey 26–28
booms 95
boot top 55 57
bulkhead 17 18 19
    bonding to the hull 9 23
    fitting a bulkhead 19

C

cabins 82–90
    insulation 83
carbon fibre 20
chain plate 24 25 100
chafing 29 62
chopper gunning 11
clevis pins 64
cockpit 76–81 controls 26
    drainage 77
    gratings 78–80
    seating 77 81
    tips 81
combination material 11 19
companionway 27
condensation 86
corrosion 28 31 183–184 185
crockery stowage 85
CSM (chopped strand mat)
    10 11 12 15 18 19 20 21 22
    23 24 44
cylinder block 28

D

deck 61–74
    fittings 24 25 29 63 66–69
    fastening to sandwich 69–99
    fastening to laminate 69
    hardware survey 62
    join with hull 17 21–24 29
    layout 107
    moulding 13
diesel engine

injection system 28
drainage system 77

E

electrics 149–163
    alternative charging
        methods 162
    battery 137 149–161
    fault finding 159–160
    interference 163–164
    wiring system 156
electronics 163–164
emergencies 186–190
engines 117–148
    access 144
    air filters 133
    air intake 27
    beds 144
    carburettor 124
    controls 139
    cooling systems 129–131
    diesel 117–121
    exhaust system 32 132–133
    fuel systems 119 123
    gearbox 138
    ignition 126
    instrumentation 146
    lubrication 136
    noise reduction 145
    oil and fuel leaks 32
    oil-pressure gauge 148
    outboard 137 146–147
    petrol 122–125
    rocker adjustment 136
    spark plugs 127
    starter 137
    survey 32
    thermostat 148
    timing 148
    turbocharger 120
    ventilation 134
engine-hours meter 148
epoxy fillers 46
epoxy resin 44

F

fairing boards 15 16 fairlead
    29
fastening wood to laminate
    44
fastenings 25
fender 27
foresail reefing 102
forestay 25 100 102
    headfoil 101
foam-core material 14 15 18
fuel system
    tank 32

G

gas installation 90
gearbox 138
    oil-pressure gauge 148
gel coat 8 12 13 17 52 62
    repairing minor damage 54

gel washing the bilge 57
generator 157
genoa 29 112 113
glassfibre
    cloth 11 12 18 19
    fastening wood to
        glassfibre laminate 44
    general construction
        methods 8
    history 7
    laminate moulding 8
    make your own storage
        box 42–43
    moulds 8 9
    qualities 7 8
    repairing light damage 41
    sandwich construction 8
        13–15
    working with 33–44
    worktable 40
grabrail 27 80–81

H

halyard
    replacing 106
    retrieving 106
hammers and pliers 37
hard spot 9 20
hatch 76
headlinings 82–83
heating 86
hole making 37
hull 16 17 20 21–24 53–60
    maintenance 30
    reinforcement 24
    repainting 58–59
humidity
    fitting a "cold wall"
        system 86

I

insulation 83
internal stiffening 9

J

jockey poles 96
joinings 21–24

K

keel 18 29 45 48
    bolts 48
    coating and painting lead
        keels 47
    external-ballast 28
    fairing an iron keel's
        surface 47
    keel-hull join 50
    stud bolts 48
    treating a rusty iron keel
        46
Kevlar 18 19 108
kicking strap 95 107

L

laminate moulding 8 12–13
leaks
    fuel 32 190

oil 32 190
    water 29 181–182
lifeline 63–65
    fender 27 65
    netting 26 65
    make your own
        terminals 65

M

mainsail reefing 103
maintenance 28 165 169–184
    deck equipment 169
    dinghies 169–170
    spring overhaul 180
    woodwork 181
    winter lay-up 171–179
mast 18 104–105
    dressing 104
    lifting 104
    stepping 105
    trimming 105 106
mast roller furling 103
masts and spars 94–98
    corrosion 28
molly nuts, how to fit 68
monocoque construction 20
motor bed 18
motor cruiser: survey 30–32
moulds and moulding 8 9 12
    13 16 40–43

N

navigation light 159
neoprene rubber adhesive
    21
Nomex 14
non-skid surfacing 26 70 71

O

outboard engines 137
    146–147

P

planes 35
plumbing 88–89
polyester filler paste 15 21
polyester resin 10 12 41
polyvinyl acetate 10
pop rivetting 24
power transmission 138–141
propeller 28 31 139–141
    care 143
    saildrive 140–141
    servicing 141
    shaft 31 139 140
prow 18
pulpit 64

R

racer-cruiser survey 26–29
radio insulation (lifeline) 64
rear-view mirror 32
reefing
    hook 94

winch 94
reinforcements 18–20
    built-in 24–25
releasing agent 8 13
rescue ladder 27
rigging 91–110
    rod and wire 99
    screws 100
    stainless-steel 91 99
    toggles 100
    tools 92
    types 93
rigs
    fractional 106
roller 12 41
roller-reefing 101
ropes and ropework 108–110
rudder 18 20 32
running rigging
    maintenance 28
rust 28 46

S
safety 165–168
safety line 26 27
sails 111–116
    cloth 111 112
    emergency repairs 116
    maintenance 28 114–115

stains 115
    types 113
sail-handling systems 101
    103 107
sandwich construction 8 9
    13–17
saws 36
seacock 32
screws 36
    machine screws 98
    self-tapping 98
sheets 29
shelves 85
skin fittings 30 32
slab reefing 95 103
spinnaker
    boom 94
    poles 96
splicing 108–110
stainless-steel fittings
    maintenance 28
stanchions 63 64
    repairing stanchion bases
    63
standing rigging
    maintenance 28
stays 100
stemhead fastening 102
step locker, making a 85
stern drive 31

stiffener 20
storage box, how to make
    42–43
stowing headsails 26
stress cracks 29
stringer 9 17 18
surface, non-skid 26 70–71
    laying teak 71–74
surfacing tissue 10 12 13
surveying a boat 26–32

T
tachometer 148
teak
    laying a teak deck 71–73
    recaulking a laid teak
    deck 74
    replacing a damaged teak
    plank 74
    seating 81
temperature gauge 148
tiller extension 27
toe rail 22 23
toggles 100
tools 33–39
    holding 34
    marking-out 34
    mechanics 38
    power 39

topsides 12 55
transom 18 24 29

U
underwater hull 45–52
unidirectional roving 11 18

V
VHF 164
voltmeter 160

W
waste tank, installing 89
waterline 55
wetting-out 10 11 12 41
winch 26 27
    repairing glassfibre at
    winch base 76
    servicing 169
winch-handle box 27
window frames 29
windows and portlights
    74–75
wiring 94
working surface, extra 85
worktop, making a 84
woven roving 10 12 44